# EXTERMINATION

## VOLUME 1: THE LAST AND DREADFUL HOUR

**BOOM!**
STUDIOS

ROSS RICHIE Chief Executive Officer • MATT GAGNON Editor-in-Chief • FILIP SABLIK VP-Publishing & Marketing • LANCE KREITER VP-Licensing & Merchandising • PHIL BARBARO Director of Finance BRYCE CARLSON Managing Editor • DAFNA PLEBAN Editor • SHANNON WATTERS Editor • ERIC HARBURN Editor • CHRIS ROSA Assistant Editor • STEPHANIE GONZAGA Graphic Designer • JASMINE AMIRI Operations Coordinator • DEVIN FUNCHES Marketing & Sales Assistant • BRIANNA HART Executive Assistant

BOOM! Studios, 5670 Wilshire Boulevard, Suite 450, Los Angeles, CA 90036-5679. Printed in China. First Printing.
ISBN: 978-1-60886-296-2

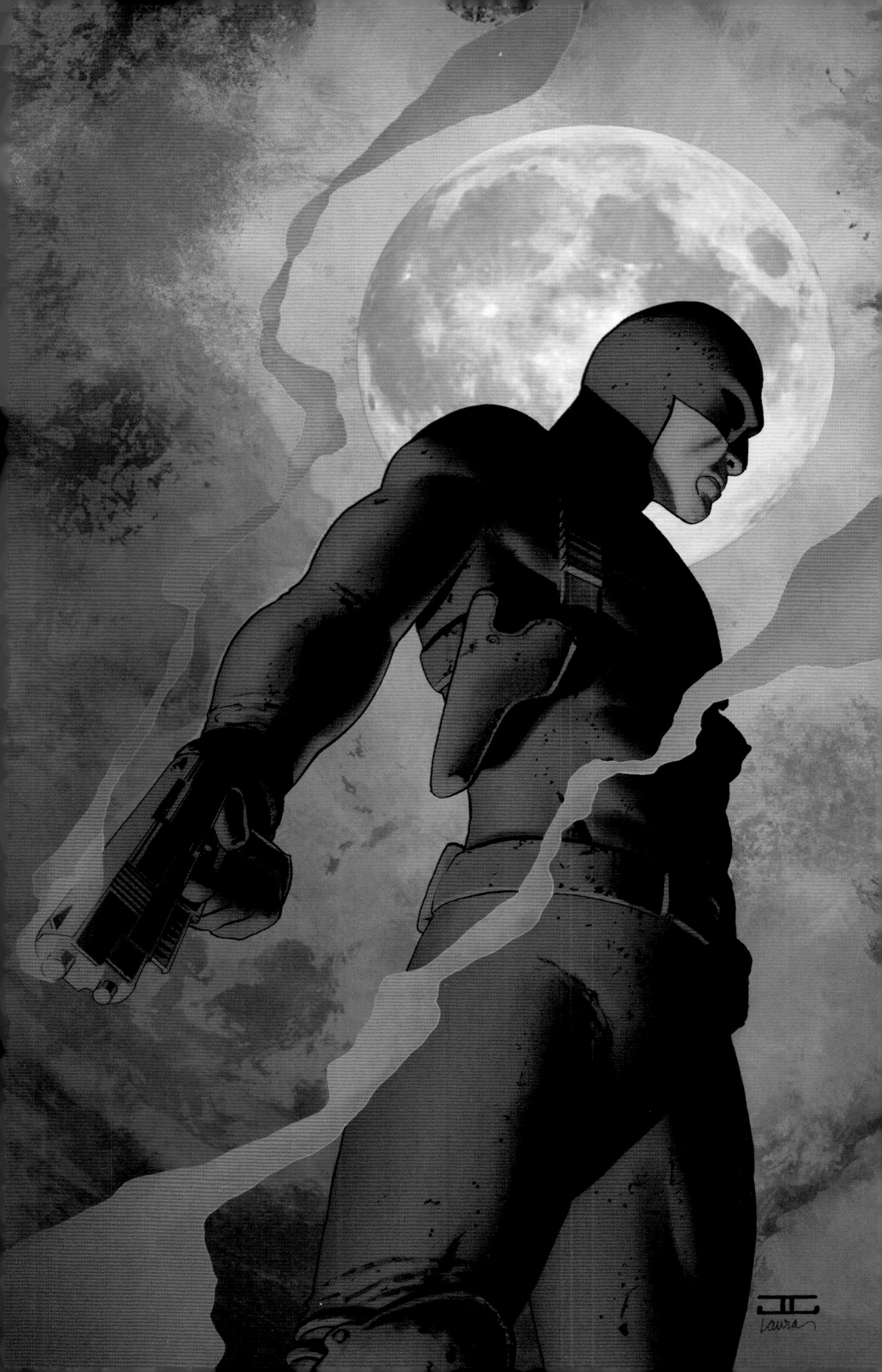
Laura

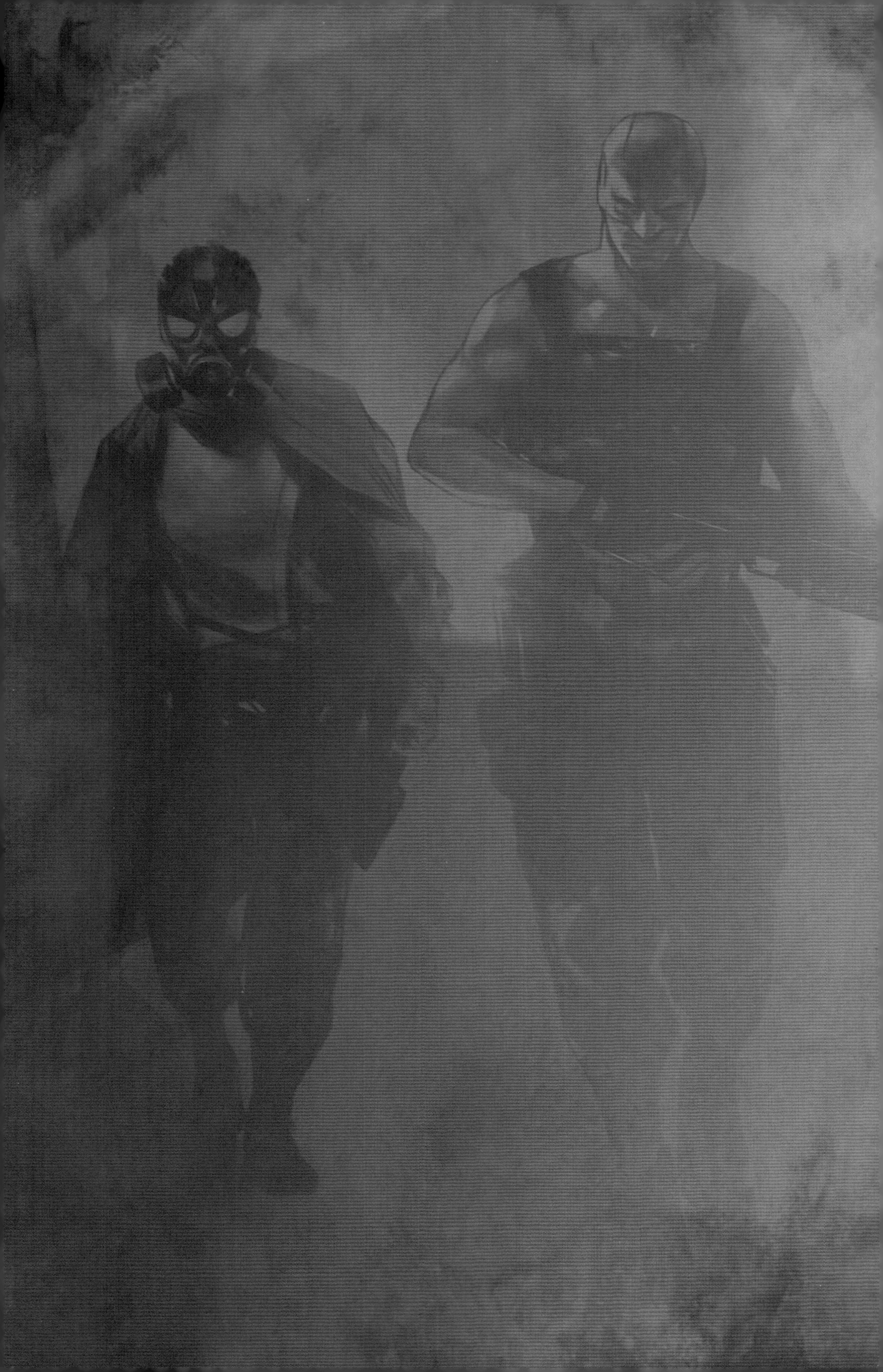

# EXTERMINATION

WRITTEN BY **SIMON SPURRIER**

ART BY **JEFFREY EDWARDS**
AND **V KEN MARION**
*(CHAPTERS 3-4)*

COLORS BY

**BLOND**
*(CHAPTERS 1-2)*

**DARRIN MOORE**
*(CHAPTER 3)*

**JOHN CHARLES**
*(CHAPTERS 3-4)*

**VLADIMIR POPOV**
*(CHAPTERS 3-4)*

LETTERS BY
**ED DUKESHIRE**

COVER BY
**TREVOR HAIRSINE**
COLORS BY **BLOND**

*EXTERMINATION CHARACTER DESIGNS BY GARRY BROWN AND JEFFREY EDWARDS*

ASSISTANT EDITOR
**ERIC HARBURN**

EDITOR
**BRYCE CARLSON**

DESIGNER
**KASSANDRA HELLER**

*EXTERMINATION CREATED BY MATT GAGNON*

# CHAPTER ONE

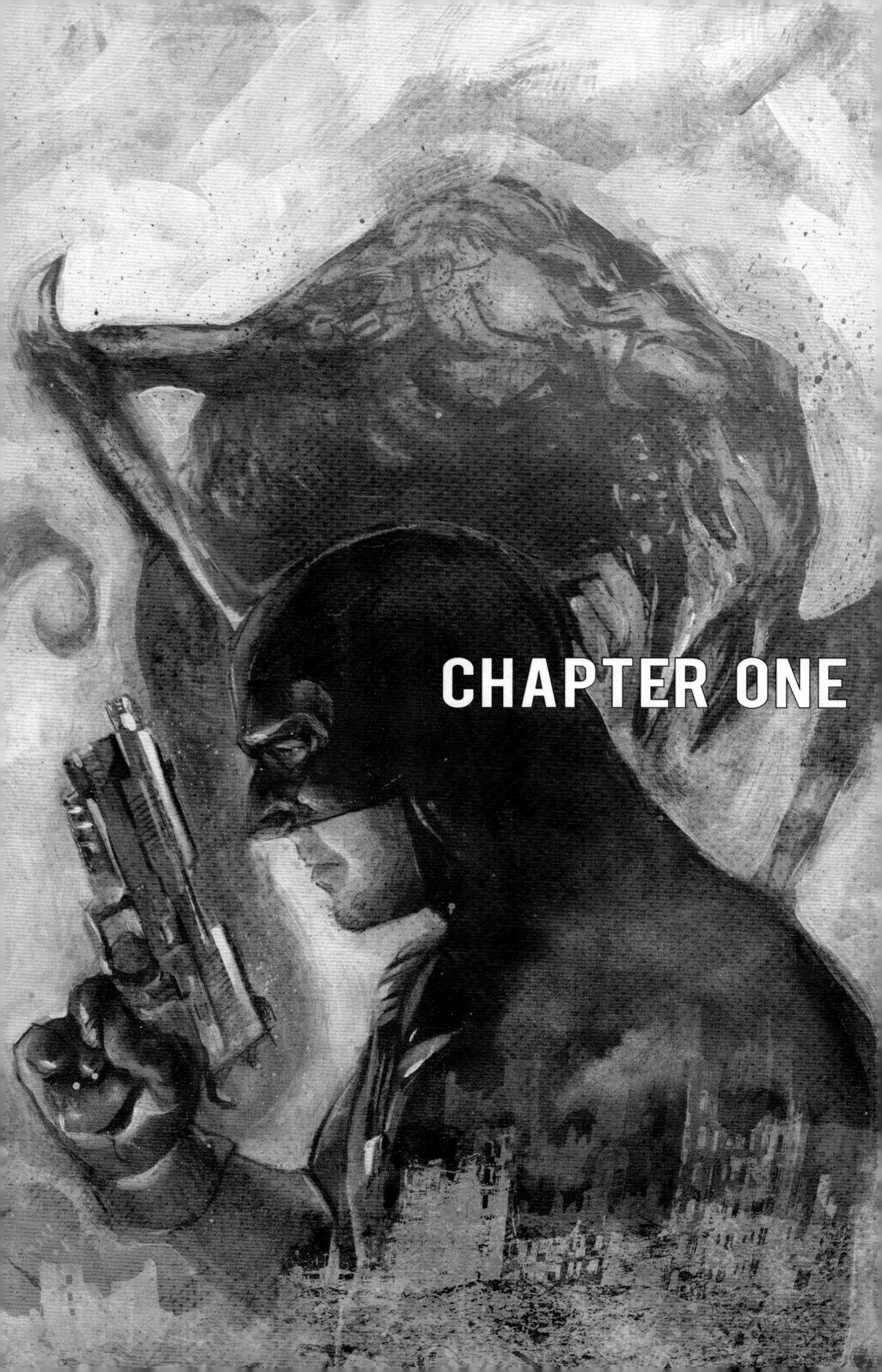

So when the last and dreadful hour
this crumbling pageant shall devour,
the trumpet shall be heard on high,
the dead shall live, the living die,
and music shall untune the sky.

--John Dryden

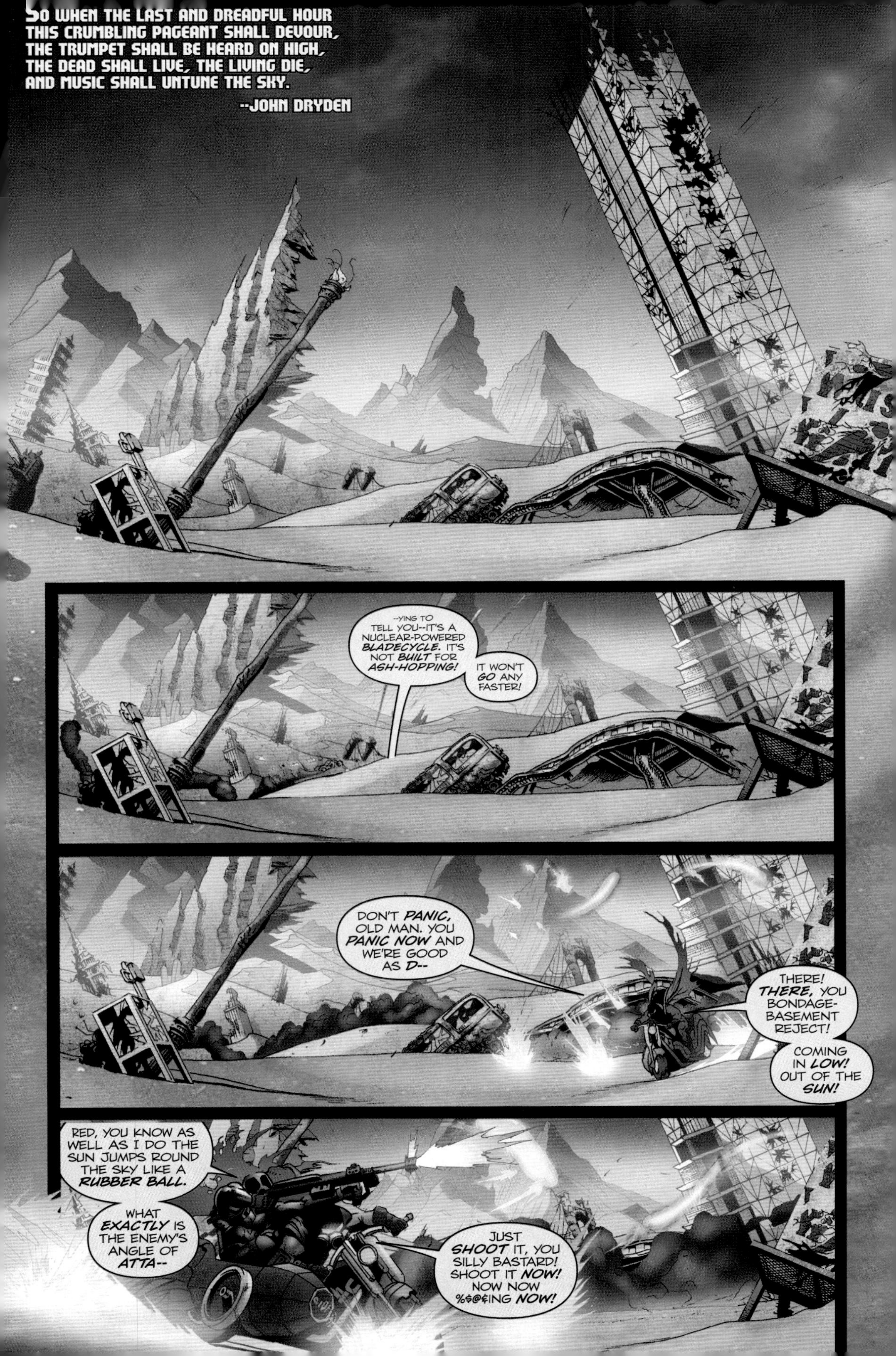

--YING TO TELL YOU--IT'S A NUCLEAR-POWERED BLADECYCLE. IT'S NOT BUILT FOR ASH-HOPPING!
IT WON'T GO ANY FASTER!
DON'T PANIC, OLD MAN. YOU PANIC NOW AND WE'RE GOOD AS D--
THERE! THERE, YOU BONDAGE-BASEMENT REJECT!
COMING IN LOW! OUT OF THE SUN!
RED, YOU KNOW AS WELL AS I DO THE SUN JUMPS ROUND THE SKY LIKE A RUBBER BALL.
WHAT EXACTLY IS THE ENEMY'S ANGLE OF ATTA--
JUST SHOOT IT, YOU SILLY BASTARD! SHOOT IT NOW! NOW NOW %$@¢ING NOW!

LANGUAGE, REAPER.
MIND IT.
NOX.
NOCTURNAL KNIGHT OF RIGHTEOUS REDEMPTION. THE GOOD GUY.
AAAA AAAA AAAA
THE RED REAPER.
MINCING MEGALOMANIACAL SCIENCE-TYRANT. EEEVIL.
STOP
KRAAOOM

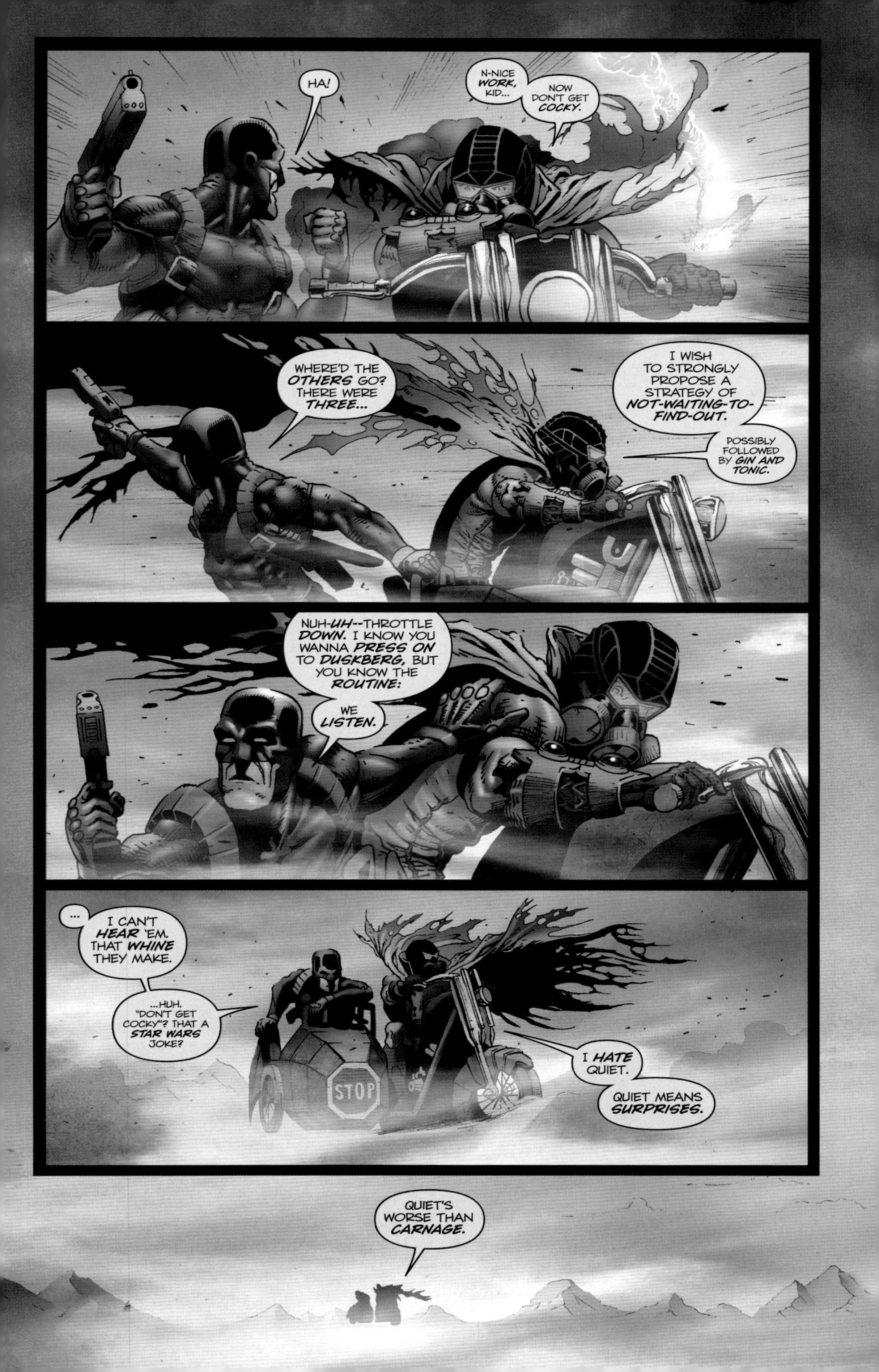
HA!
N-NICE WORK, KID...
NOW DON'T GET COCKY.
WHERE'D THE OTHERS GO? THERE WERE THREE...
I WISH TO STRONGLY PROPOSE A STRATEGY OF NOT-WAITING-TO-FIND-OUT.
POSSIBLY FOLLOWED BY GIN AND TONIC.
NUH-UH--THROTTLE DOWN. I KNOW YOU WANNA PRESS ON TO DUSKBERG, BUT YOU KNOW THE ROUTINE:
WE LISTEN.
...
I CAN'T HEAR 'EM. THAT WHINE THEY MAKE.
...HUH. "DON'T GET COCKY"? THAT A STAR WARS JOKE?
I HATE QUIET.
QUIET MEANS SURPRISES.
STOP
QUIET'S WORSE THAN CARNAGE.

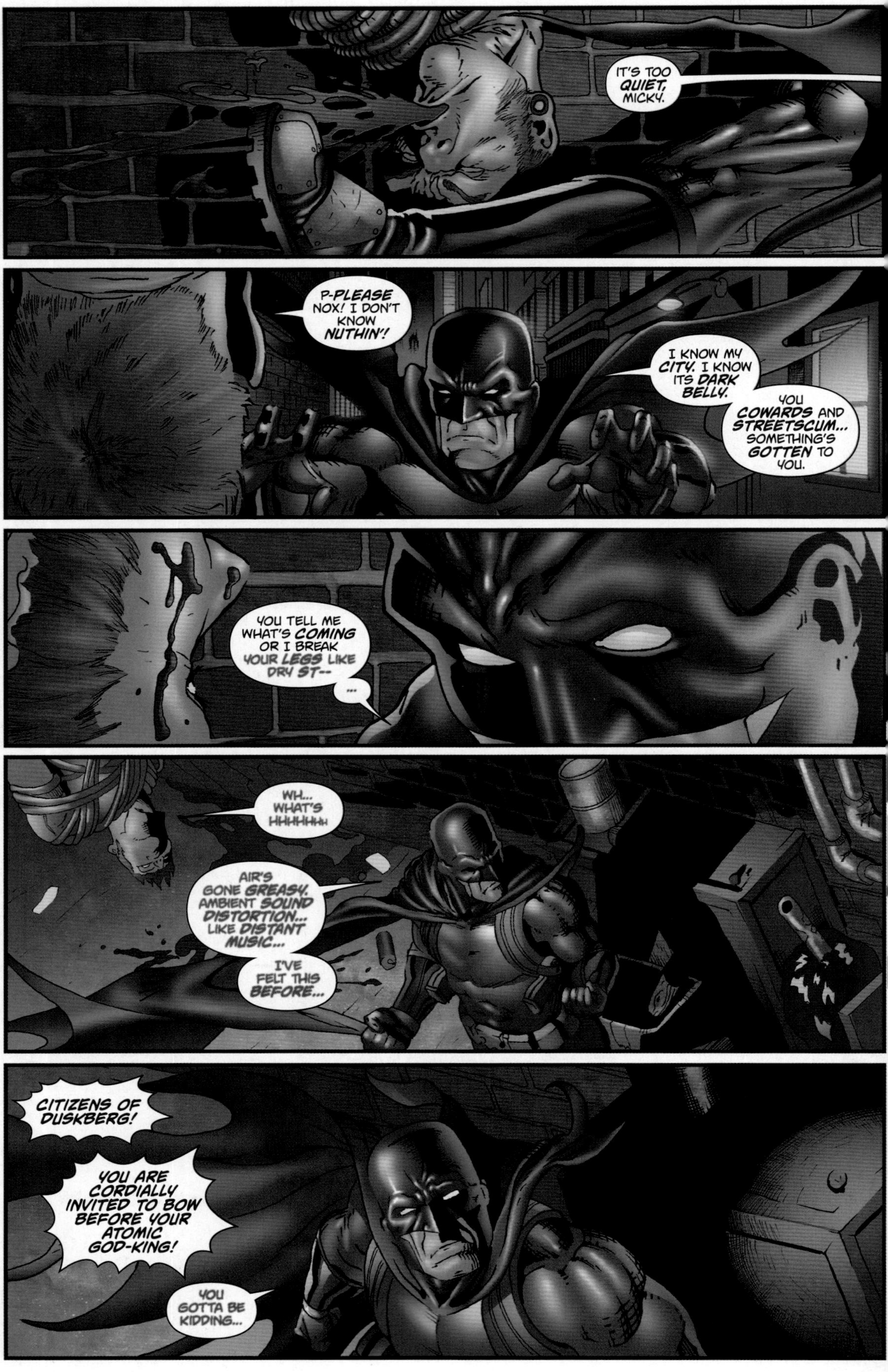
IT'S TOO QUIET, MICKY.
P-PLEASE NOX! I DON'T KNOW NUTHIN'!
I KNOW MY CITY. I KNOW ITS DARK BELLY.
YOU COWARDS AND STREETSCUM... SOMETHING'S GOTTEN TO YOU.
YOU TELL ME WHAT'S COMING OR I BREAK YOUR LEGS LIKE DRY ST--
...
WH... WHAT'S HHHHHHH
AIR'S GONE GREASY. AMBIENT SOUND DISTORTION... LIKE DISTANT MUSIC...
I'VE FELT THIS BEFORE...
CITIZENS OF DUSKBERG!
YOU ARE CORDIALLY INVITED TO BOW BEFORE YOUR ATOMIC GOD-KING!
YOU GOTTA BE KIDDING...

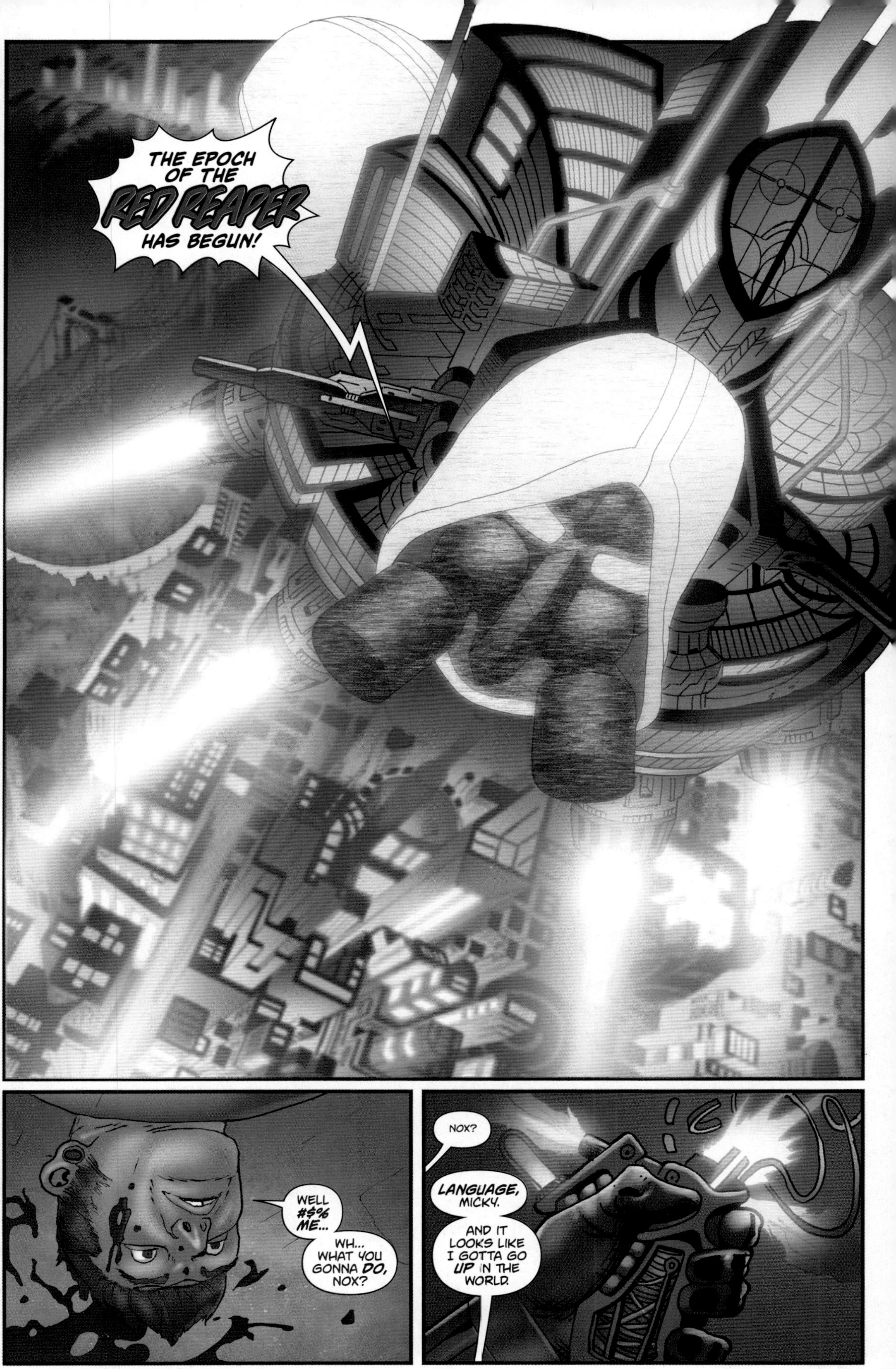
THE EPOCH OF THE RED REAPER HAS BEGUN!
WELL #$% ME...
WH... WHAT YOU GONNA DO, NOX?
NOX?
LANGUAGE, MICKY.
AND IT LOOKS LIKE I GOTTA GO UP IN THE WORLD.

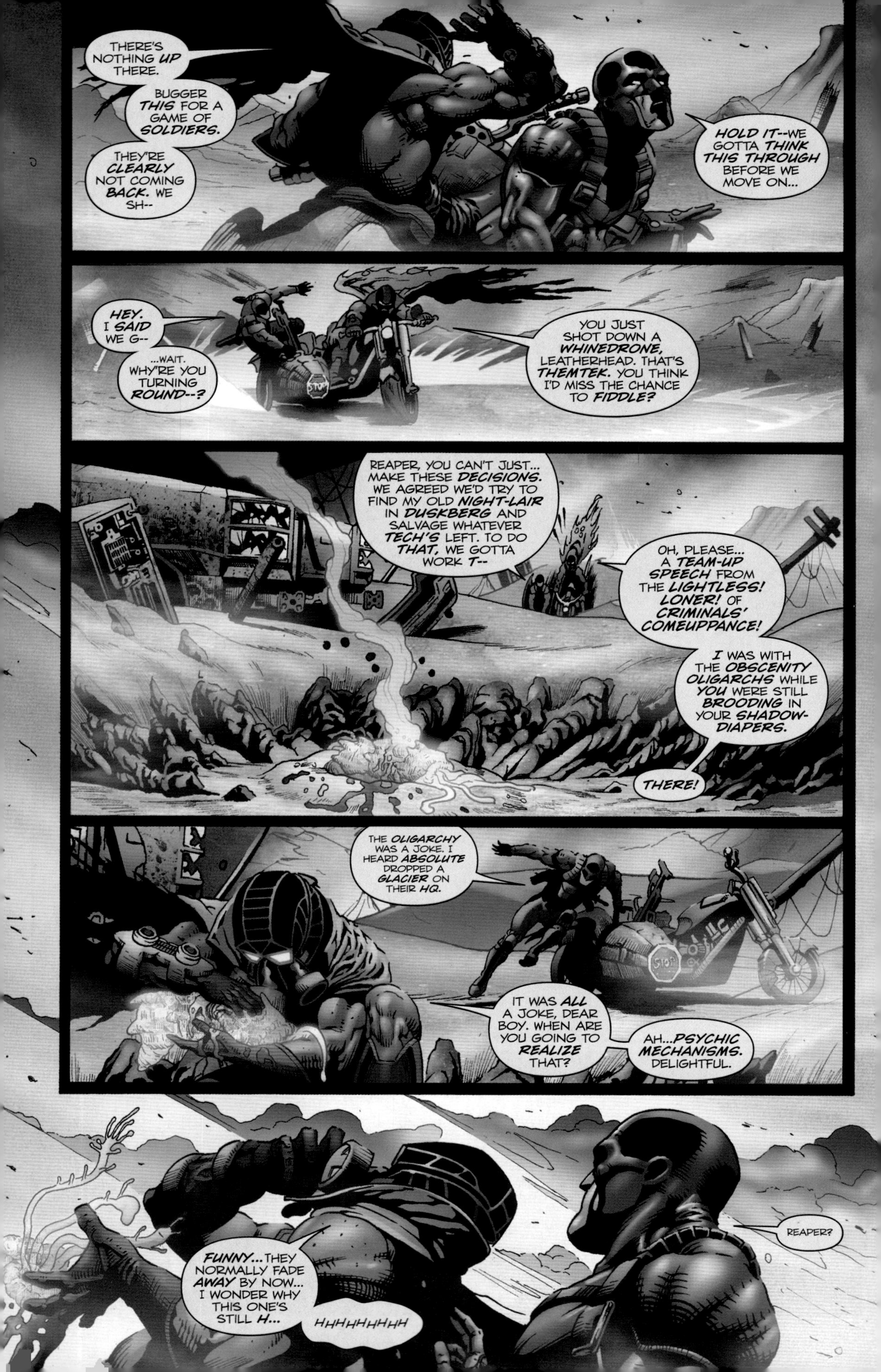
THERE'S NOTHING UP THERE.
BUGGER THIS FOR A GAME OF SOLDIERS.
THEY'RE CLEARLY NOT COMING BACK. WE SH--
HOLD IT--WE GOTTA THINK THIS THROUGH BEFORE WE MOVE ON...
HEY. I SAID WE G--
...WAIT. WHY'RE YOU TURNING ROUND--?
YOU JUST SHOT DOWN A WHINEDRONE, LEATHERHEAD. THAT'S THEMTEK. YOU THINK I'D MISS THE CHANCE TO FIDDLE?
REAPER, YOU CAN'T JUST... MAKE THESE DECISIONS. WE AGREED WE'D TRY TO FIND MY OLD NIGHT-LAIR IN DUSKBERG AND SALVAGE WHATEVER TECH'S LEFT. TO DO THAT, WE GOTTA WORK T--
OH, PLEASE... A TEAM-UP SPEECH FROM THE LIGHTLESS! LONER! OF CRIMINALS' COMEUPPANCE!
I WAS WITH THE OBSCENITY OLIGARCHS WHILE YOU WERE STILL BROODING IN YOUR SHADOW-DIAPERS.
THERE!
THE OLIGARCHY WAS A JOKE. I HEARD ABSOLUTE DROPPED A GLACIER ON THEIR HQ.
IT WAS ALL A JOKE, DEAR BOY. WHEN ARE YOU GOING TO REALIZE THAT?
AH...PSYCHIC MECHANISMS. DELIGHTFUL.
REAPER?
FUNNY...THEY NORMALLY FADE AWAY BY NOW... I WONDER WHY THIS ONE'S STILL H...
HHHHHHHHH

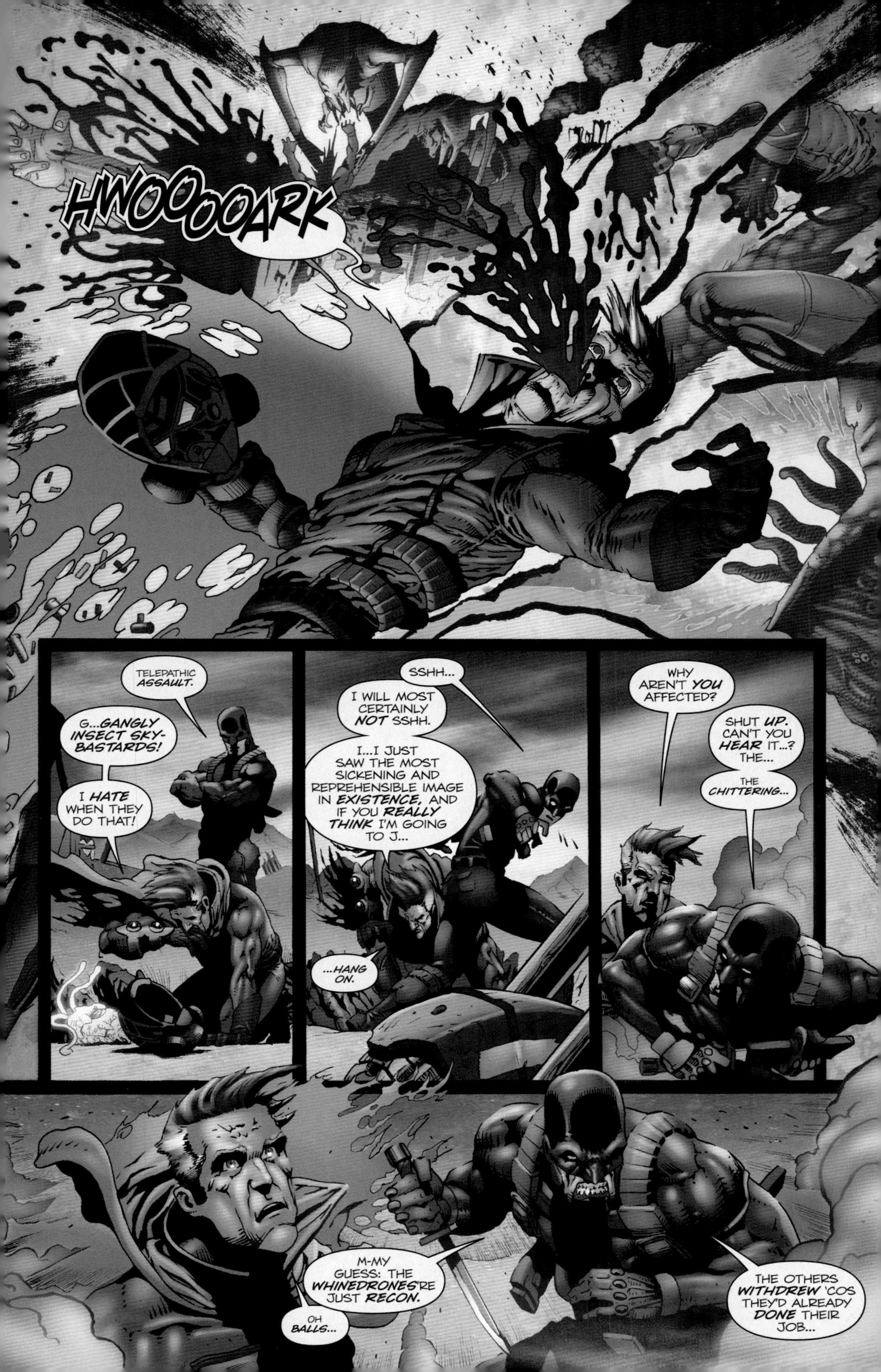
HWOOOOOARK
TELEPATHIC ASSAULT.
G...GANGLY INSECT SKY-BASTARDS!
I HATE WHEN THEY DO THAT!
SSHH...
I WILL MOST CERTAINLY NOT SSHH.
I...I JUST SAW THE MOST SICKENING AND REPREHENSIBLE IMAGE IN EXISTENCE, AND IF YOU REALLY THINK I'M GOING TO J...
...HANG ON.
WHY AREN'T YOU AFFECTED?
SHUT UP. CAN'T YOU HEAR IT...? THE...
THE CHITTERING...
M-MY GUESS: THE WHINEDRONES'RE JUST RECON.
OH BALLS...
THE OTHERS WITHDREW 'COS THEY'D ALREADY DONE THEIR JOB...

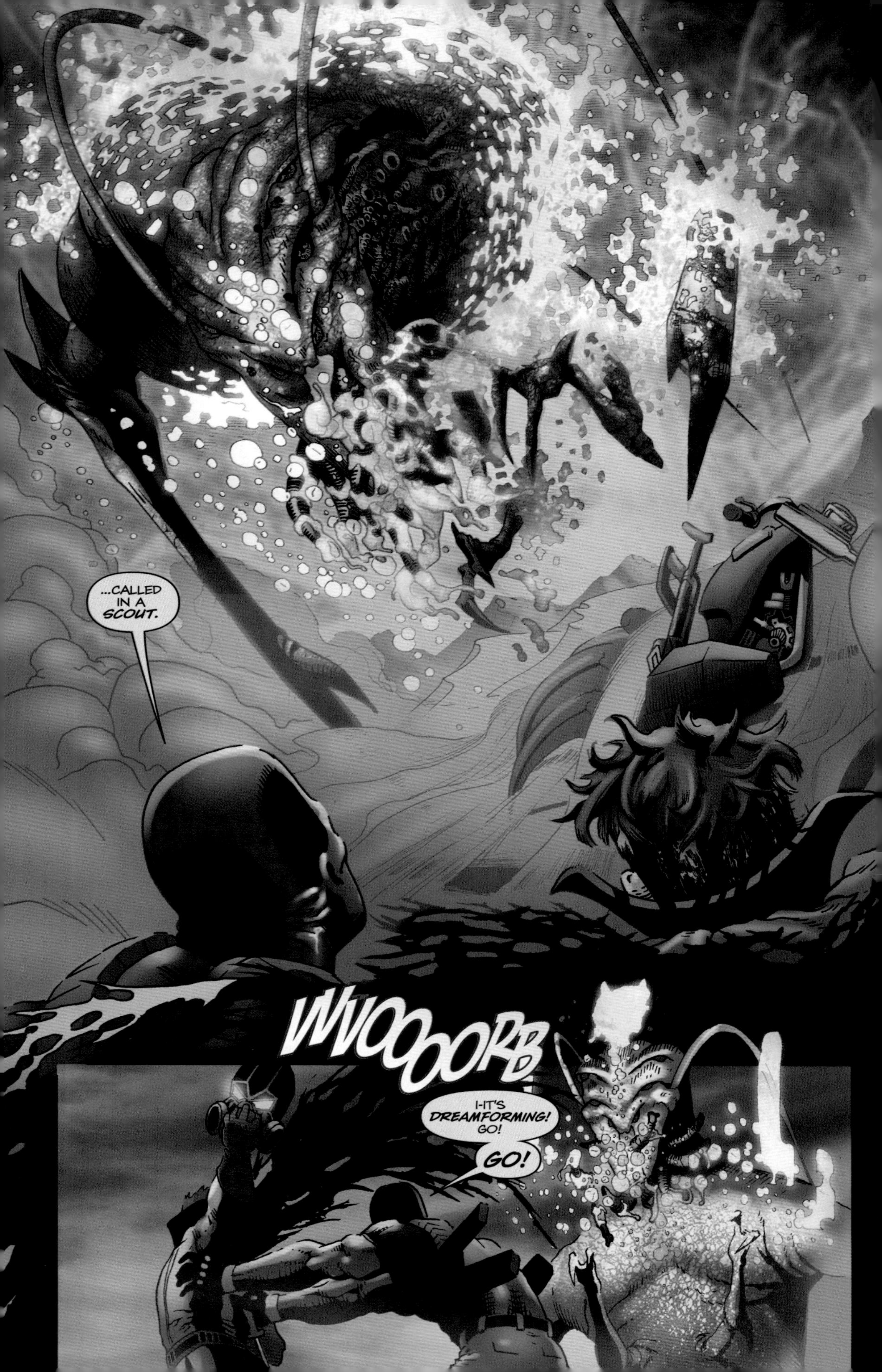
...CALLED IN A SCOUT.
VVVOOOORB
I-IT'S DREAMFORMING! GO!
GO!

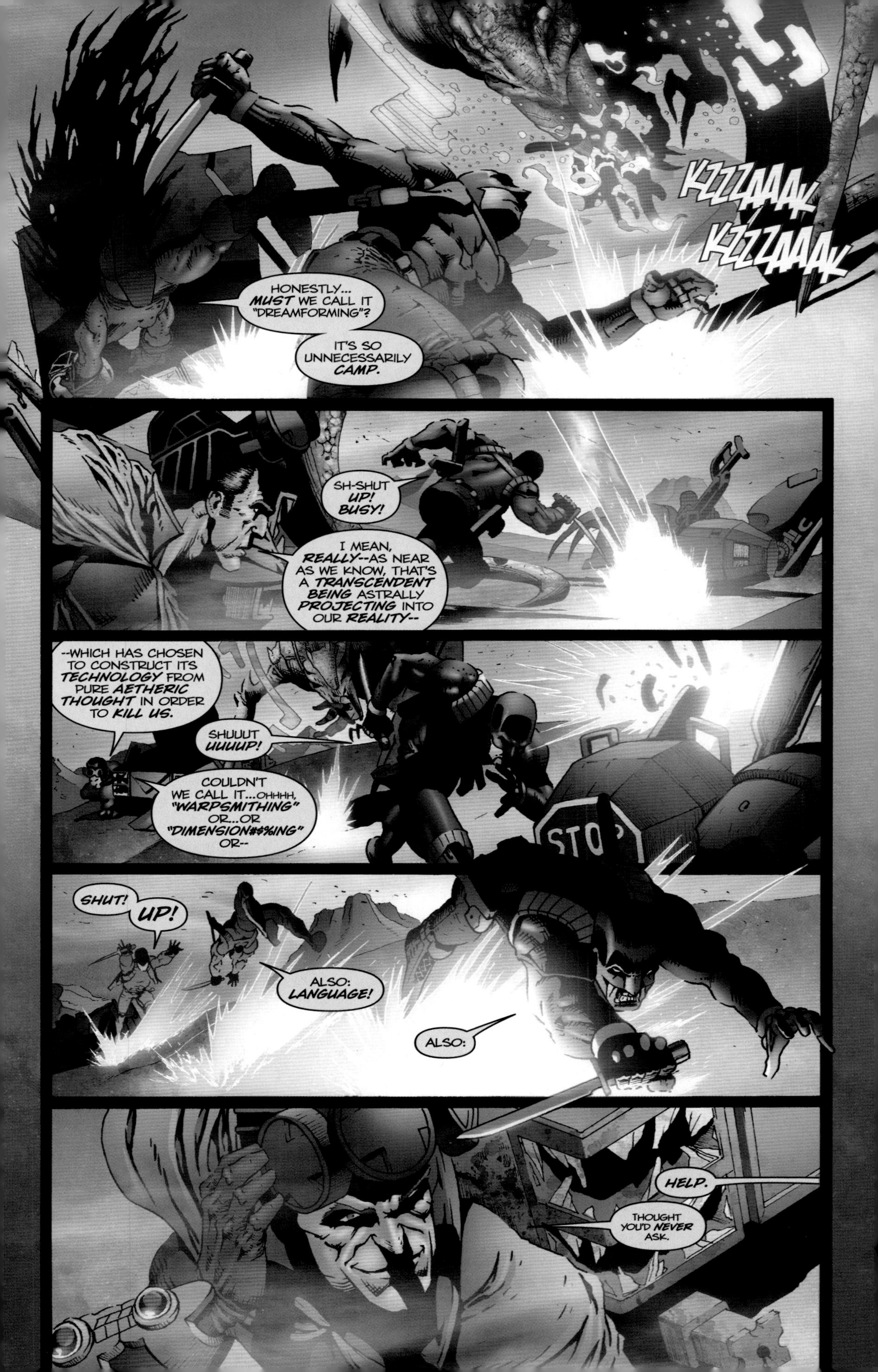
KZZZAAAK
KZZZAAAK
HONESTLY... MUST WE CALL IT "DREAMFORMING"?
IT'S SO UNNECESSARILY CAMP.
SH-SHUT UP! BUSY!
I MEAN, REALLY--AS NEAR AS WE KNOW, THAT'S A TRANSCENDENT BEING ASTRALLY PROJECTING INTO OUR REALITY--
--WHICH HAS CHOSEN TO CONSTRUCT ITS TECHNOLOGY FROM PURE AETHERIC THOUGHT IN ORDER TO KILL US.
SHUUUT UUUUP!
COULDN'T WE CALL IT...OHHHH, "WARPSMITHING" OR...OR "DIMENSION#$%ING" OR--
STOP
SHUT! UP!
ALSO: LANGUAGE!
ALSO:
HELP.
THOUGHT YOU'D NEVER ASK.

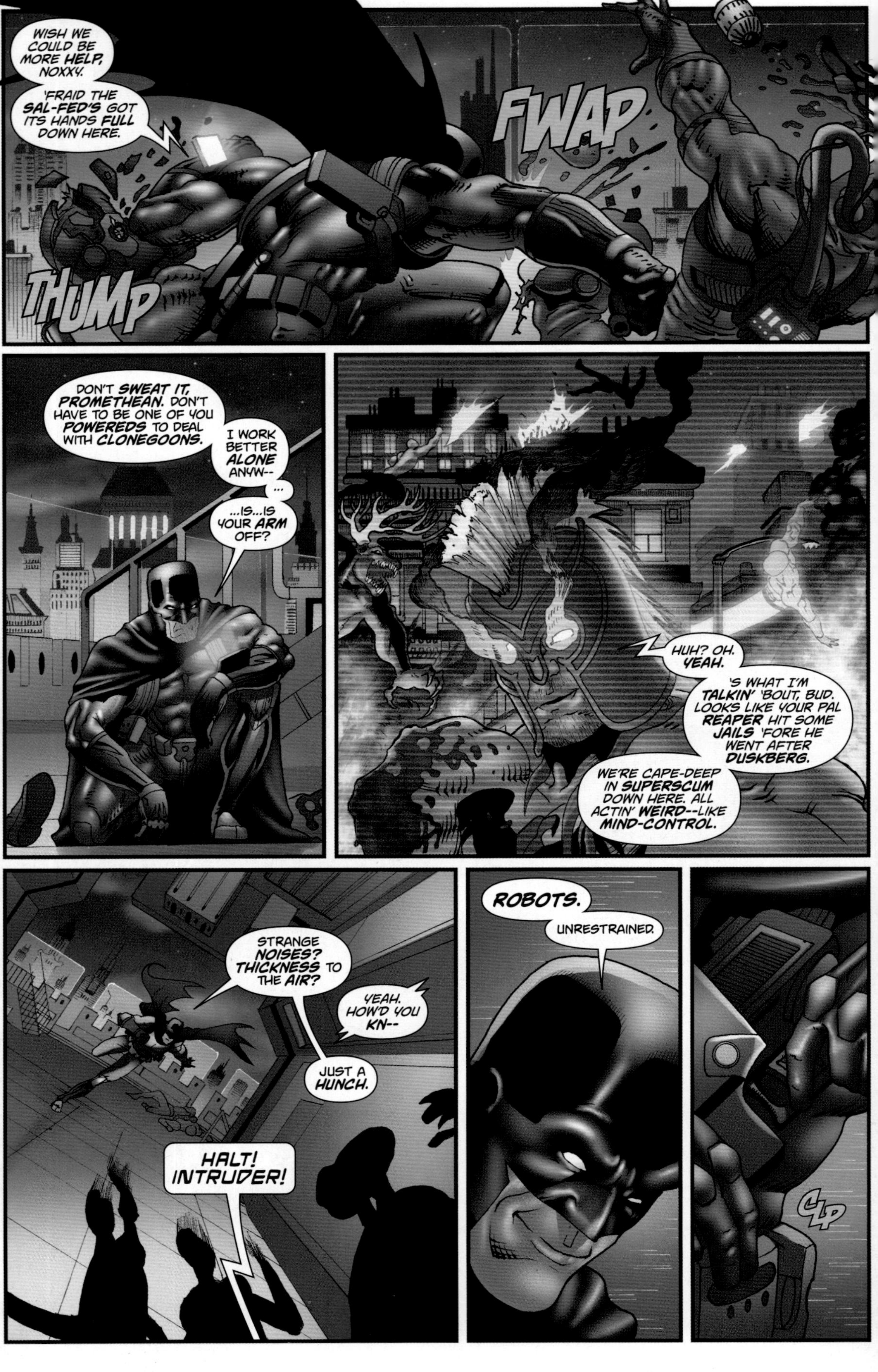
WISH WE COULD BE MORE HELP, NOXXY.
'FRAID THE SAL-FED'S GOT ITS HANDS FULL DOWN HERE.
FWAP
THUMP
DON'T SWEAT IT, PROMETHEAN. DON'T HAVE TO BE ONE OF YOU POWEREDS TO DEAL WITH CLONEGOONS.
I WORK BETTER ALONE ANYW--
...
...IS...IS YOUR ARM OFF?
HUH? OH. YEAH.
'S WHAT I'M TALKIN' 'BOUT, BUD. LOOKS LIKE YOUR PAL REAPER HIT SOME JAILS 'FORE HE WENT AFTER DUSKBERG.
WE'RE CAPE-DEEP IN SUPERSCUM DOWN HERE. ALL ACTIN' WEIRD--LIKE MIND-CONTROL.
STRANGE NOISES? THICKNESS TO THE AIR?
YEAH. HOW'D YOU KN--
JUST A HUNCH.
HALT! INTRUDER!
ROBOTS.
UNRESTRAINED.
CLP

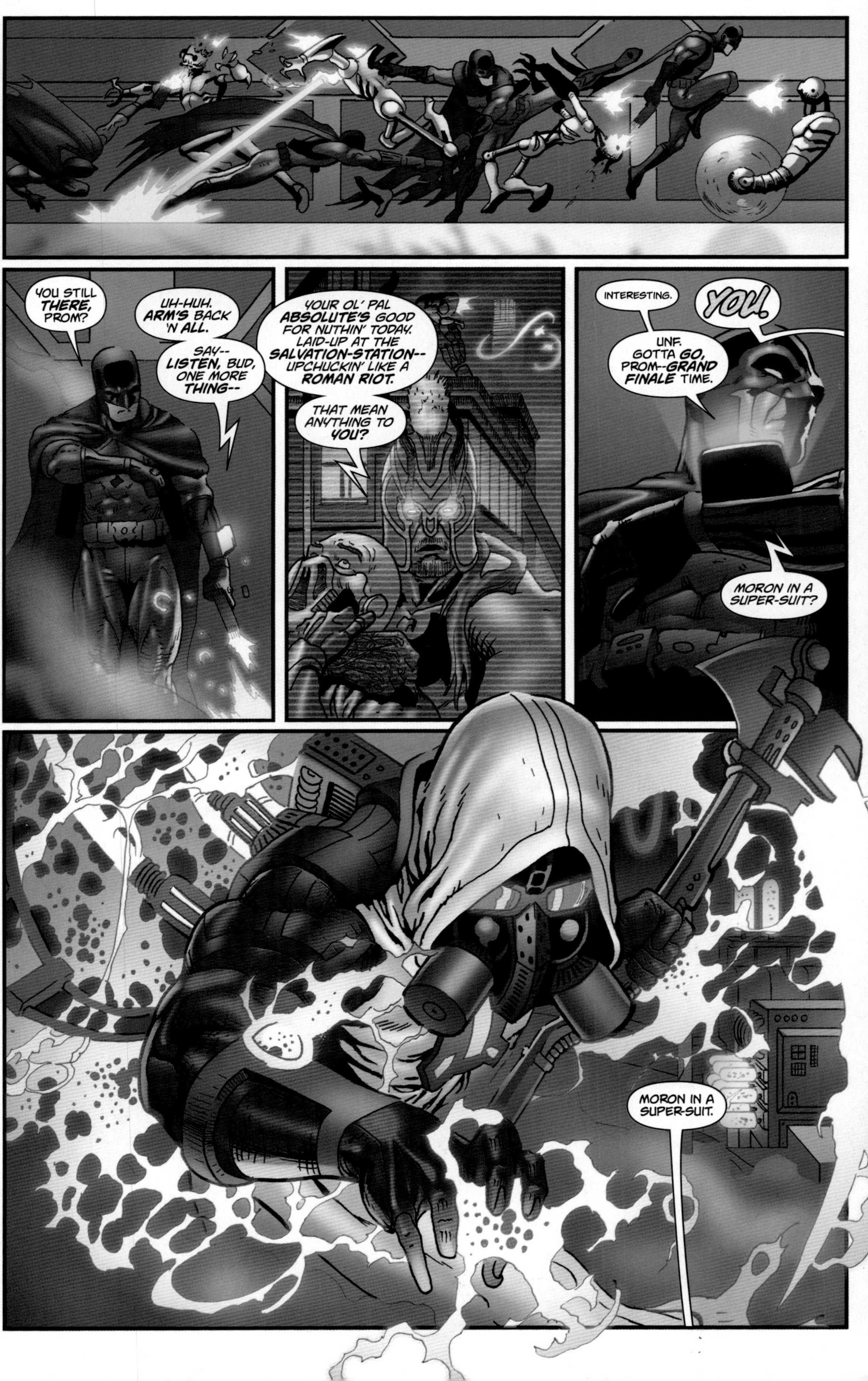
YOU STILL THERE, PROM?
UH-HUH. ARM'S BACK 'N ALL.
SAY-- LISTEN, BUD, ONE MORE THING--
YOUR OL' PAL ABSOLUTE'S GOOD FOR NUTHIN' TODAY. LAID-UP AT THE SALVATION-STATION-- UPCHUCKIN' LIKE A ROMAN RIOT.
THAT MEAN ANYTHING TO YOU?
INTERESTING.
YOU.
UNF. GOTTA GO, PROM--GRAND FINALE TIME.
MORON IN A SUPER-SUIT?
MORON IN A SUPER-SUIT.

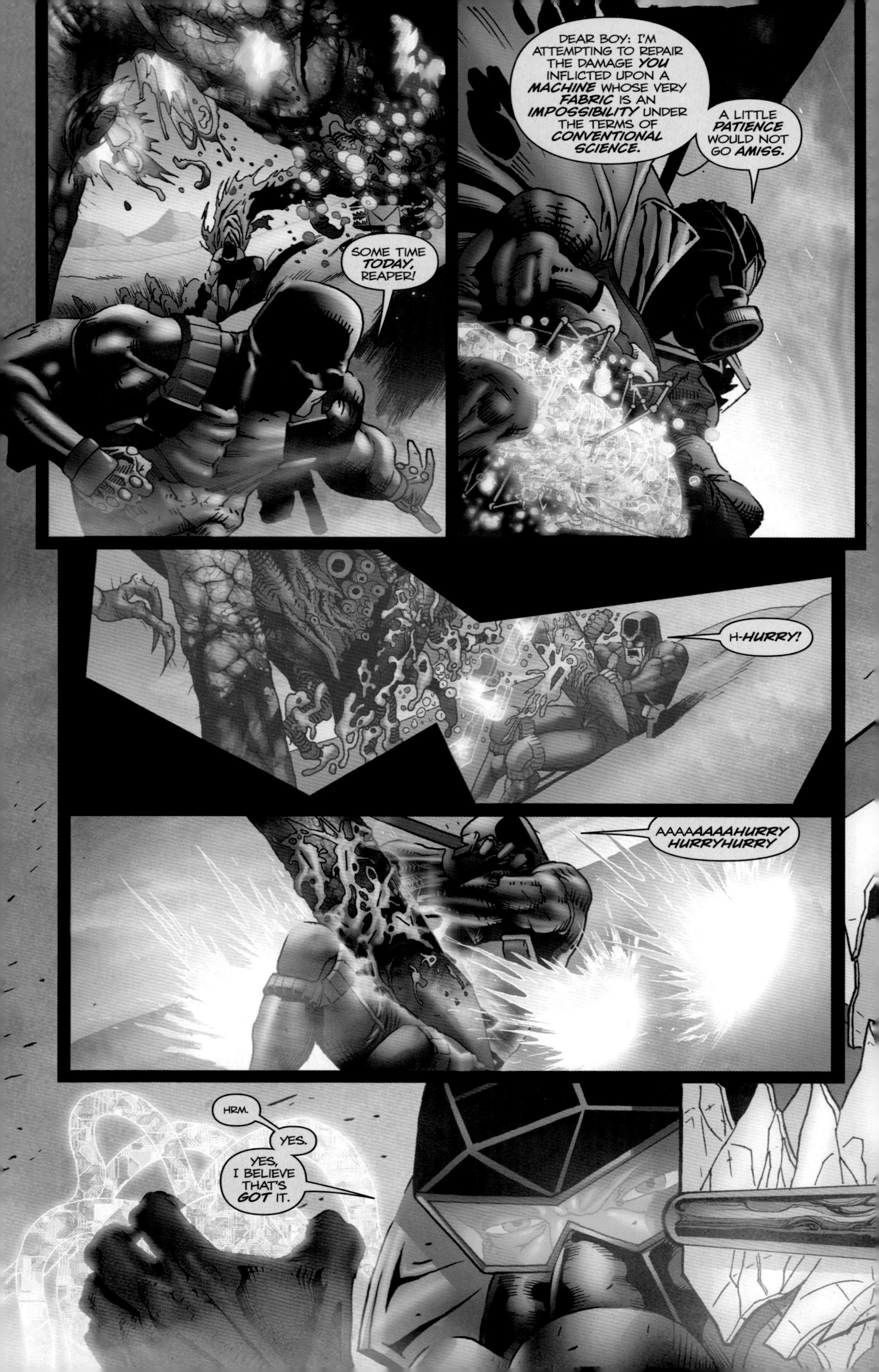

SOME TIME TODAY, REAPER!
DEAR BOY: I'M ATTEMPTING TO REPAIR THE DAMAGE YOU INFLICTED UPON A MACHINE WHOSE VERY FABRIC IS AN IMPOSSIBILITY UNDER THE TERMS OF CONVENTIONAL SCIENCE.
A LITTLE PATIENCE WOULD NOT GO AMISS.
H-HURRY!
AAAAAAAAHURRY HURRYHURRY
HRM.
YES.
YES, I BELIEVE THAT'S GOT IT.

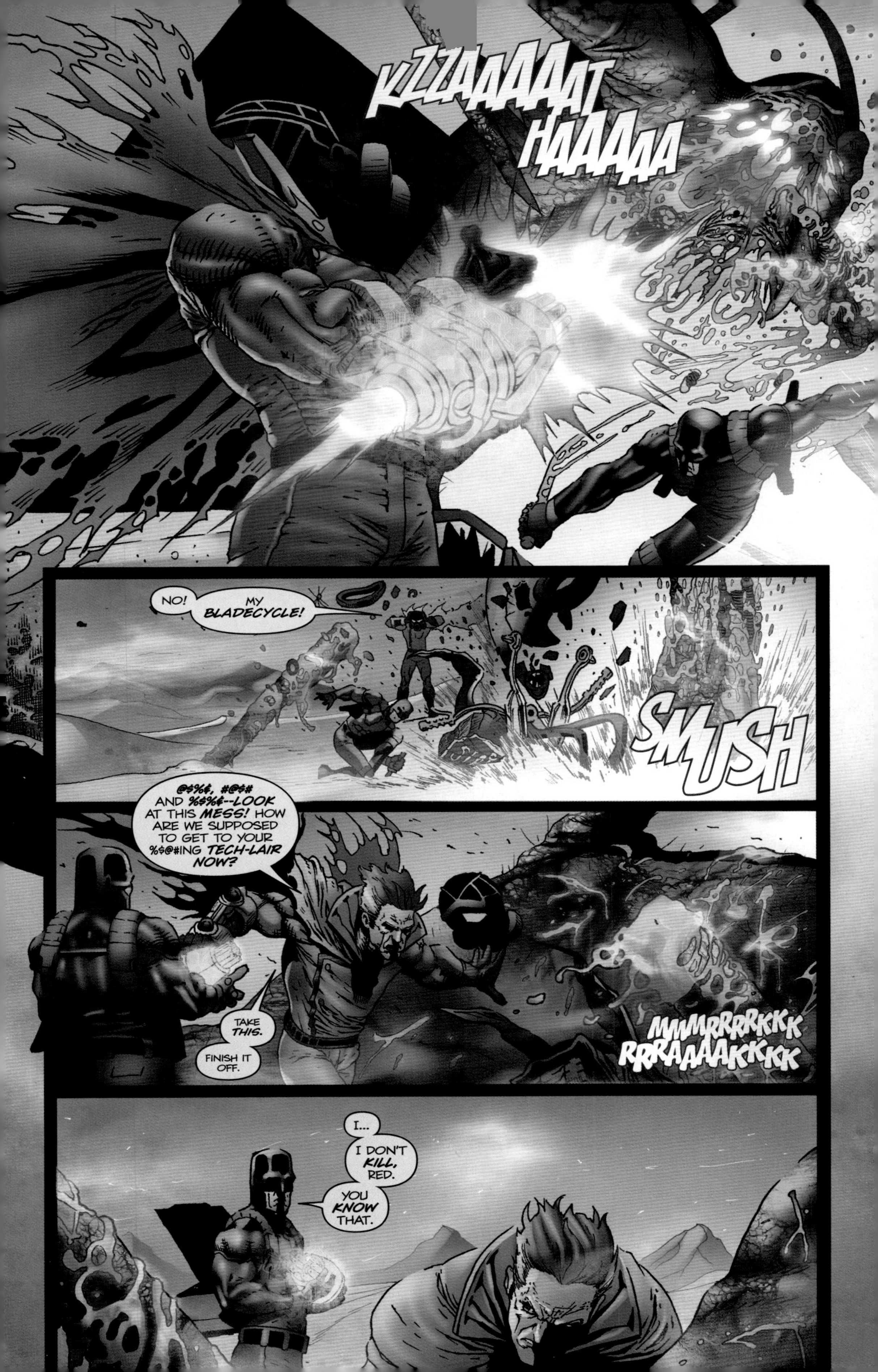
KZZAAAAAAT
HAAAAAA
NO! MY BLADECYCLE!
SMUSH
@$%¢, #@$# AND %$%¢--LOOK AT THIS MESS! HOW ARE WE SUPPOSED TO GET TO YOUR %$@#ING TECH-LAIR NOW?
TAKE THIS.
FINISH IT OFF.
MMMRRRRKKK RRRAAAAKKKK
I...
I DON'T KILL, RED.
YOU KNOW THAT.

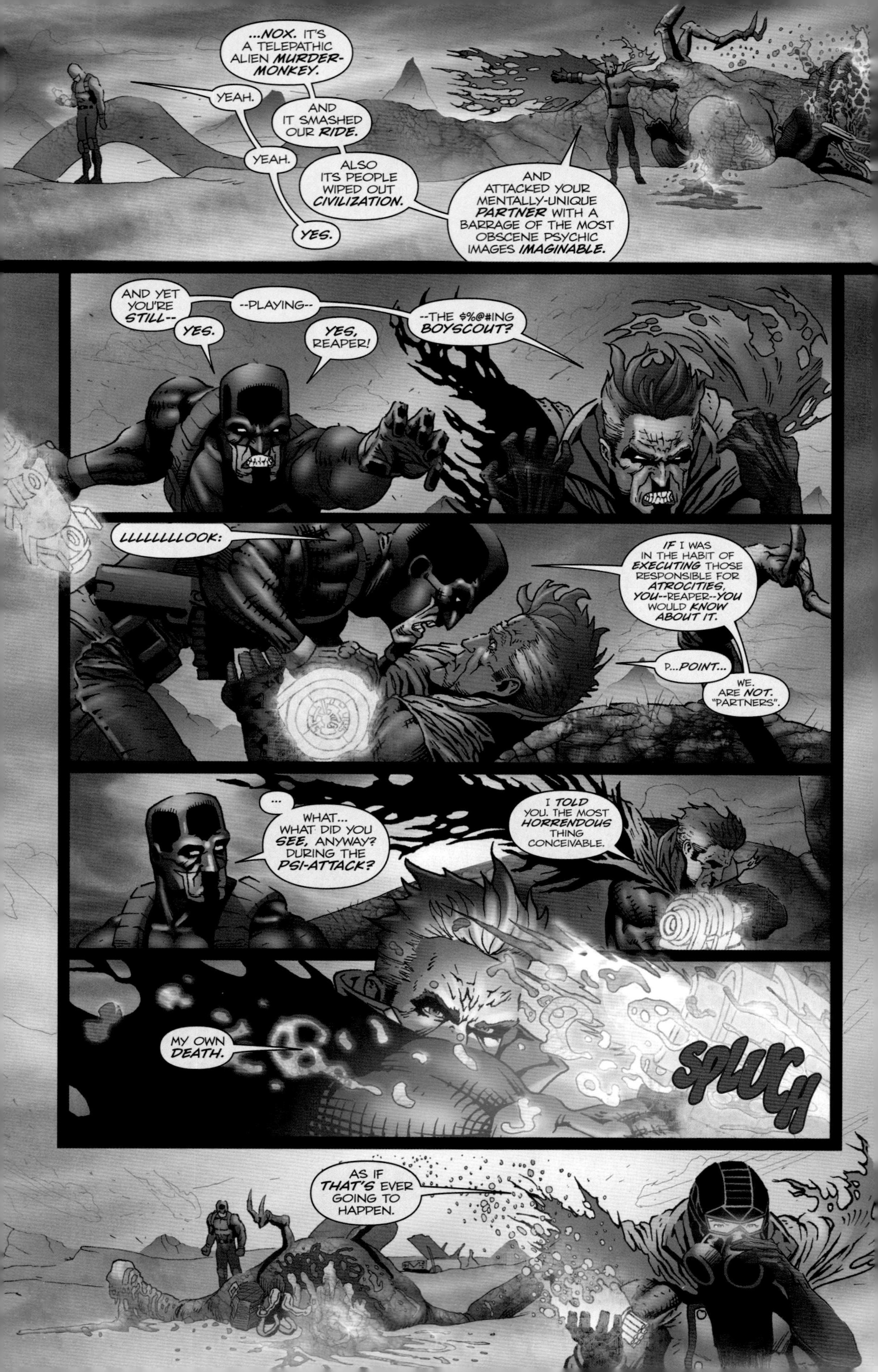
...NOX. IT'S A TELEPATHIC ALIEN MURDER-MONKEY.
YEAH.
AND IT SMASHED OUR RIDE.
YEAH.
ALSO ITS PEOPLE WIPED OUT CIVILIZATION.
YES.
AND ATTACKED YOUR MENTALLY-UNIQUE PARTNER WITH A BARRAGE OF THE MOST OBSCENE PSYCHIC IMAGES IMAGINABLE.
AND YET YOU'RE STILL--
YES.
--PLAYING--
YES, REAPER!
--THE $%@#ING BOYSCOUT?
LLLLLLLLOOK:
IF I WAS IN THE HABIT OF EXECUTING THOSE RESPONSIBLE FOR ATROCITIES, YOU--REAPER--YOU WOULD KNOW ABOUT IT.
P...POINT...
WE. ARE NOT. "PARTNERS".
...
WHAT... WHAT DID YOU SEE, ANYWAY? DURING THE PSI-ATTACK?
I TOLD YOU. THE MOST HORRENDOUS THING CONCEIVABLE.
MY OWN DEATH.
SPLUCH
AS IF THAT'S EVER GOING TO HAPPEN.

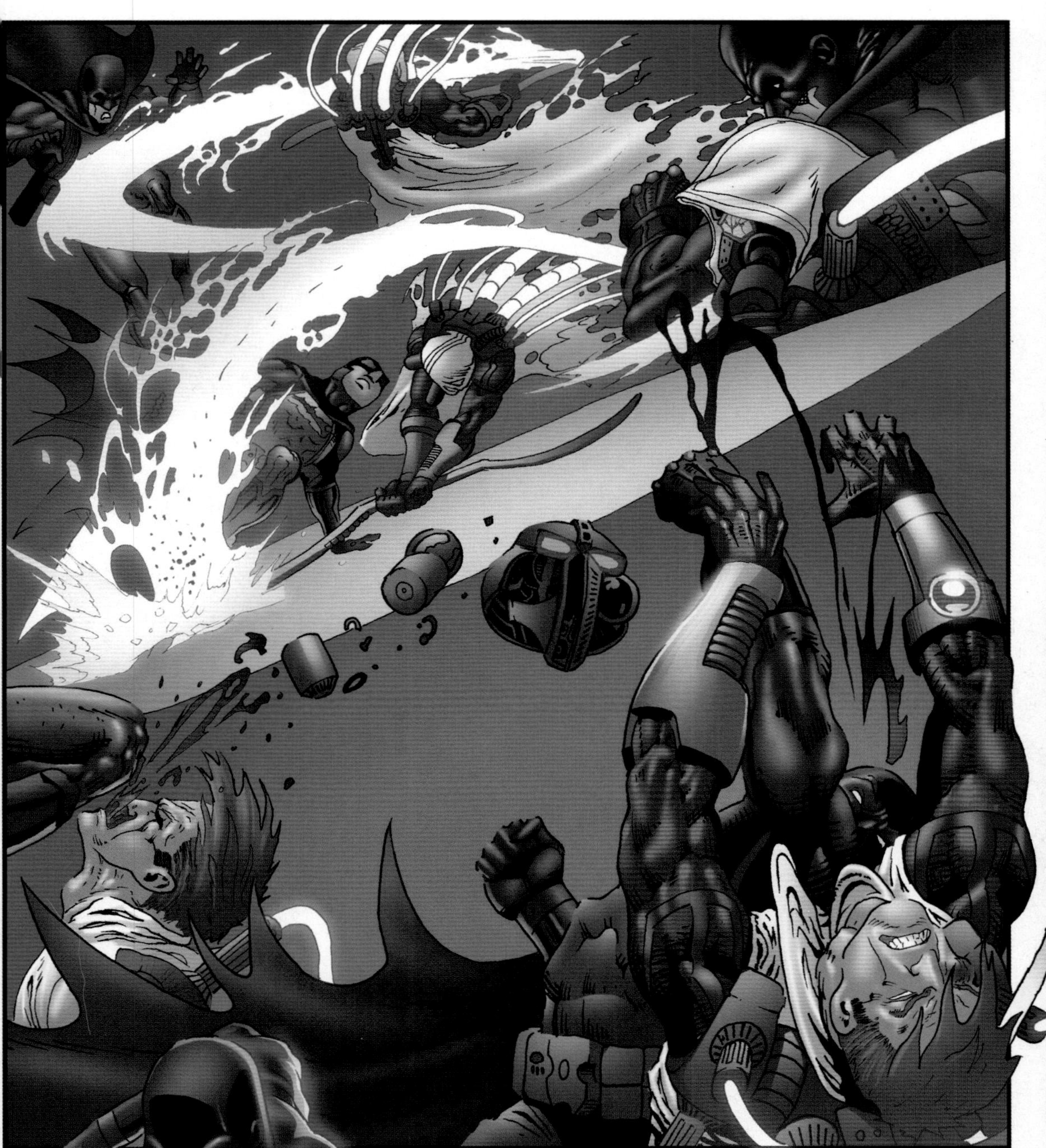

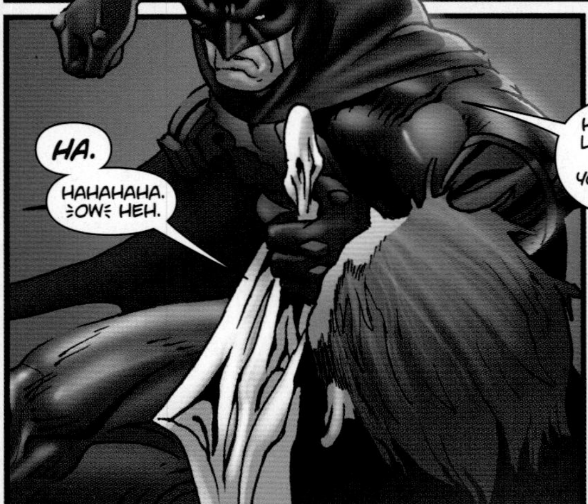
HA.
HAHAHAHA. OW HEH.
HELL'RE YOU LAUGHING AT, VILLAIN? YOU'RE GOING TO JAIL.

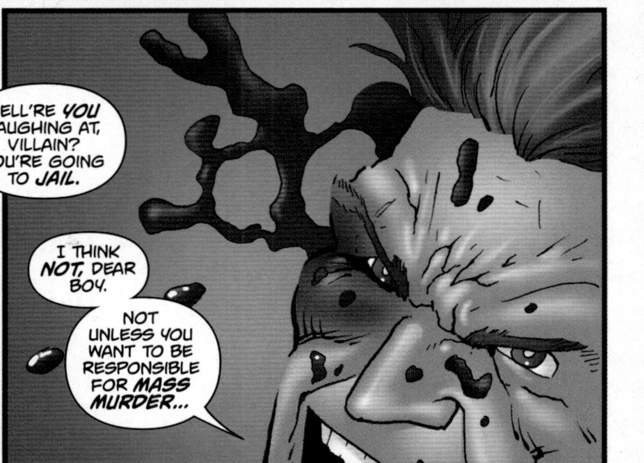
I THINK NOT, DEAR BOY.
NOT UNLESS YOU WANT TO BE RESPONSIBLE FOR MASS MURDER...

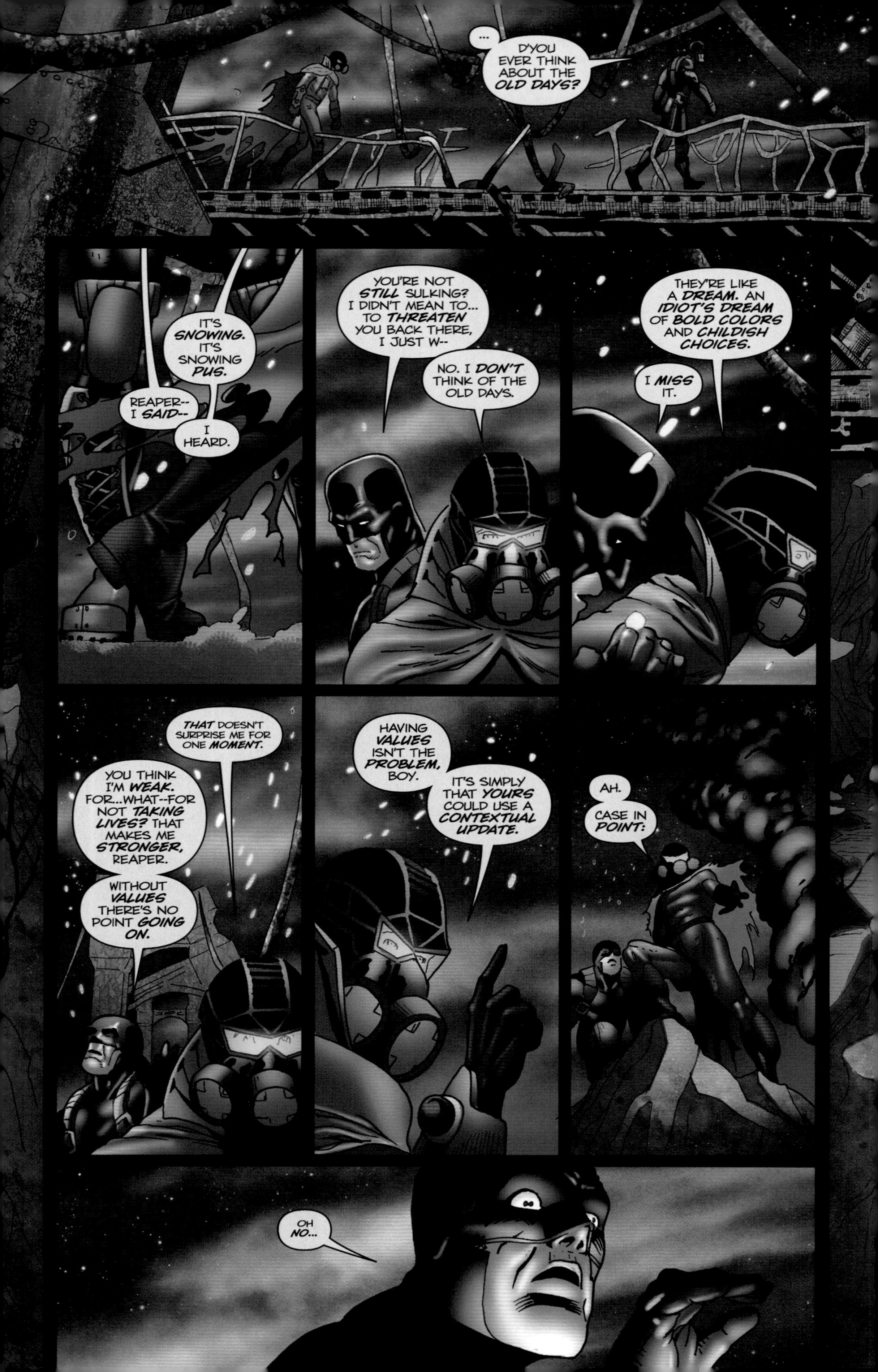
...
D'YOU EVER THINK ABOUT THE OLD DAYS?
IT'S SNOWING. IT'S SNOWING PUS.
REAPER-- I SAID--
I HEARD.
YOU'RE NOT STILL SULKING? I DIDN'T MEAN TO... TO THREATEN YOU BACK THERE, I JUST W--
NO. I DON'T THINK OF THE OLD DAYS.
THEY'RE LIKE A DREAM. AN IDIOT'S DREAM OF BOLD COLORS AND CHILDISH CHOICES.
I MISS IT.
THAT DOESN'T SURPRISE ME FOR ONE MOMENT.
YOU THINK I'M WEAK. FOR...WHAT--FOR NOT TAKING LIVES? THAT MAKES ME STRONGER, REAPER.
WITHOUT VALUES THERE'S NO POINT GOING ON.
HAVING VALUES ISN'T THE PROBLEM, BOY.
IT'S SIMPLY THAT YOURS COULD USE A CONTEXTUAL UPDATE.
AH.
CASE IN POINT:
OH NO...

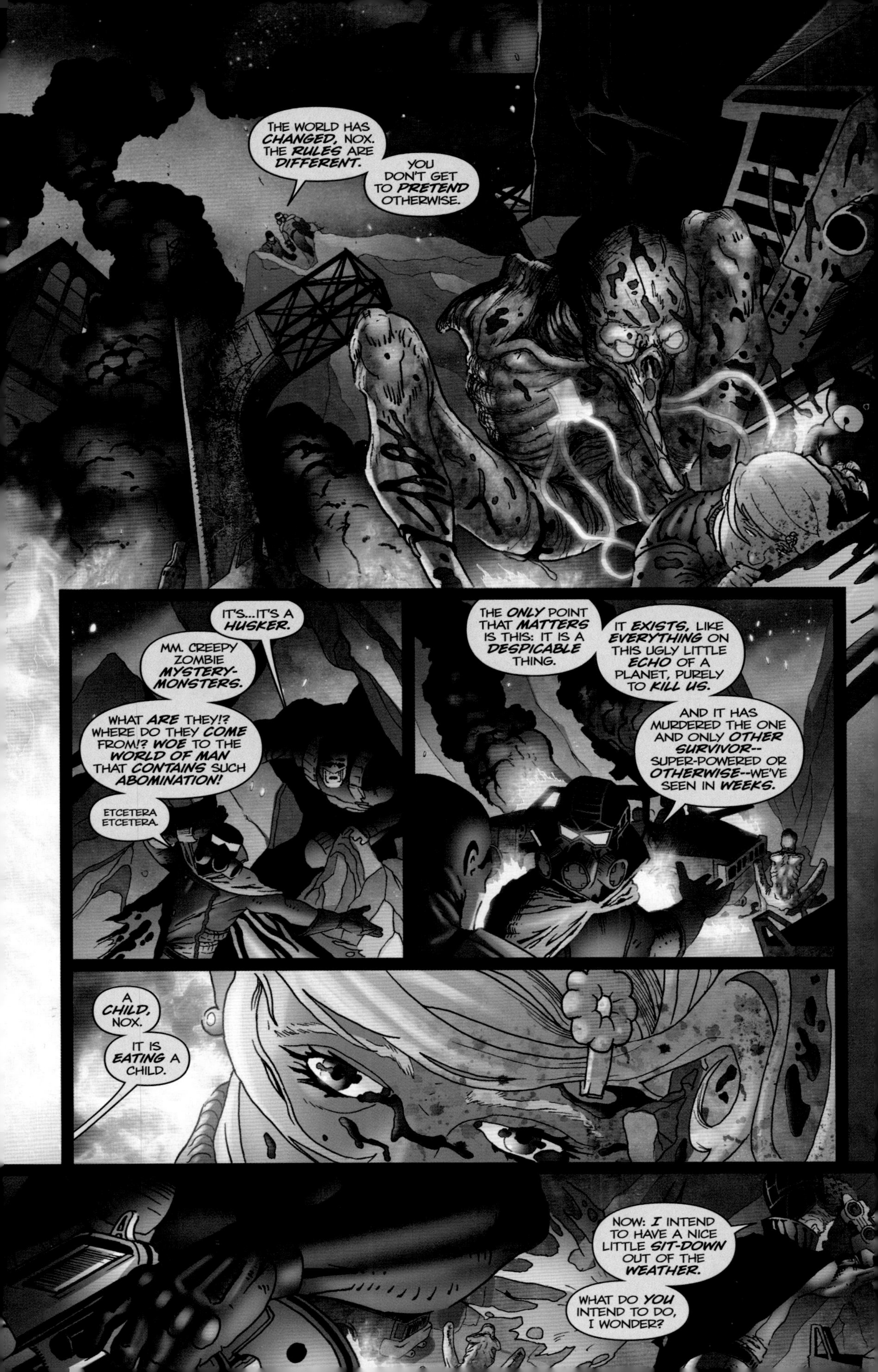

THE WORLD HAS CHANGED, NOX. THE RULES ARE DIFFERENT.
YOU DON'T GET TO PRETEND OTHERWISE.
IT'S...IT'S A HUSKER.
MM. CREEPY ZOMBIE MYSTERY-MONSTERS.
WHAT ARE THEY!? WHERE DO THEY COME FROM!? WOE TO THE WORLD OF MAN THAT CONTAINS SUCH ABOMINATION!
ETCETERA ETCETERA.
THE ONLY POINT THAT MATTERS IS THIS: IT IS A DESPICABLE THING.
IT EXISTS, LIKE EVERYTHING ON THIS UGLY LITTLE ECHO OF A PLANET, PURELY TO KILL US.
AND IT HAS MURDERED THE ONE AND ONLY OTHER SURVIVOR-- SUPER-POWERED OR OTHERWISE--WE'VE SEEN IN WEEKS.
A CHILD, NOX.
IT IS EATING A CHILD.
NOW: I INTEND TO HAVE A NICE LITTLE SIT-DOWN OUT OF THE WEATHER.
WHAT DO YOU INTEND TO DO, I WONDER?

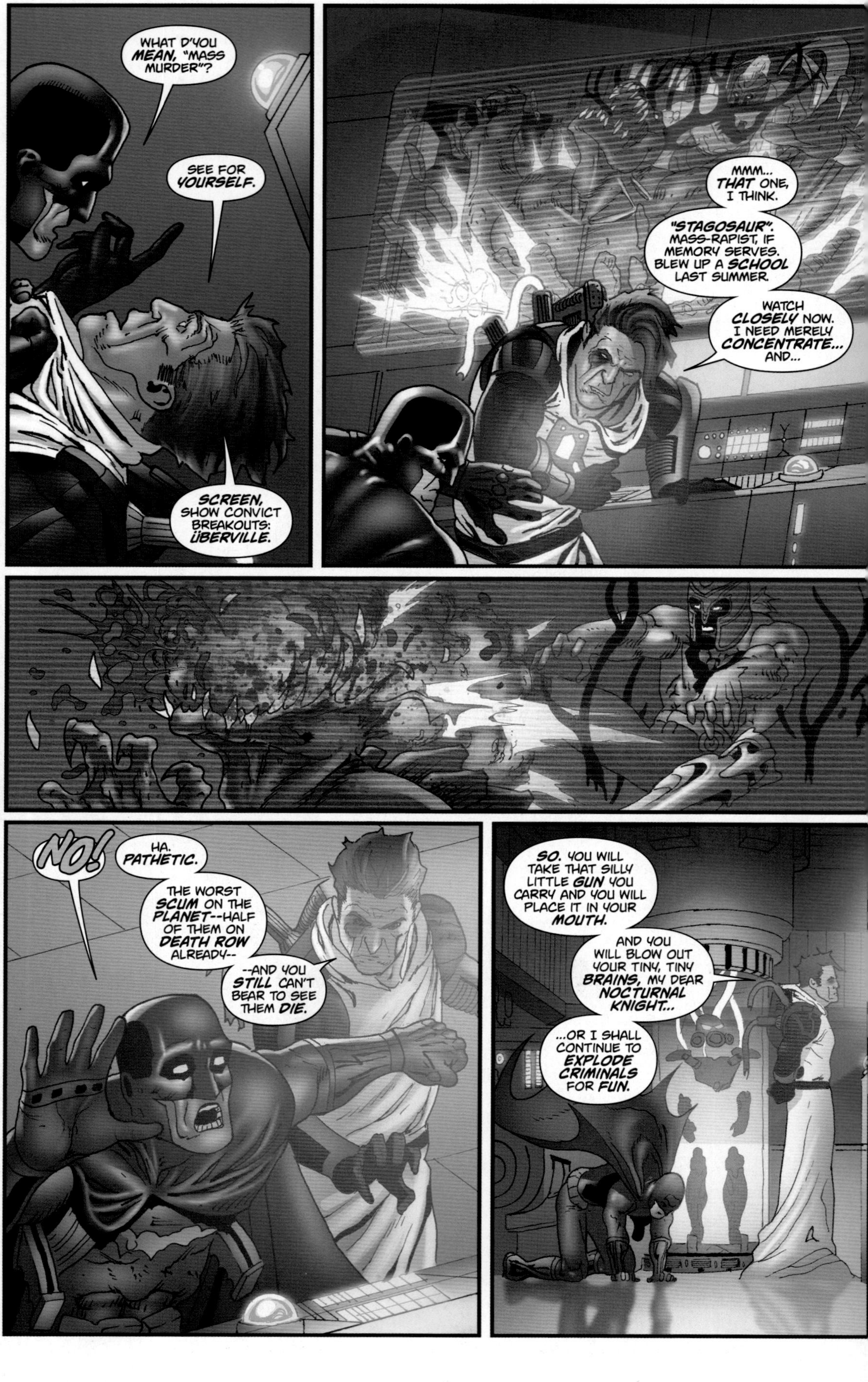
WHAT D'YOU MEAN, "MASS MURDER"?
SEE FOR YOURSELF.
SCREEN, SHOW CONVICT BREAKOUTS: ÜBERVILLE.
MMM... THAT ONE, I THINK.
"STAGOSAUR". MASS-RAPIST, IF MEMORY SERVES. BLEW UP A SCHOOL LAST SUMMER.
WATCH CLOSELY NOW. I NEED MERELY CONCENTRATE... AND...
NO!
HA. PATHETIC.
THE WORST SCUM ON THE PLANET--HALF OF THEM ON DEATH ROW ALREADY--
--AND YOU STILL CAN'T BEAR TO SEE THEM DIE.
SO. YOU WILL TAKE THAT SILLY LITTLE GUN YOU CARRY AND YOU WILL PLACE IT IN YOUR MOUTH.
AND YOU WILL BLOW OUT YOUR TINY, TINY BRAINS, MY DEAR NOCTURNAL KNIGHT...
...OR I SHALL CONTINUE TO EXPLODE CRIMINALS FOR FUN.

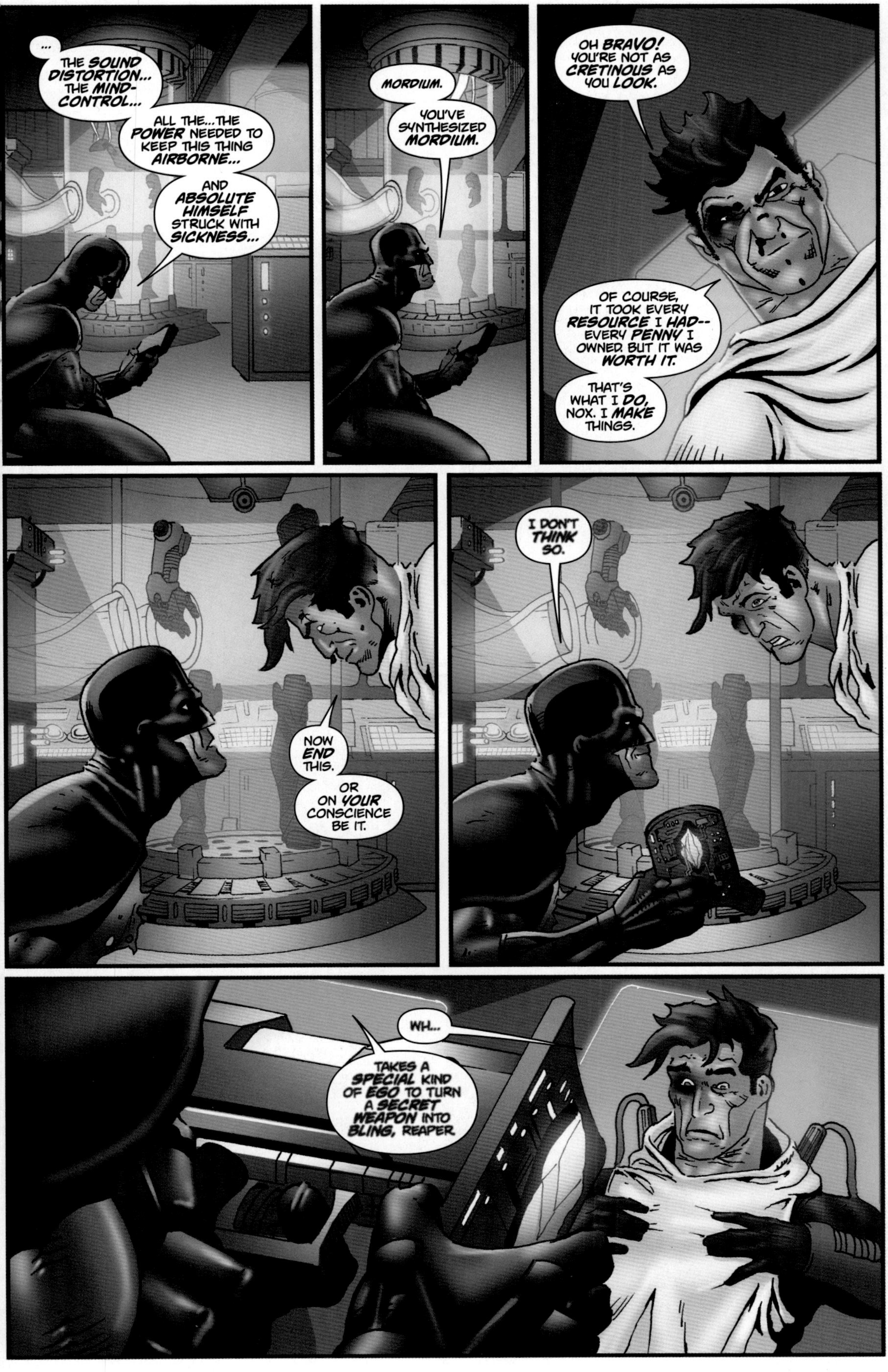
...
THE SOUND DISTORTION... THE MIND-CONTROL...
ALL THE...THE POWER NEEDED TO KEEP THIS THING AIRBORNE...
AND ABSOLUTE HIMSELF STRUCK WITH SICKNESS...
MORDIUM.
YOU'VE SYNTHESIZED MORDIUM.
OH BRAVO! YOU'RE NOT AS CRETINOUS AS YOU LOOK.
OF COURSE, IT TOOK EVERY RESOURCE I HAD-- EVERY PENNY I OWNED. BUT IT WAS WORTH IT.
THAT'S WHAT I DO, NOX. I MAKE THINGS.
NOW END THIS.
OR ON YOUR CONSCIENCE BE IT.
I DON'T THINK SO.
WH...
TAKES A SPECIAL KIND OF EGO TO TURN A SECRET WEAPON INTO BLING, REAPER

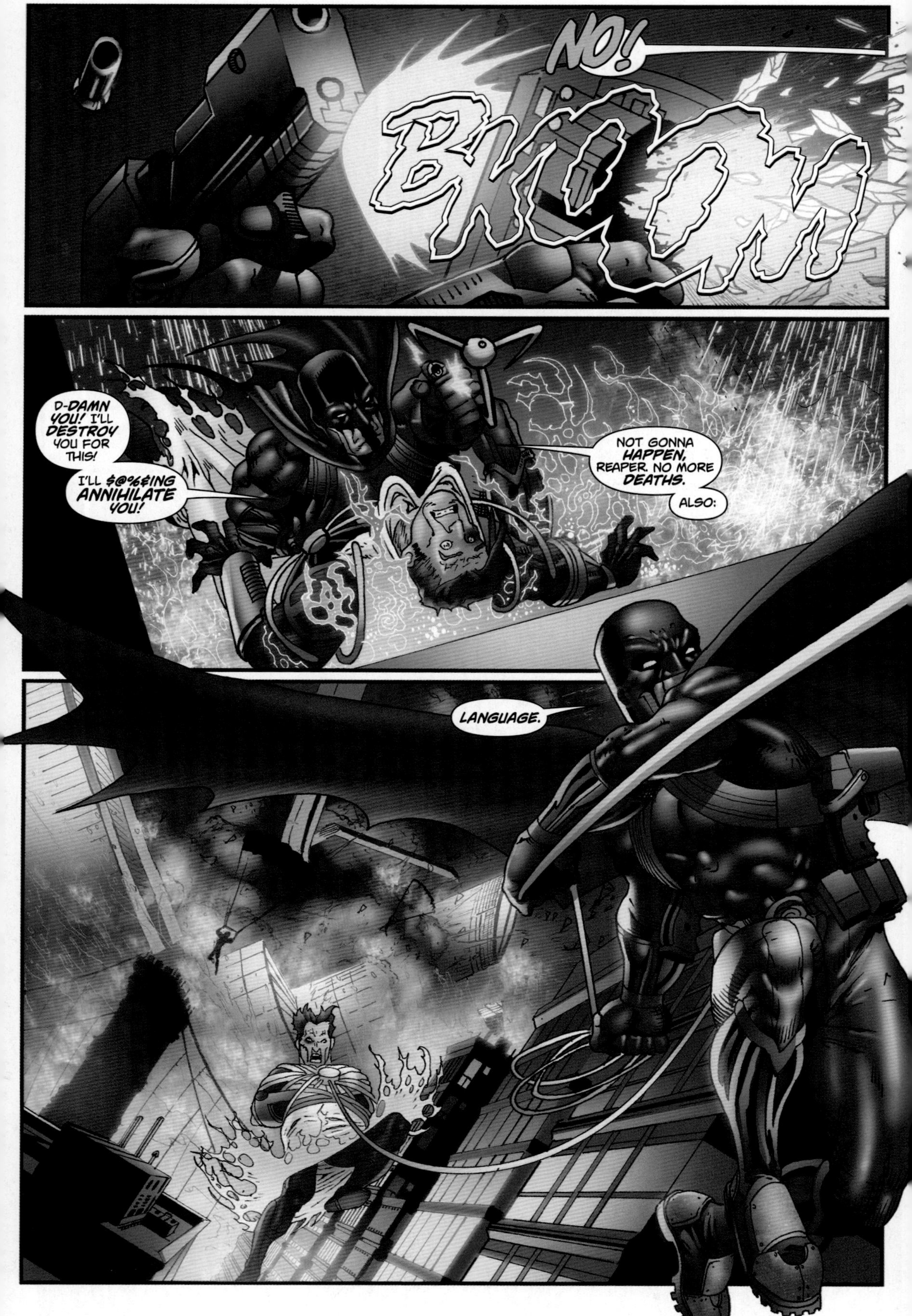
NO!
BKOOM
D-DAMN YOU! I'LL DESTROY YOU FOR THIS!
I'LL $@%&ING ANNIHILATE YOU!
NOT GONNA HAPPEN, REAPER. NO MORE DEATHS.
ALSO:
LANGUAGE.

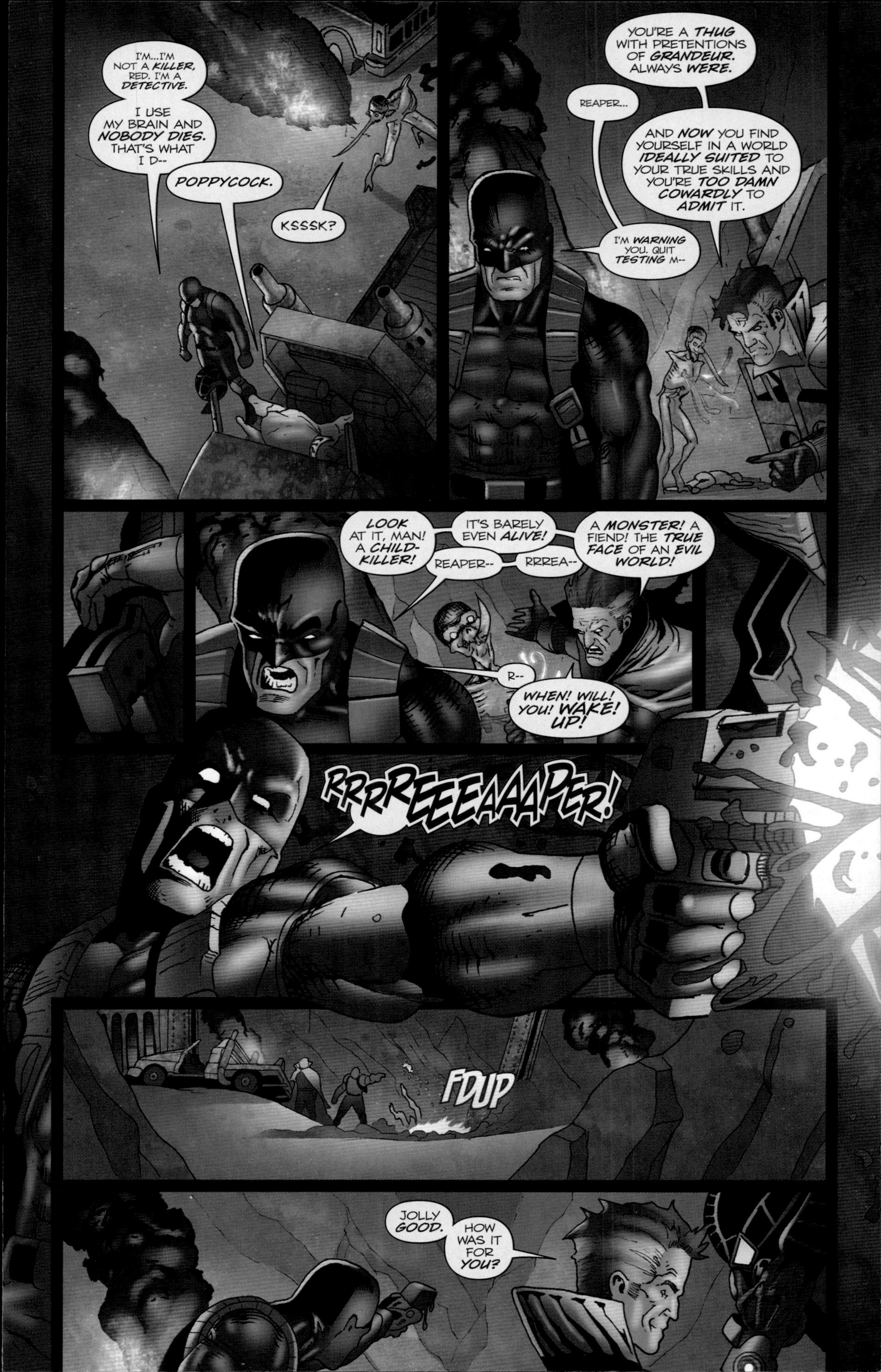

I'M...I'M NOT A *KILLER*, RED. I'M A *DETECTIVE*.
I USE MY BRAIN AND *NOBODY DIES*. THAT'S WHAT I D--
*POPPYCOCK*.
KSSSK?
REAPER...
YOU'RE A *THUG* WITH PRETENTIONS OF *GRANDEUR*. ALWAYS *WERE*.
AND *NOW* YOU FIND YOURSELF IN A WORLD *IDEALLY SUITED* TO YOUR TRUE SKILLS AND YOU'RE *TOO DAMN COWARDLY* TO *ADMIT* IT.
I'M *WARNING* YOU. QUIT *TESTING* M--
*LOOK* AT IT, MAN! A *CHILD-KILLER*!
IT'S BARELY EVEN *ALIVE*!
A *MONSTER*! A FIEND! THE *TRUE FACE* OF AN *EVIL WORLD*!
REAPER--
RRREA--
R--
*WHEN! WILL! YOU! WAKE! UP!*
RRRREEEAAAPER!
FDUP
JOLLY *GOOD*.
HOW WAS IT FOR *YOU*?

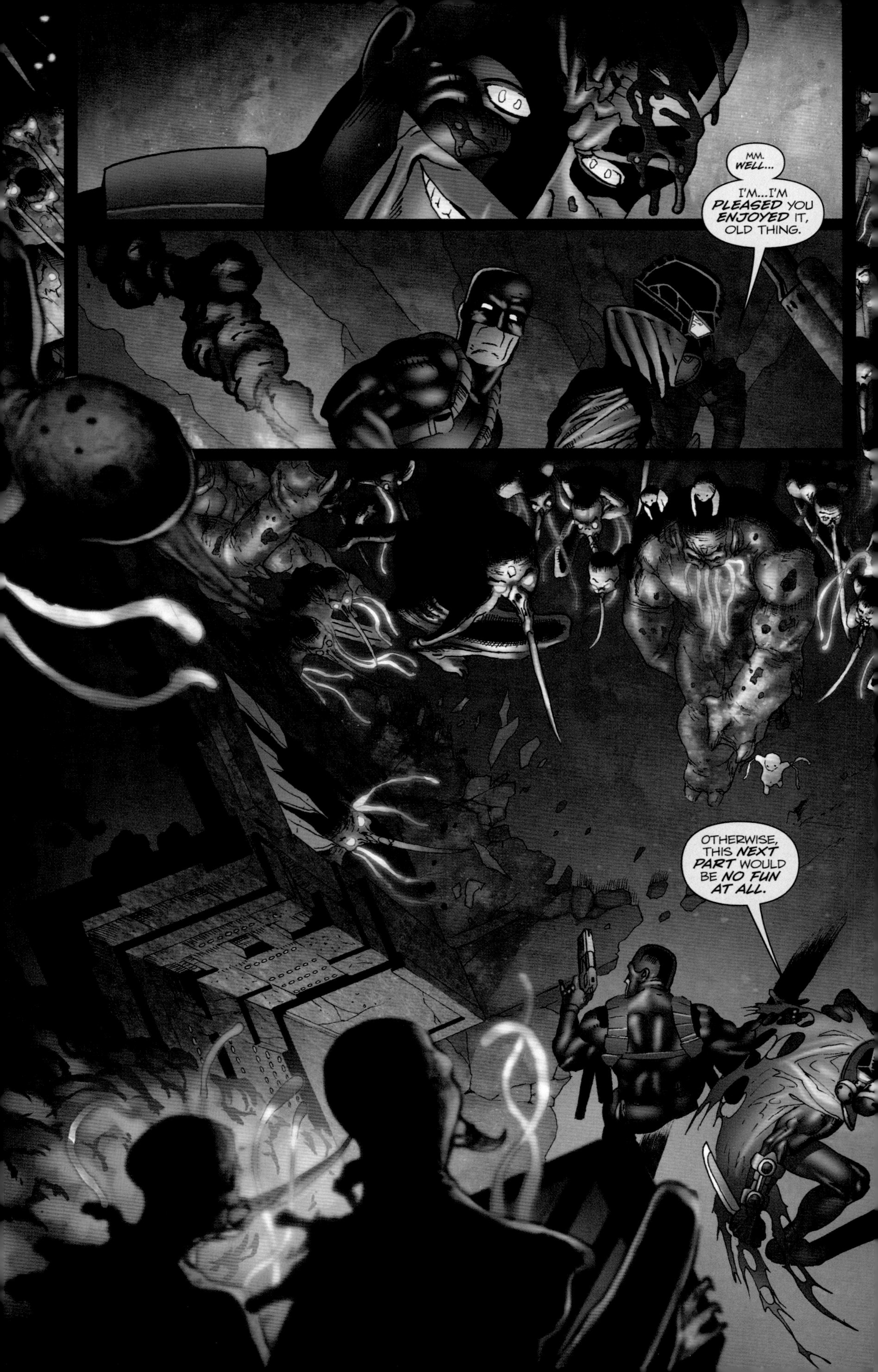
MM. WELL...
I'M...I'M PLEASED YOU ENJOYED IT, OLD THING.
OTHERWISE, THIS NEXT PART WOULD BE NO FUN AT ALL.

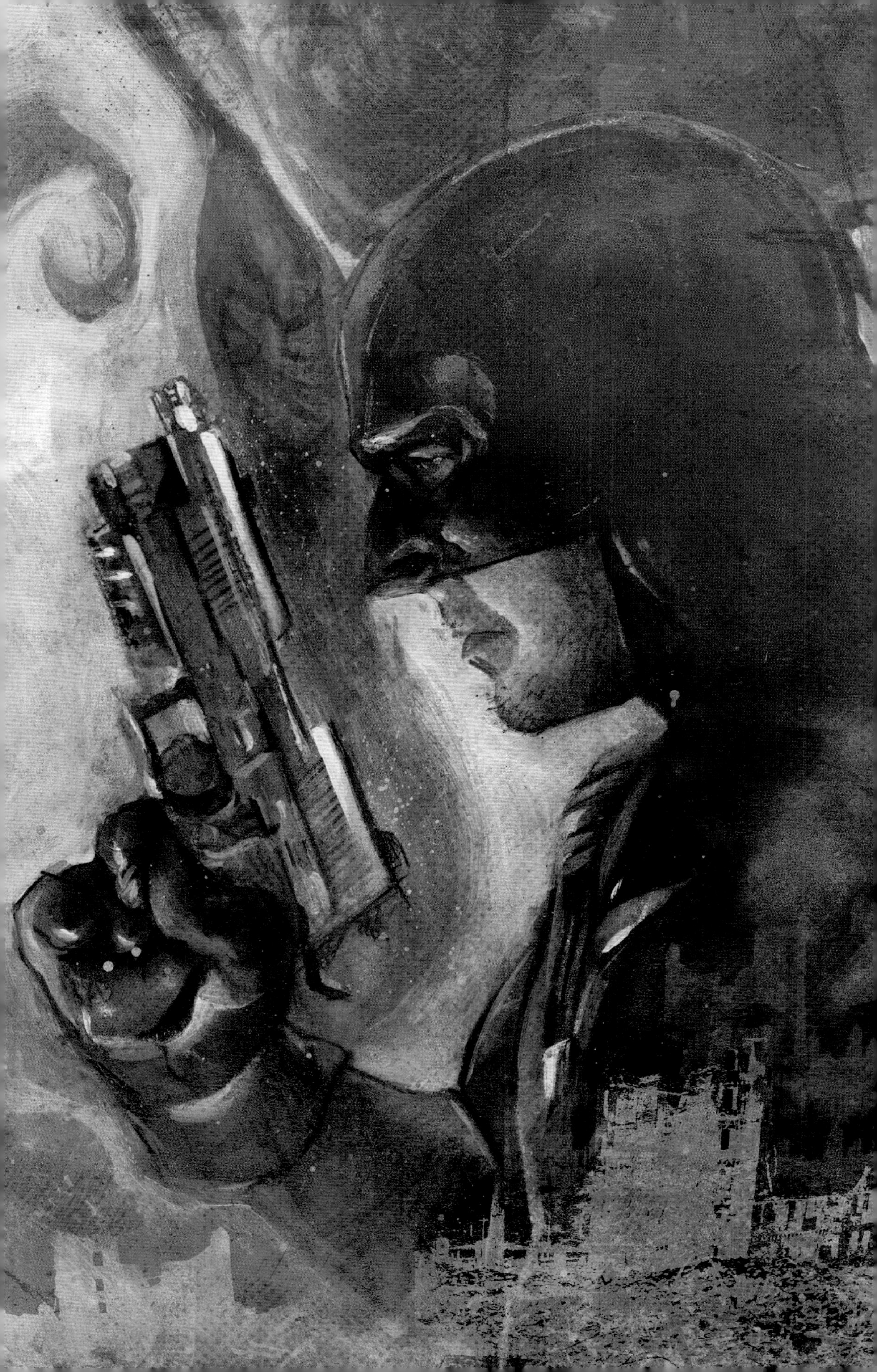

# CHAPTER TWO

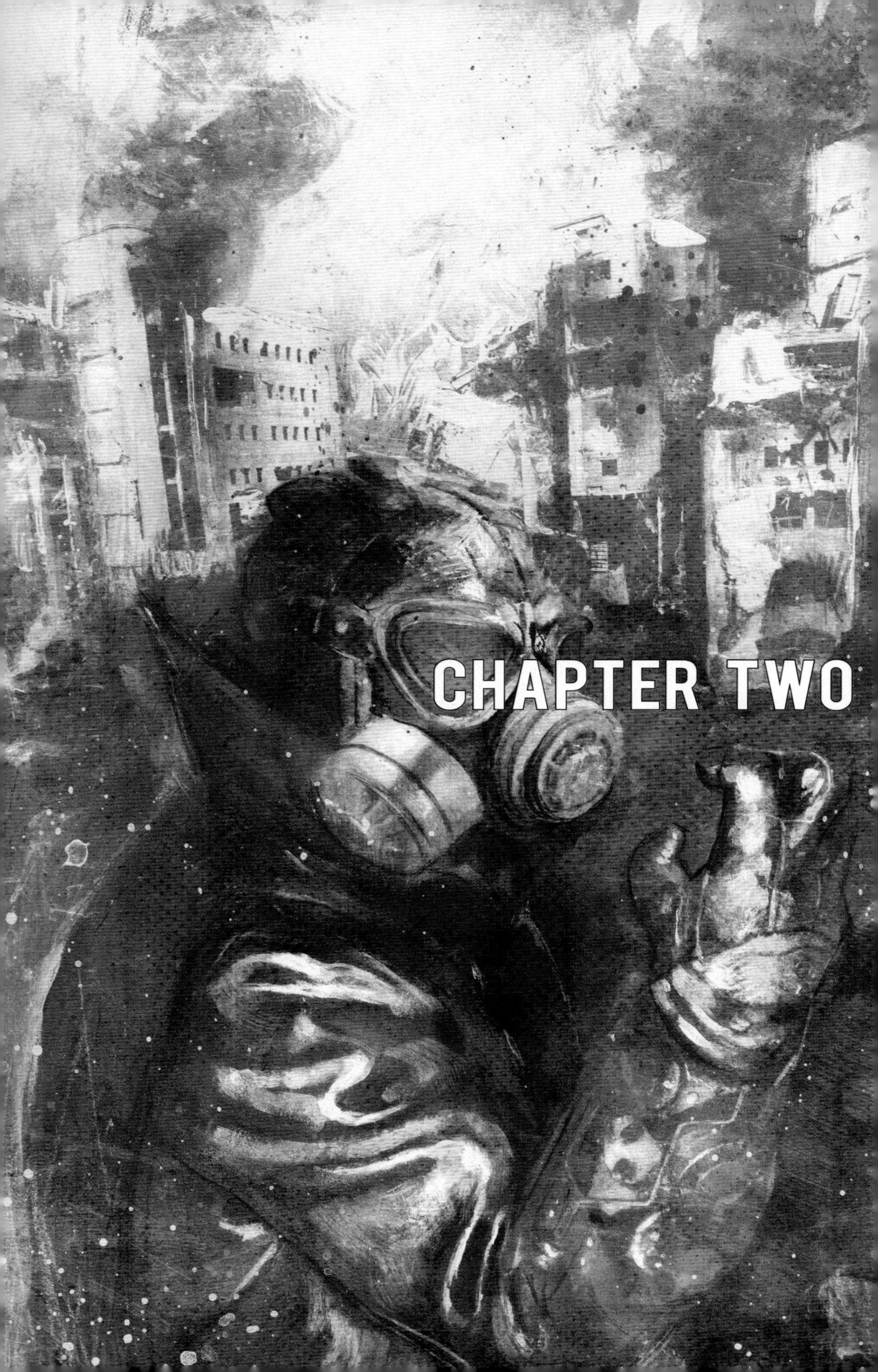

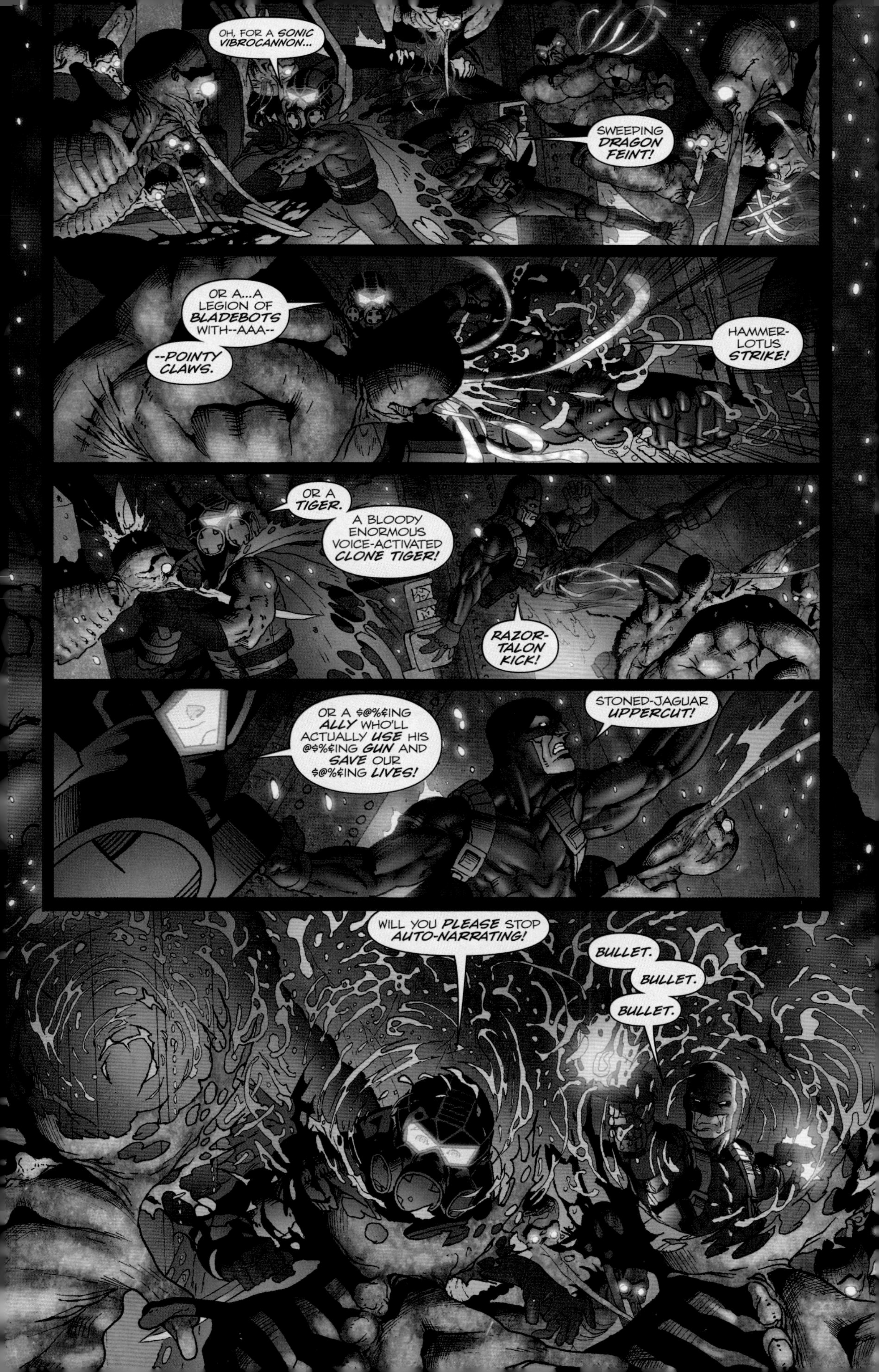
OH, FOR A SONIC VIBROCANNON...
SWEEPING DRAGON FEINT!
OR A...A LEGION OF BLADEBOTS WITH--AAA--
--POINTY CLAWS.
HAMMER-LOTUS STRIKE!
OR A TIGER.
A BLOODY ENORMOUS VOICE-ACTIVATED CLONE TIGER!
RAZOR-TALON KICK!
OR A $@%¢ING ALLY WHO'LL ACTUALLY USE HIS @$%¢ING GUN AND SAVE OUR $@%¢ING LIVES!
STONED-JAGUAR UPPERCUT!
WILL YOU PLEASE STOP AUTO-NARRATING!
BULLET.
BULLET.
BULLET.

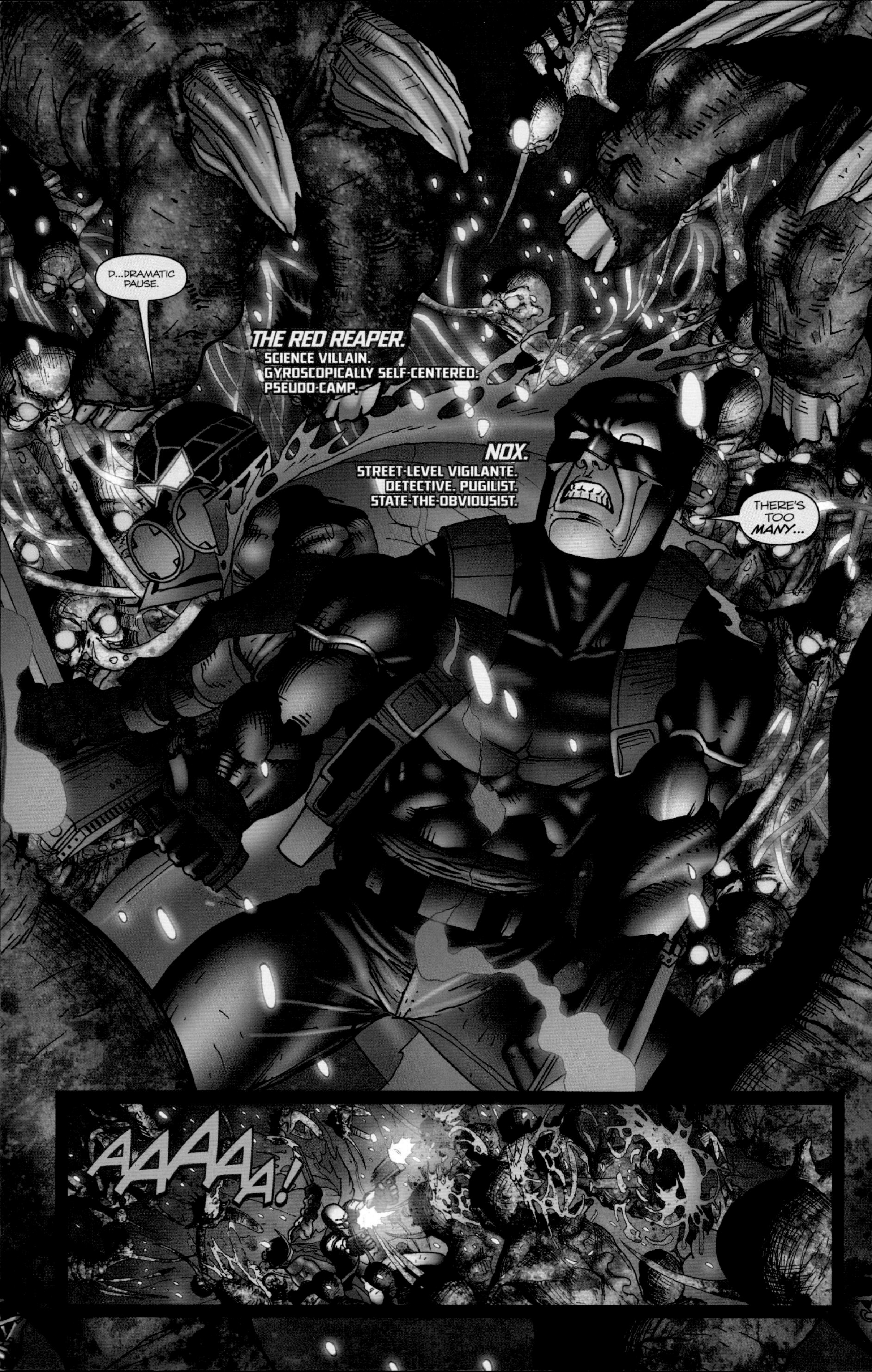

D...DRAMATIC PAUSE.
THE RED REAPER.
SCIENCE VILLAIN.
GYROSCOPICALLY SELF-CENTERED.
PSEUDO-CAMP.
NOX.
STREET-LEVEL VIGILANTE.
DETECTIVE. PUGILIST.
STATE-THE-OBVIOUSIST.
THERE'S TOO MANY...
AAAAA!

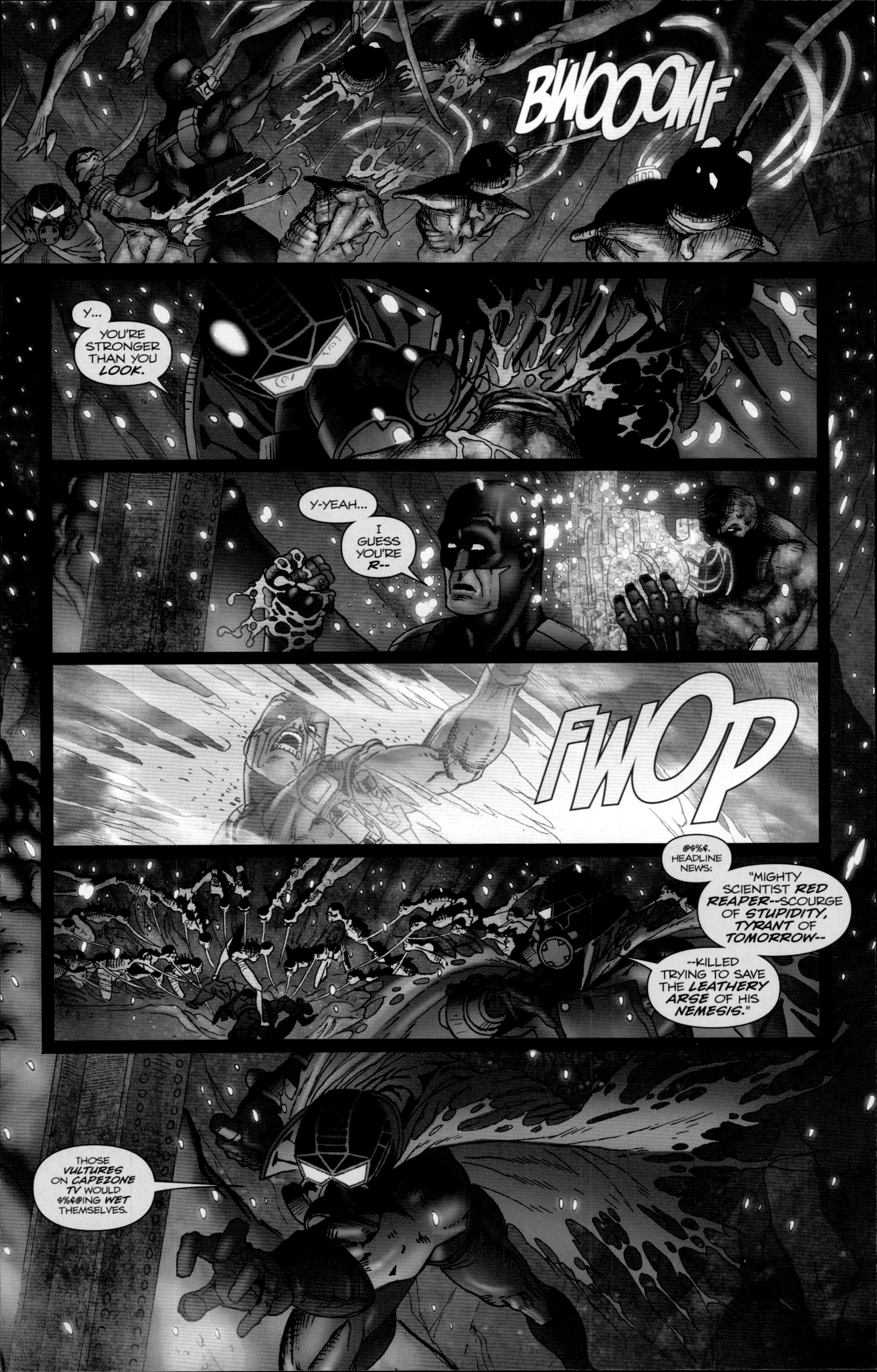

BWOOOMF
Y... YOU'RE STRONGER THAN YOU LOOK.
Y-YEAH... I GUESS YOU'RE R--
FWOP
@$%$. HEADLINE NEWS:
"MIGHTY SCIENTIST RED REAPER--SCOURGE OF STUPIDITY, TYRANT OF TOMORROW--
--KILLED TRYING TO SAVE THE LEATHERY ARSE OF HIS NEMESIS."
THOSE VULTURES ON CAPEZONE TV WOULD $%$@ING WET THEMSELVES.

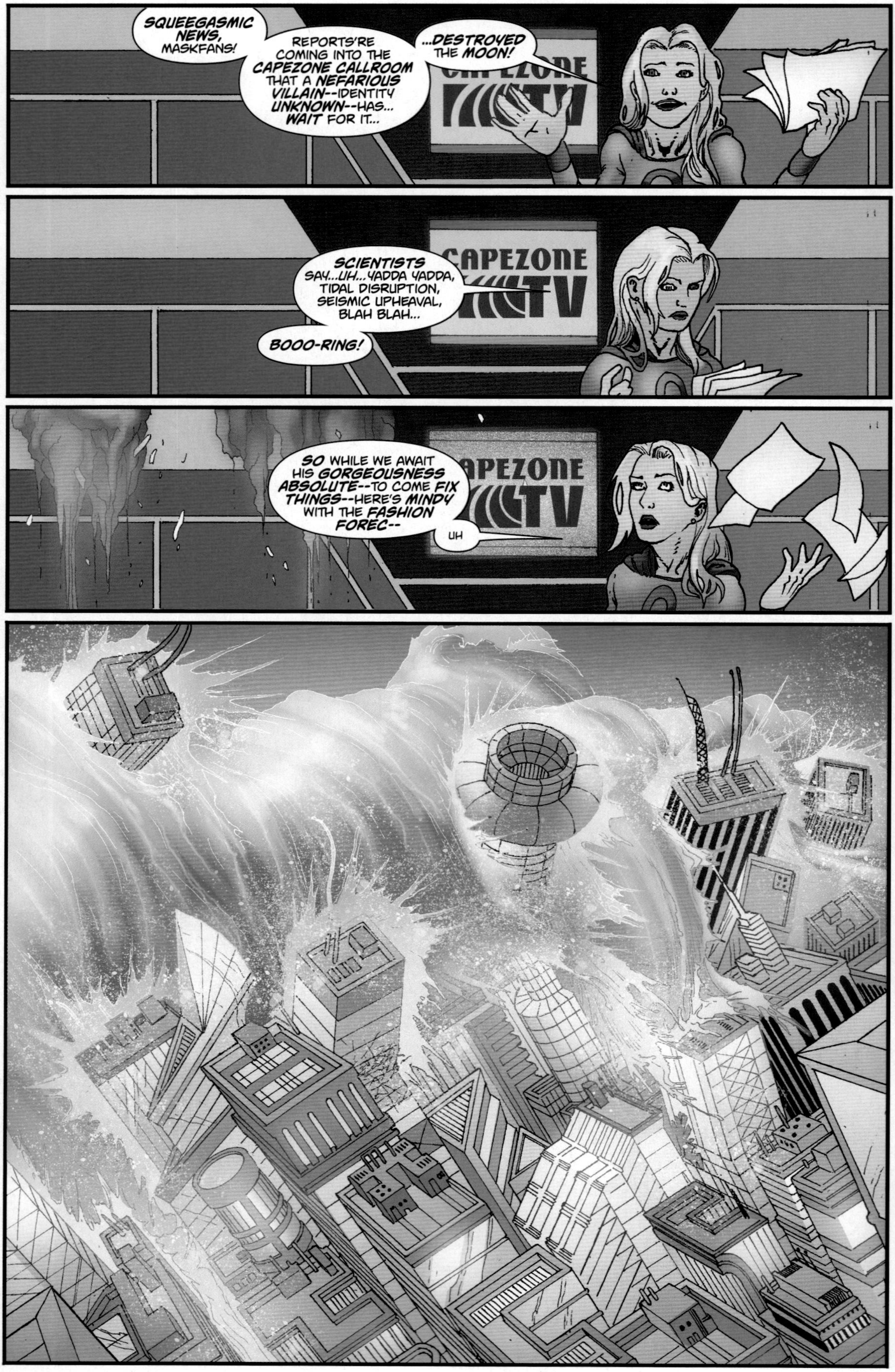

SQUEEGASMIC NEWS, MASKFANS!
REPORTS'RE COMING INTO THE CAPEZONE CALLROOM THAT A NEFARIOUS VILLAIN--IDENTITY UNKNOWN--HAS... WAIT FOR IT...
...DESTROYED THE MOON!
CAPEZONE TV
SCIENTISTS SAY...UH...YADDA YADDA, TIDAL DISRUPTION, SEISMIC UPHEAVAL, BLAH BLAH...
BOOO-RING!
SO WHILE WE AWAIT HIS GORGEOUSNESS ABSOLUTE--TO COME FIX THINGS--HERE'S MINDY WITH THE FASHION FOREC--
UH

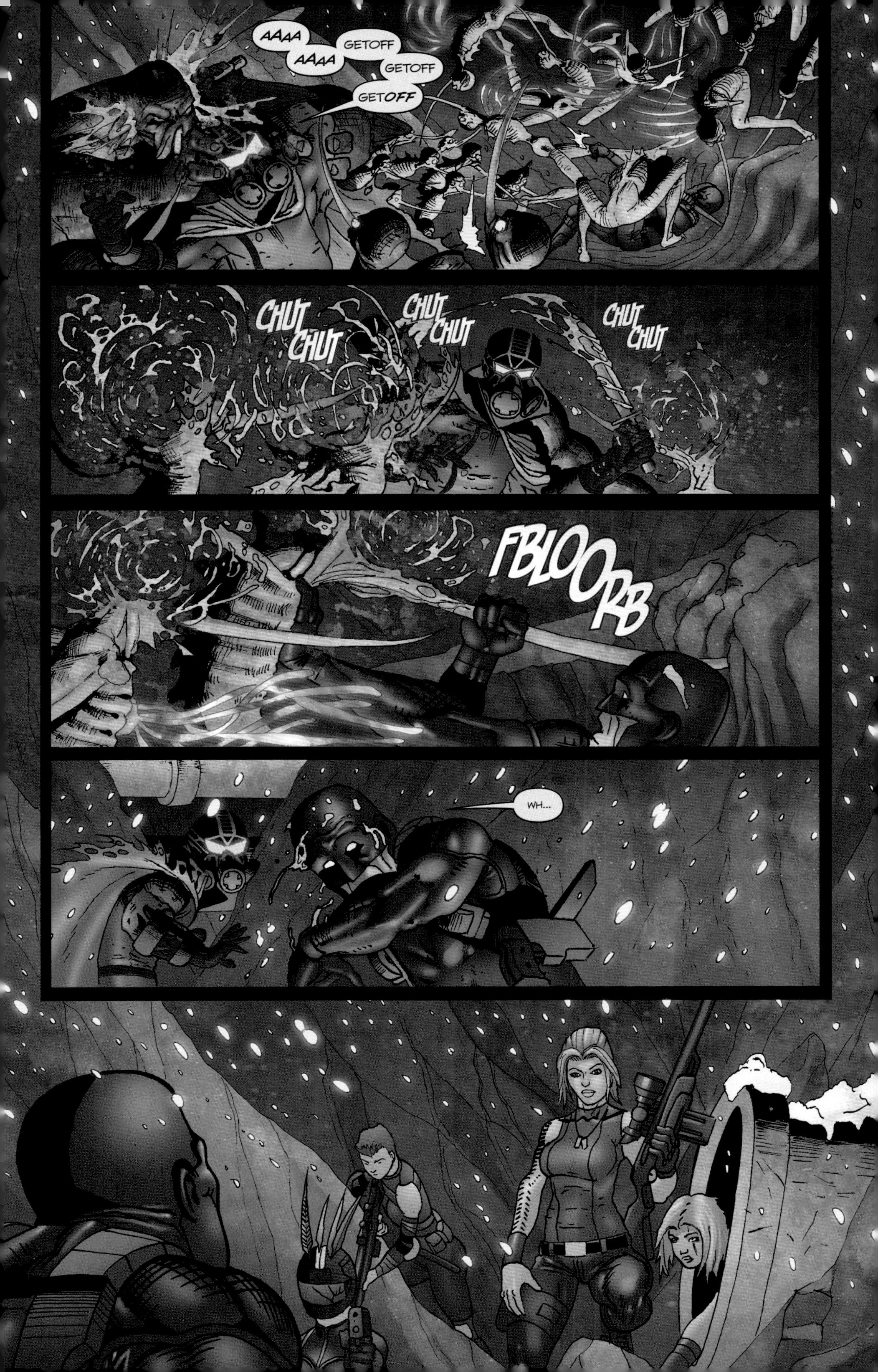
AAAA
AAAA
GETOFF
GETOFF
GETOFF
CHUT CHUT
CHUT CHUT
CHUT CHUT
FBLOORB
WH...

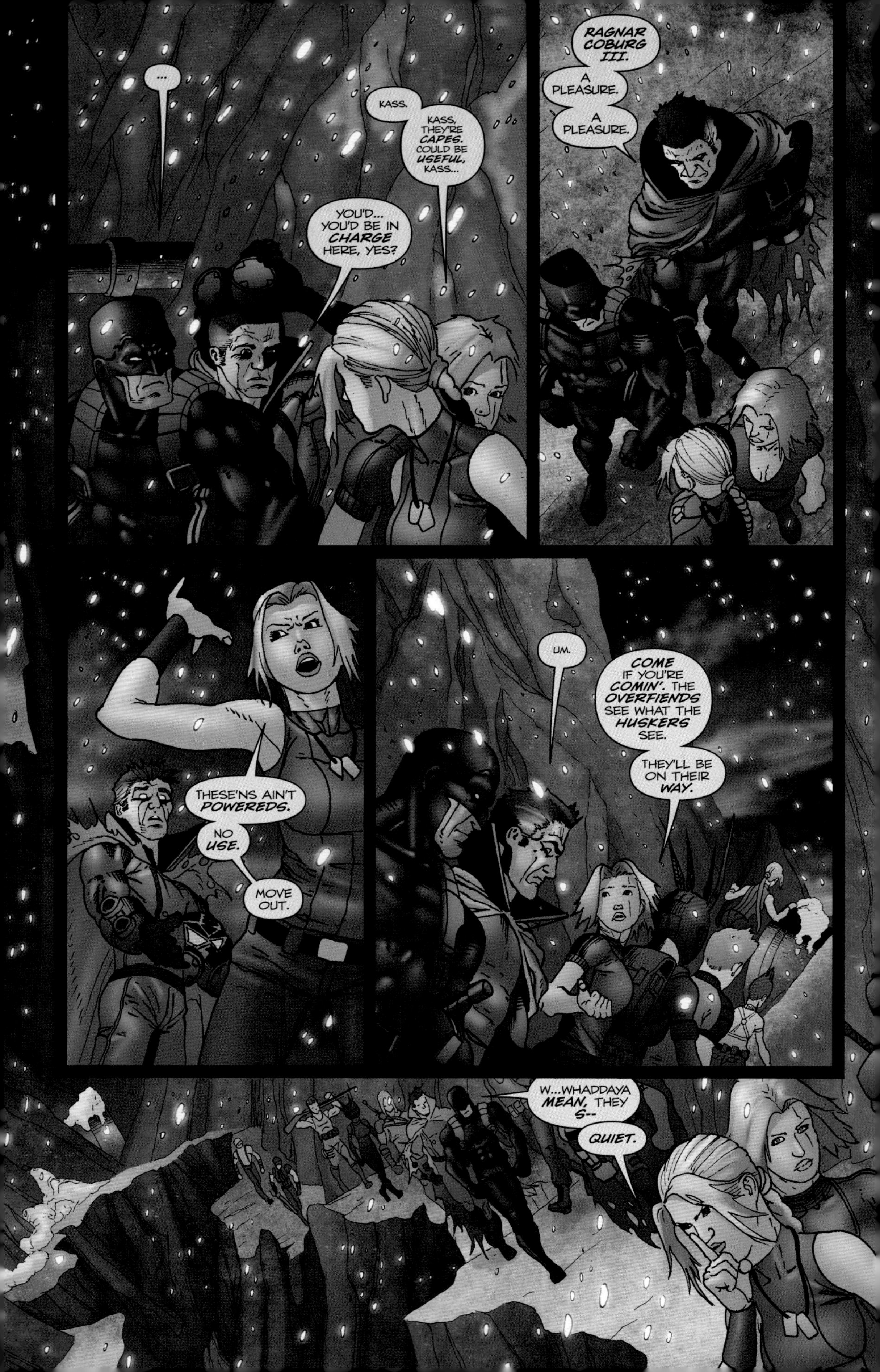
...
KASS.
KASS, THEY'RE CAPES. COULD BE USEFUL, KASS...
YOU'D... YOU'D BE IN CHARGE HERE, YES?
RAGNAR COBURG III.
A PLEASURE.
A PLEASURE.
THESE'NS AIN'T POWEREDS.
NO USE.
MOVE OUT.
UM.
COME IF YOU'RE COMIN'. THE OVERFIENDS SEE WHAT THE HUSKERS SEE.
THEY'LL BE ON THEIR WAY.
W...WHADDAYA MEAN, THEY S--
QUIET.

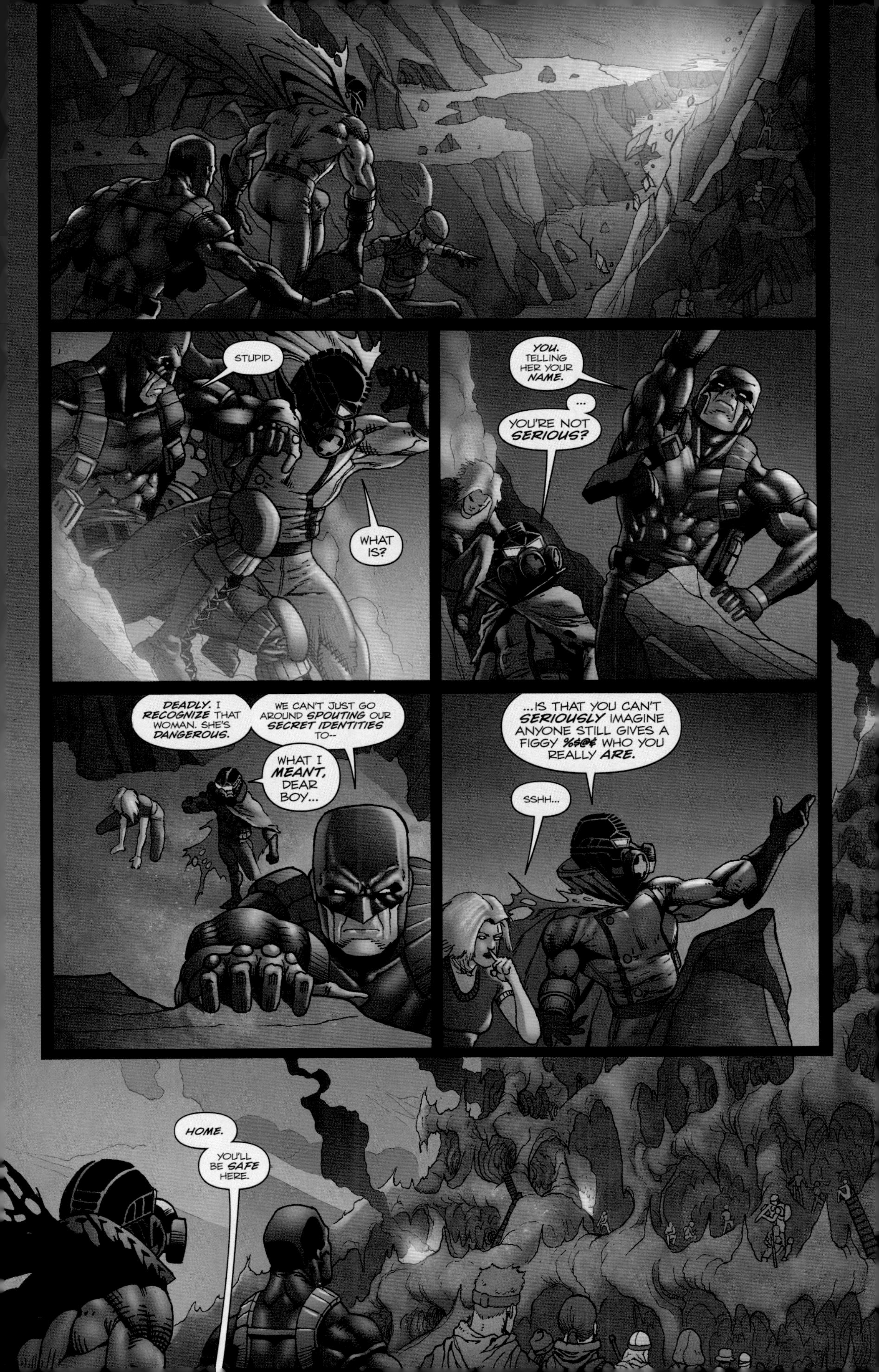
STUPID.
WHAT IS?
YOU. TELLING HER YOUR NAME.
...
YOU'RE NOT SERIOUS?
DEADLY. I RECOGNIZE THAT WOMAN. SHE'S DANGEROUS.
WE CAN'T JUST GO AROUND SPOUTING OUR SECRET IDENTITIES TO--
WHAT I MEANT, DEAR BOY...
...IS THAT YOU CAN'T SERIOUSLY IMAGINE ANYONE STILL GIVES A FIGGY %$@¢ WHO YOU REALLY ARE.
SSHH...
HOME.
YOU'LL BE SAFE HERE.

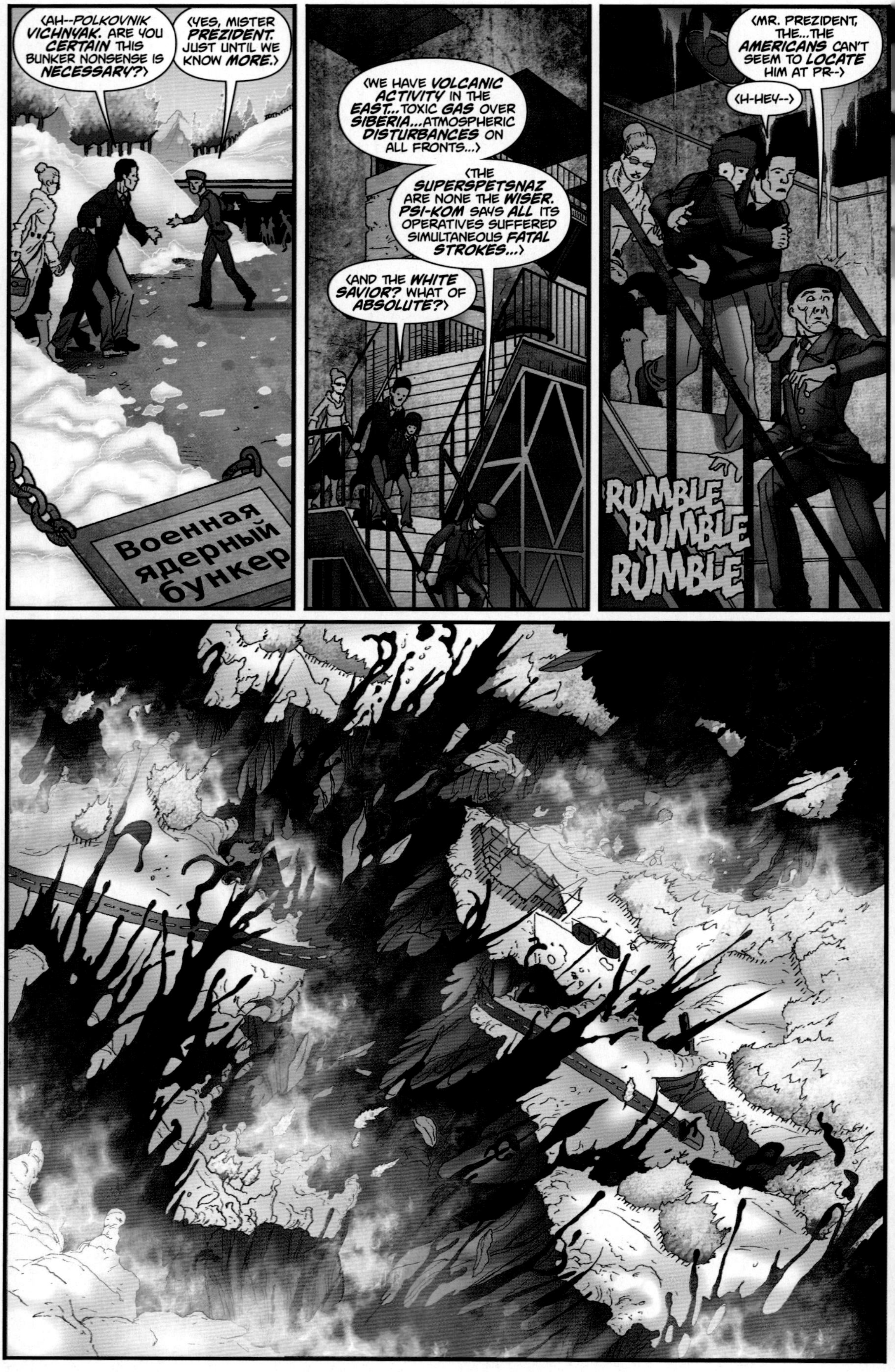

‹AH--POLKOVNIK VICHNYAK. ARE YOU CERTAIN THIS BUNKER NONSENSE IS NECESSARY?›
‹YES, MISTER PREZIDENT. JUST UNTIL WE KNOW MORE.›
Военная ядерный бункер
‹WE HAVE VOLCANIC ACTIVITY IN THE EAST...TOXIC GAS OVER SIBERIA...ATMOSPHERIC DISTURBANCES ON ALL FRONTS...›
‹THE SUPERSPETSNAZ ARE NONE THE WISER. PSI-KOM SAYS ALL ITS OPERATIVES SUFFERED SIMULTANEOUS FATAL STROKES...›
‹AND THE WHITE SAVIOR? WHAT OF ABSOLUTE?›
‹MR. PREZIDENT, THE...THE AMERICANS CAN'T SEEM TO LOCATE HIM AT PR--›
‹H-HEY--›
RUMBLE RUMBLE RUMBLE

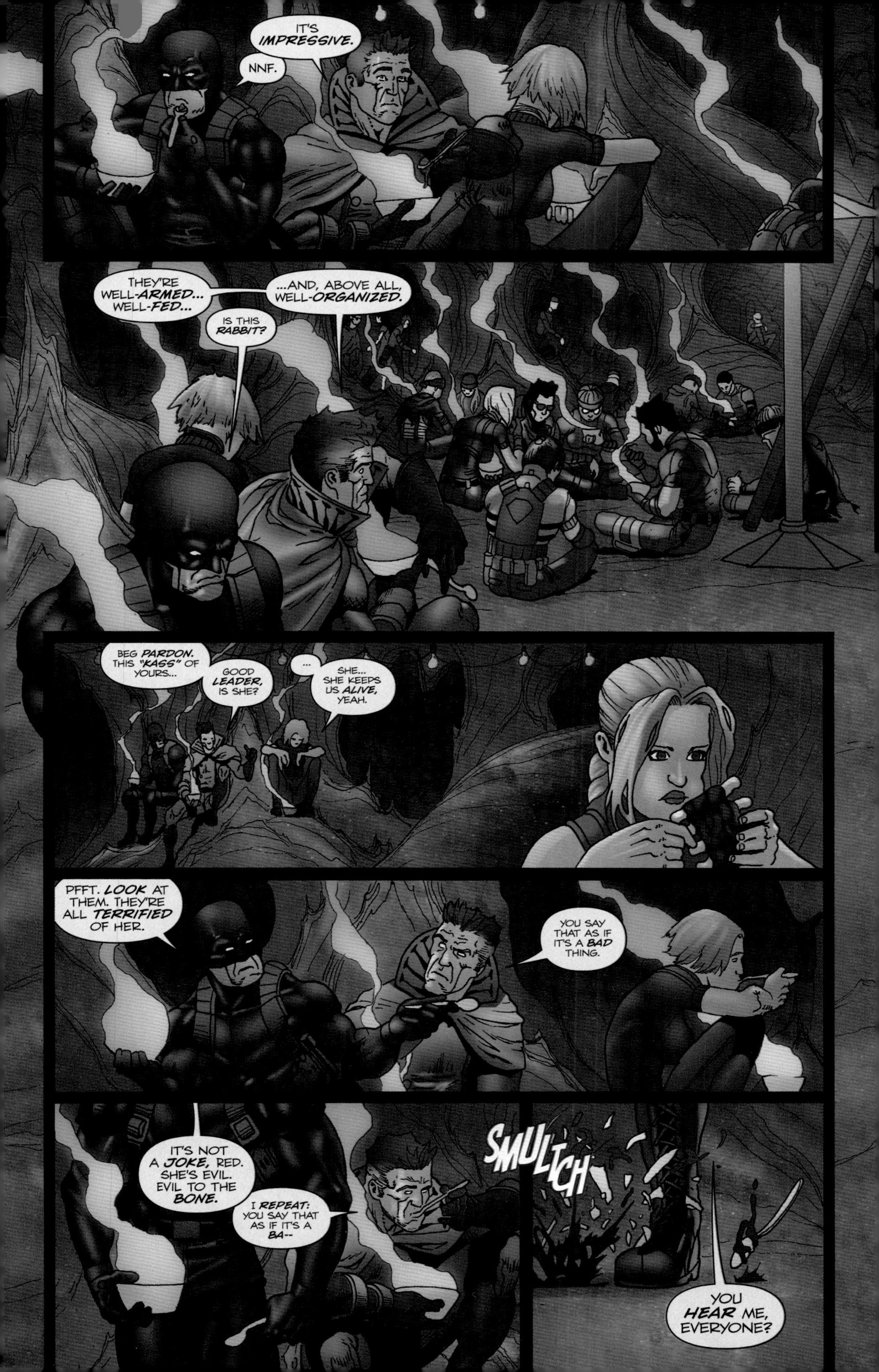

IT'S IMPRESSIVE.
NNF.
THEY'RE WELL-ARMED... WELL-FED...
...AND, ABOVE ALL, WELL-ORGANIZED.
IS THIS RABBIT?
BEG PARDON. THIS "KASS" OF YOURS...
GOOD LEADER, IS SHE?
...
SHE... SHE KEEPS US ALIVE, YEAH.
PFFT. LOOK AT THEM. THEY'RE ALL TERRIFIED OF HER.
YOU SAY THAT AS IF IT'S A BAD THING.
IT'S NOT A JOKE, RED. SHE'S EVIL. EVIL TO THE BONE.
I REPEAT: YOU SAY THAT AS IF IT'S A BA--
SMULTCH
YOU HEAR ME, EVERYONE?

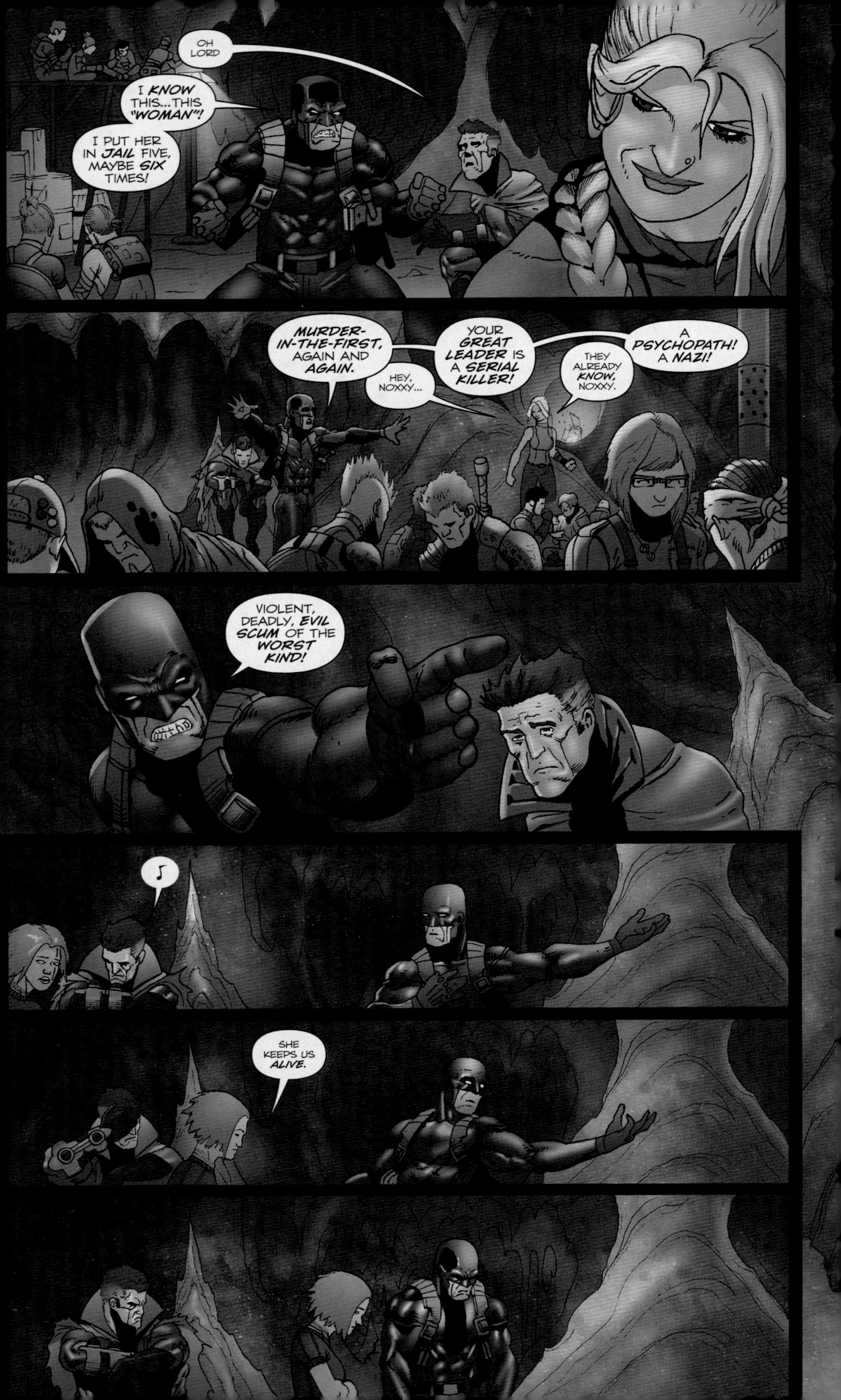
OH LORD
I KNOW THIS...THIS "WOMAN"!
I PUT HER IN JAIL FIVE, MAYBE SIX TIMES!
MURDER-IN-THE-FIRST, AGAIN AND AGAIN.
YOUR GREAT LEADER IS A SERIAL KILLER!
A PSYCHOPATH! A NAZI!
HEY, NOXXY...
THEY ALREADY KNOW, NOXXY.
VIOLENT, DEADLY, EVIL SCUM OF THE WORST KIND!
♪
SHE KEEPS US ALIVE.

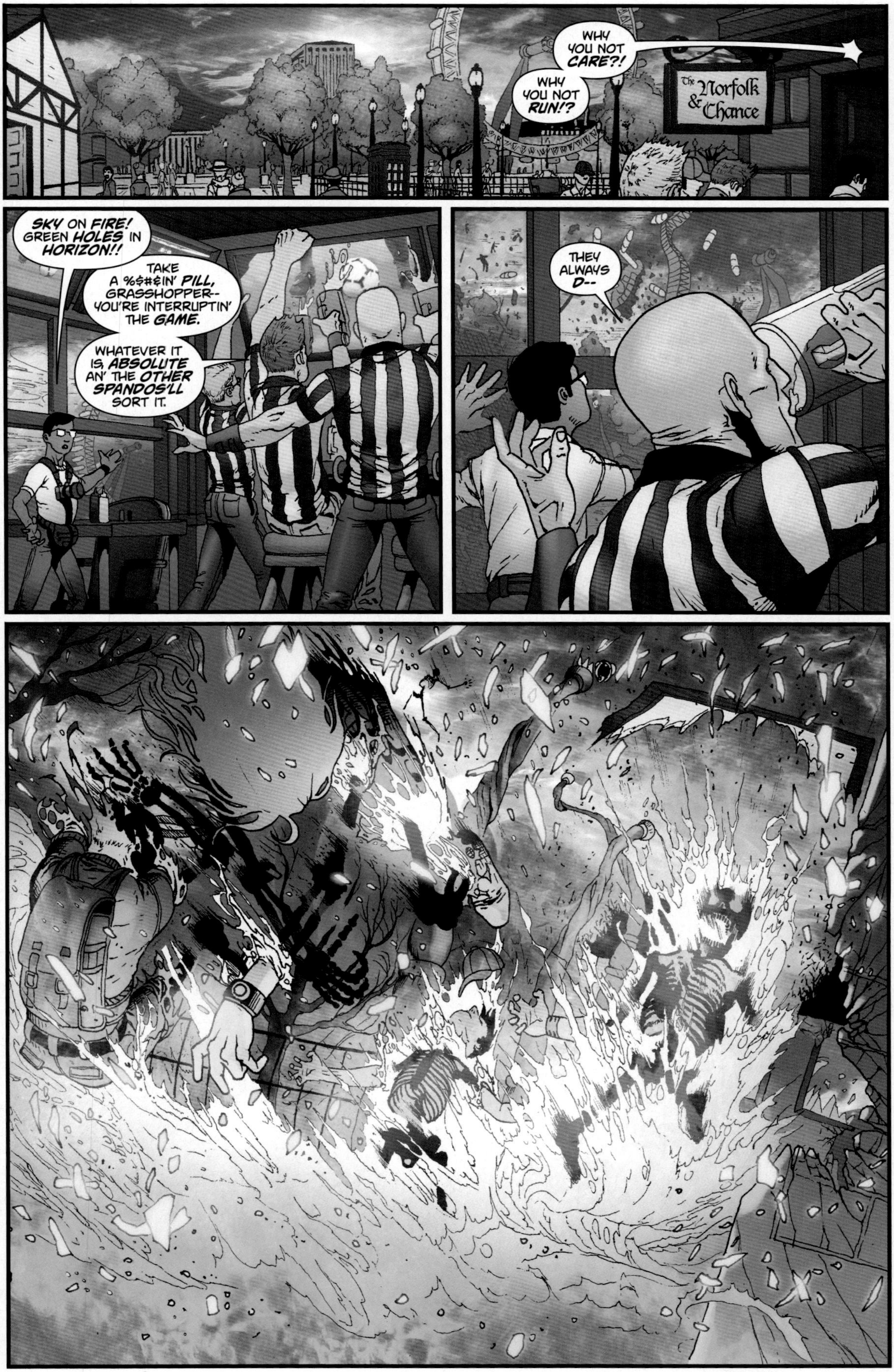
WHY YOU NOT CARE?!
WHY YOU NOT RUN!?
The Norfolk & Chance
SKY ON FIRE! GREEN HOLES IN HORIZON!!
TAKE A %$#&IN' PILL, GRASSHOPPER-- YOU'RE INTERRUPTIN' THE GAME.
WHATEVER IT IS, ABSOLUTE AN' THE OTHER SPANDOS'LL SORT IT.
THEY ALWAYS D--

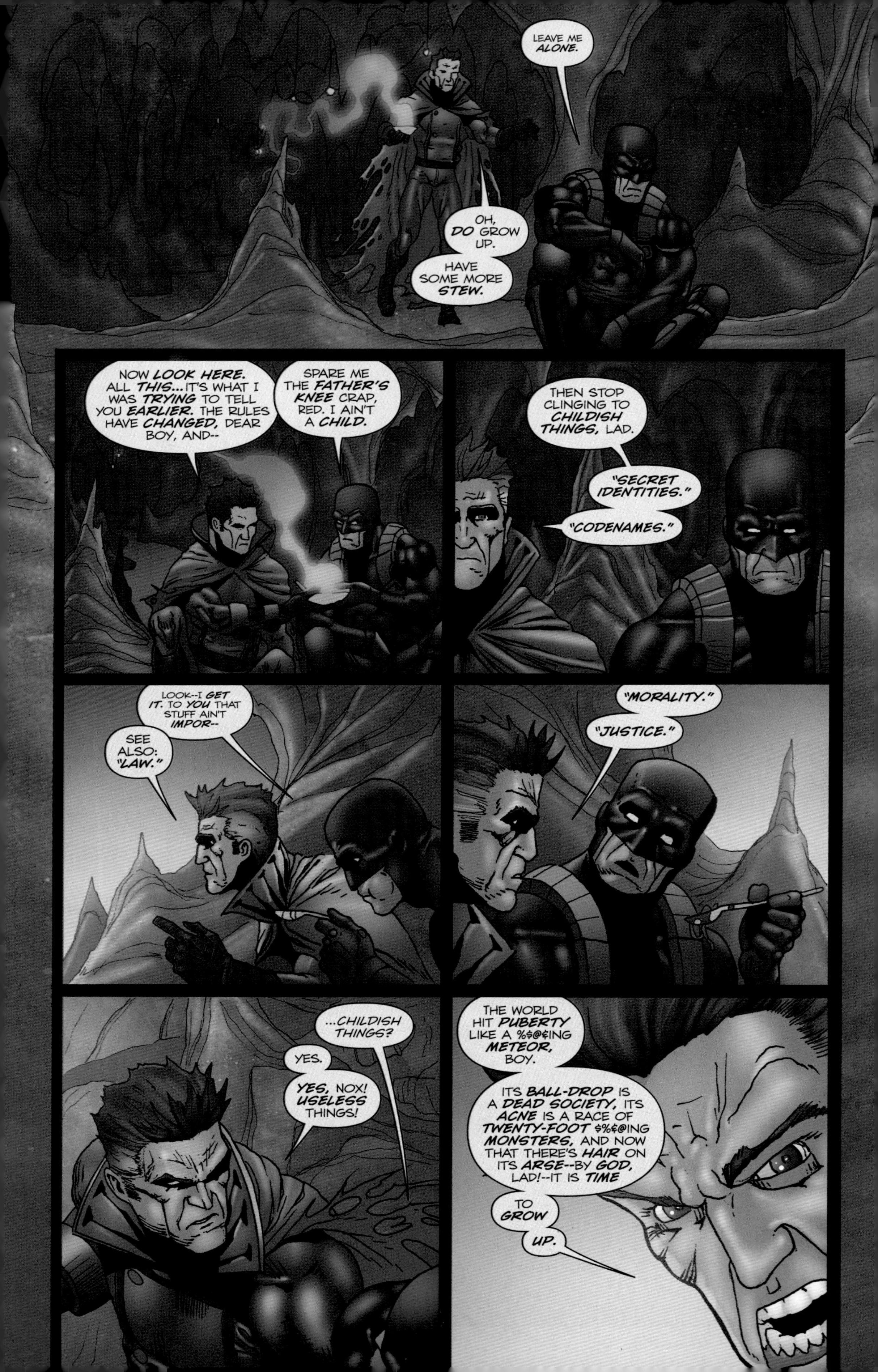
LEAVE ME ALONE.
OH, DO GROW UP.
HAVE SOME MORE STEW.
NOW LOOK HERE. ALL THIS... IT'S WHAT I WAS TRYING TO TELL YOU EARLIER. THE RULES HAVE CHANGED, DEAR BOY, AND--
SPARE ME THE FATHER'S KNEE CRAP, RED. I AIN'T A CHILD.
THEN STOP CLINGING TO CHILDISH THINGS, LAD.
"SECRET IDENTITIES."
"CODENAMES."
LOOK--I GET IT. TO YOU THAT STUFF AIN'T IMPOR--
SEE ALSO: "LAW."
"MORALITY."
"JUSTICE."
...CHILDISH THINGS?
YES.
YES, NOX! USELESS THINGS!
THE WORLD HIT PUBERTY LIKE A %$@¢ING METEOR, BOY.
ITS BALL-DROP IS A DEAD SOCIETY, ITS ACNE IS A RACE OF TWENTY-FOOT $%¢@ING MONSTERS, AND NOW THAT THERE'S HAIR ON ITS ARSE--BY GOD, LAD!--IT IS TIME
TO GROW
UP.

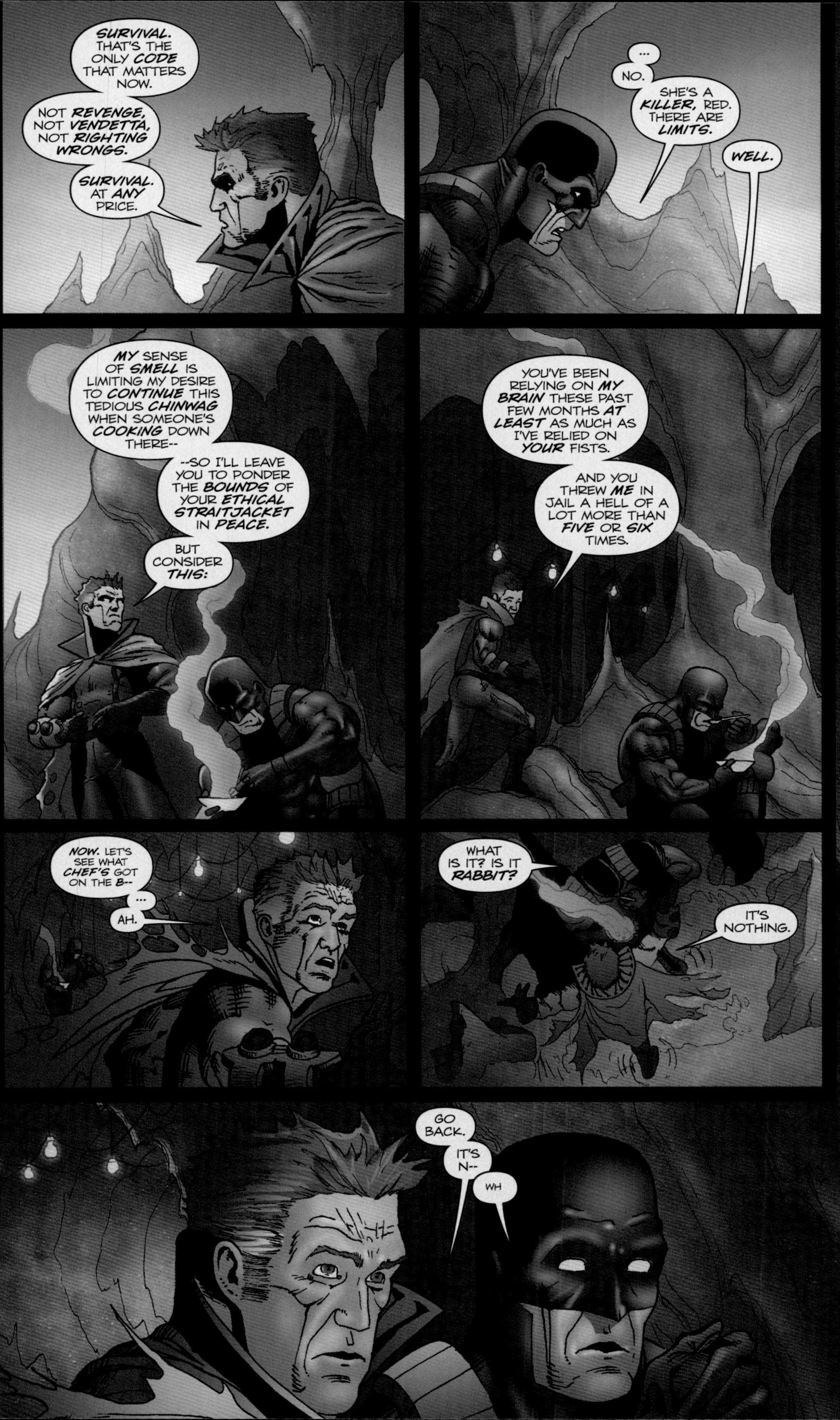
SURVIVAL. THAT'S THE ONLY CODE THAT MATTERS NOW.
NOT REVENGE, NOT VENDETTA, NOT RIGHTING WRONGS.
SURVIVAL. AT ANY PRICE.
...
NO.
SHE'S A KILLER, RED. THERE ARE LIMITS.
WELL.
MY SENSE OF SMELL IS LIMITING MY DESIRE TO CONTINUE THIS TEDIOUS CHINWAG WHEN SOMEONE'S COOKING DOWN THERE--
--SO I'LL LEAVE YOU TO PONDER THE BOUNDS OF YOUR ETHICAL STRAITJACKET IN PEACE.
BUT CONSIDER THIS:
YOU'VE BEEN RELYING ON MY BRAIN THESE PAST FEW MONTHS AT LEAST AS MUCH AS I'VE RELIED ON YOUR FISTS.
AND YOU THREW ME IN JAIL A HELL OF A LOT MORE THAN FIVE OR SIX TIMES.
NOW. LET'S SEE WHAT CHEF'S GOT ON THE B--
...
AH.
WHAT IS IT? IS IT RABBIT?
IT'S NOTHING.
GO BACK.
IT'S N--
WH

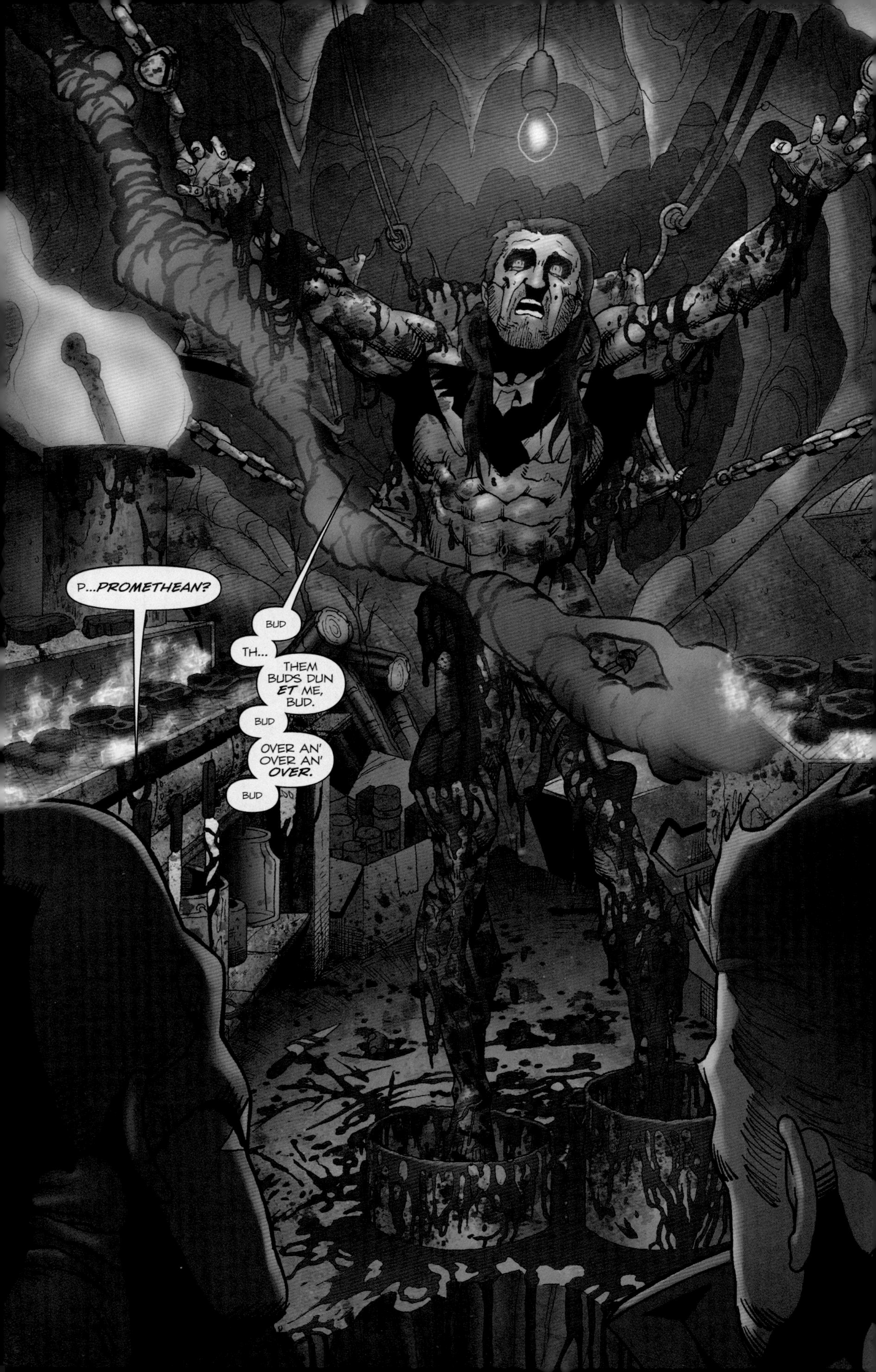
P...PROMETHEAN?
BUD
TH...
THEM BUDS DUN ET ME, BUD.
BUD
OVER AN' OVER AN' OVER.
BUD

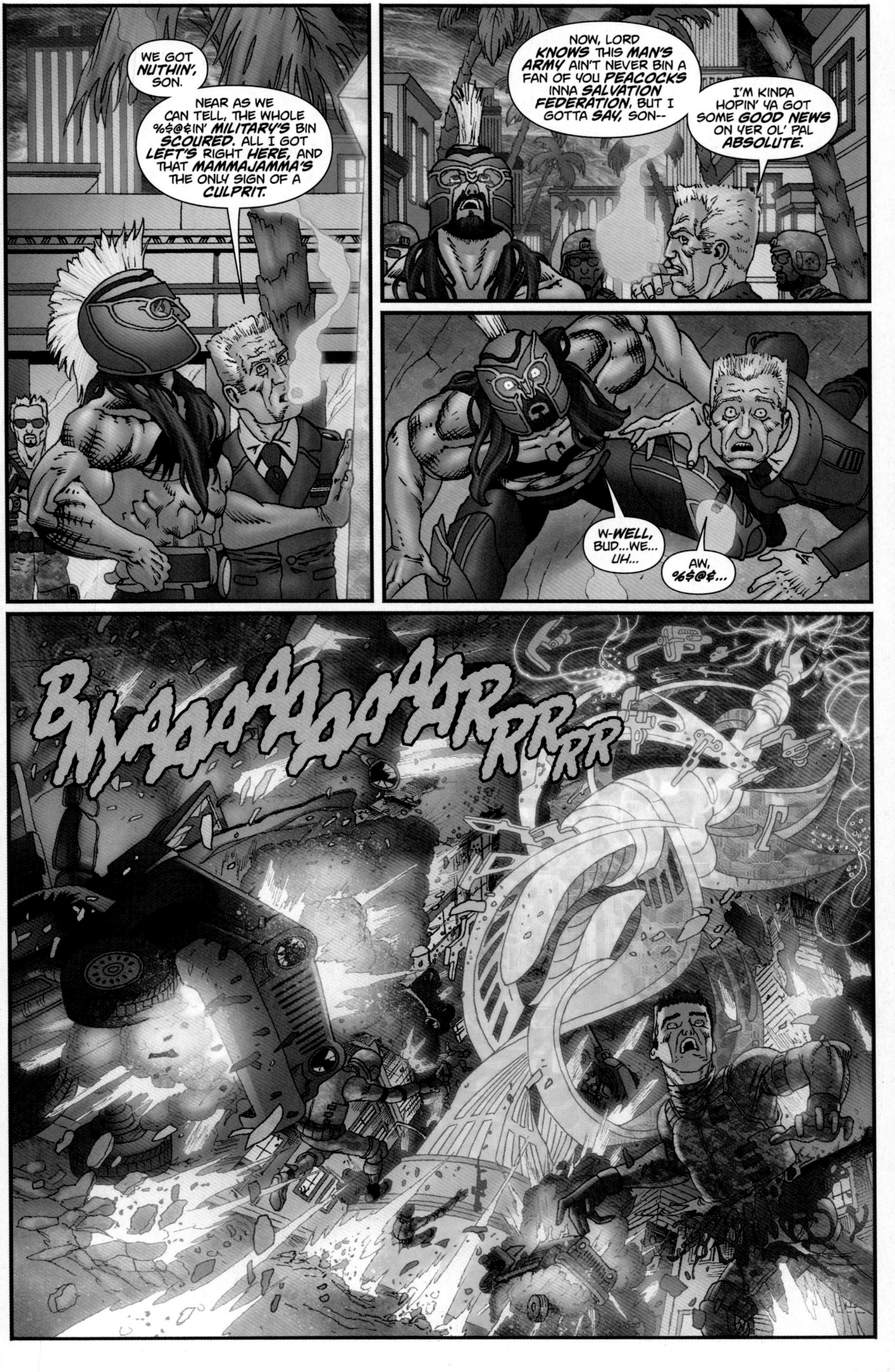
WE GOT NUTHIN', SON.
NEAR AS WE CAN TELL, THE WHOLE %$@¢IN' MILITARY'S BIN SCOURED. ALL I GOT LEFT'S RIGHT HERE, AND THAT MAMMAJAMMA'S THE ONLY SIGN OF A CULPRIT.
NOW, LORD KNOWS THIS MAN'S ARMY AIN'T NEVER BIN A FAN OF YOU PEACOCKS INNA SALVATION FEDERATION, BUT I GOTTA SAY, SON--
I'M KINDA HOPIN' YA GOT SOME GOOD NEWS ON YER OL' PAL ABSOLUTE.
W-WELL, BUD...WE... UH...
AW, %$@¢...
BWAAAAAAAARRRRR

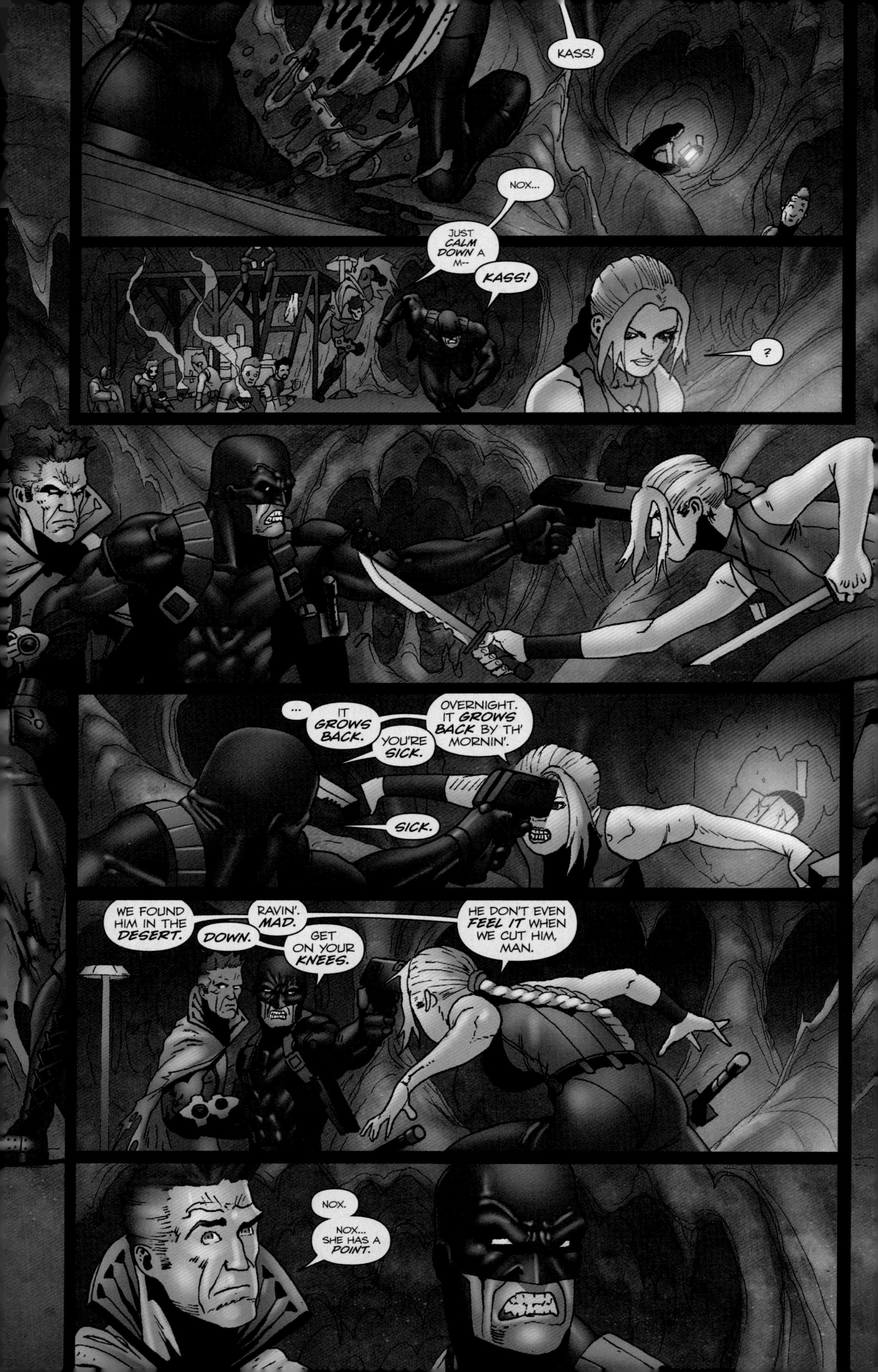
KASS!
NOX...
JUST CALM DOWN A M--
KASS!
?
...
IT GROWS BACK.
YOU'RE SICK.
OVERNIGHT. IT GROWS BACK BY TH' MORNIN'.
SICK.
WE FOUND HIM IN THE DESERT.
RAVIN'. MAD.
DOWN.
GET ON YOUR KNEES.
HE DON'T EVEN FEEL IT WHEN WE CUT HIM, MAN.
NOX.
NOX... SHE HAS A POINT.

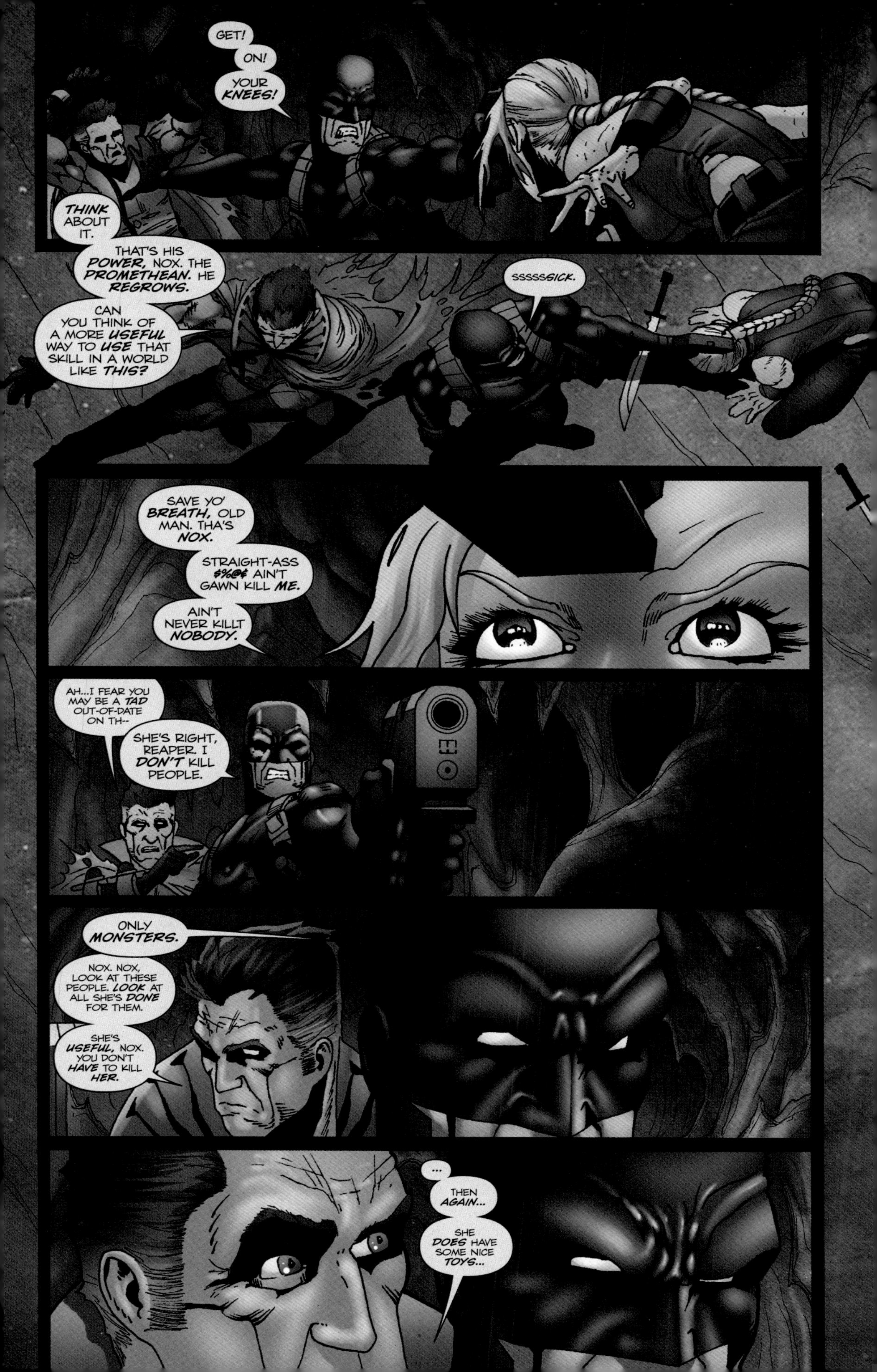
GET!
ON!
YOUR KNEES!
THINK ABOUT IT.
THAT'S HIS POWER, NOX. THE PROMETHEAN. HE REGROWS.
CAN YOU THINK OF A MORE USEFUL WAY TO USE THAT SKILL IN A WORLD LIKE THIS?
SSSSSSICK.
SAVE YO' BREATH, OLD MAN. THA'S NOX.
STRAIGHT-ASS $%@¢ AIN'T GAWN KILL ME.
AIN'T NEVER KILLT NOBODY.
AH...I FEAR YOU MAY BE A TAD OUT-OF-DATE ON TH--
SHE'S RIGHT, REAPER. I DON'T KILL PEOPLE.
ONLY MONSTERS.
NOX. NOX, LOOK AT THESE PEOPLE. LOOK AT ALL SHE'S DONE FOR THEM.
SHE'S USEFUL, NOX. YOU DON'T HAVE TO KILL HER.
...
THEN AGAIN...
SHE DOES HAVE SOME NICE TOYS...

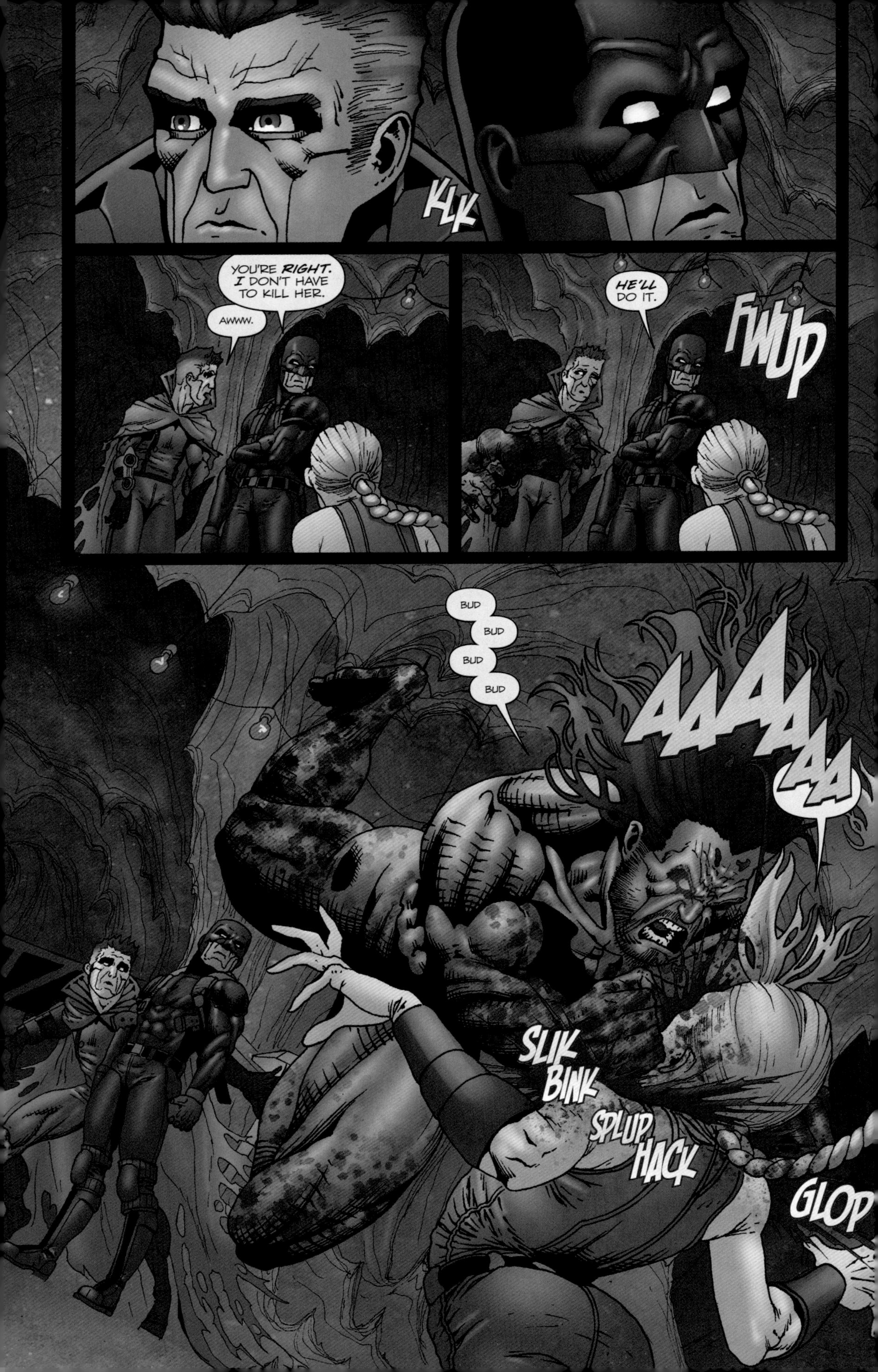
KLK
YOU'RE **RIGHT.** *I* DON'T HAVE TO KILL HER.
AWWW.
*HE'LL* DO IT.
FWUP
BUD
BUD
BUD
BUD
AAAAAAA
SLIK
BINK
SPLUP
HACK
GLOP

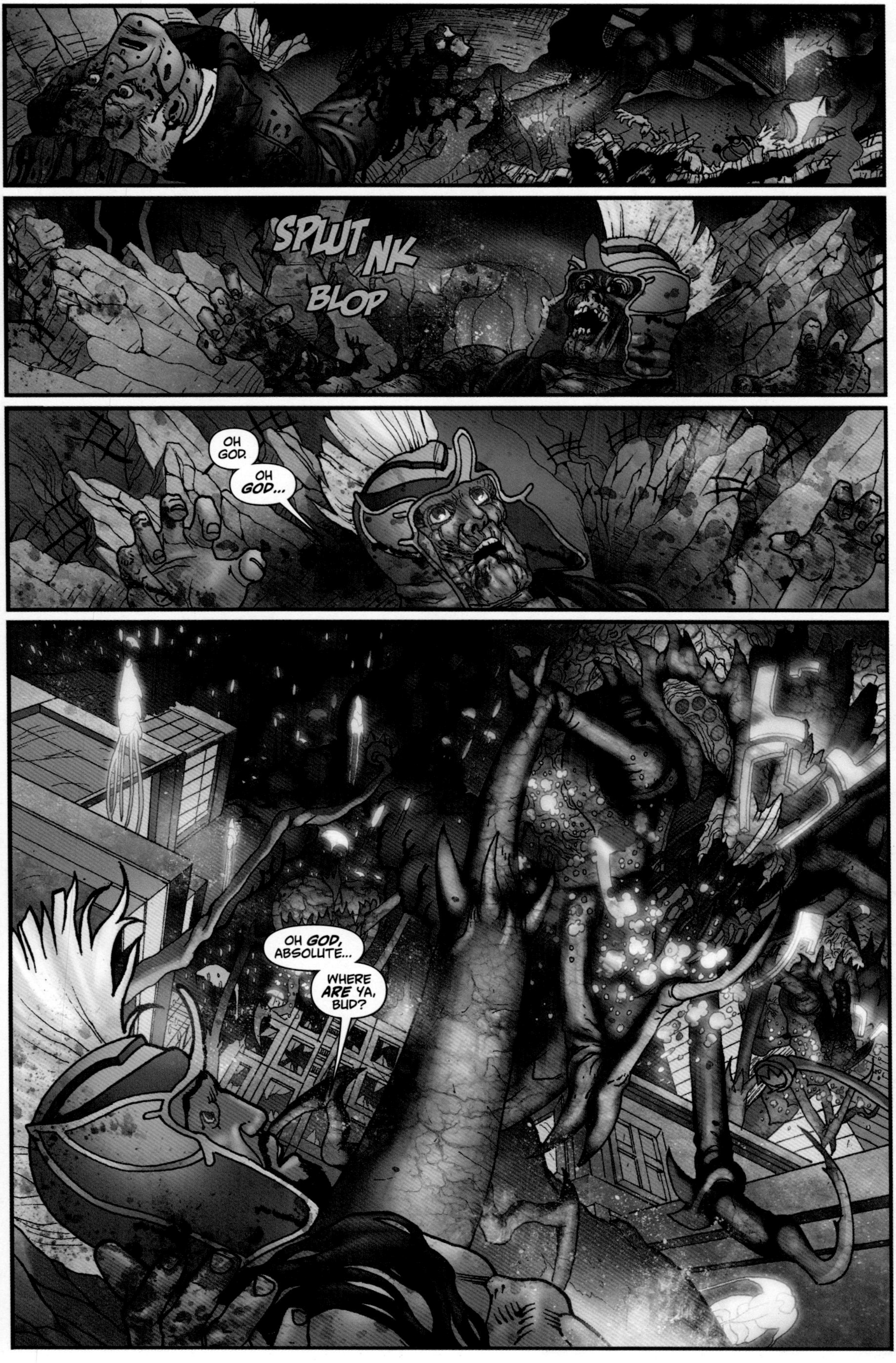
SPLUT
NK
BLOP
OH GOD.
OH GOD...
OH GOD, ABSOLUTE...
WHERE ARE YA, BUD?

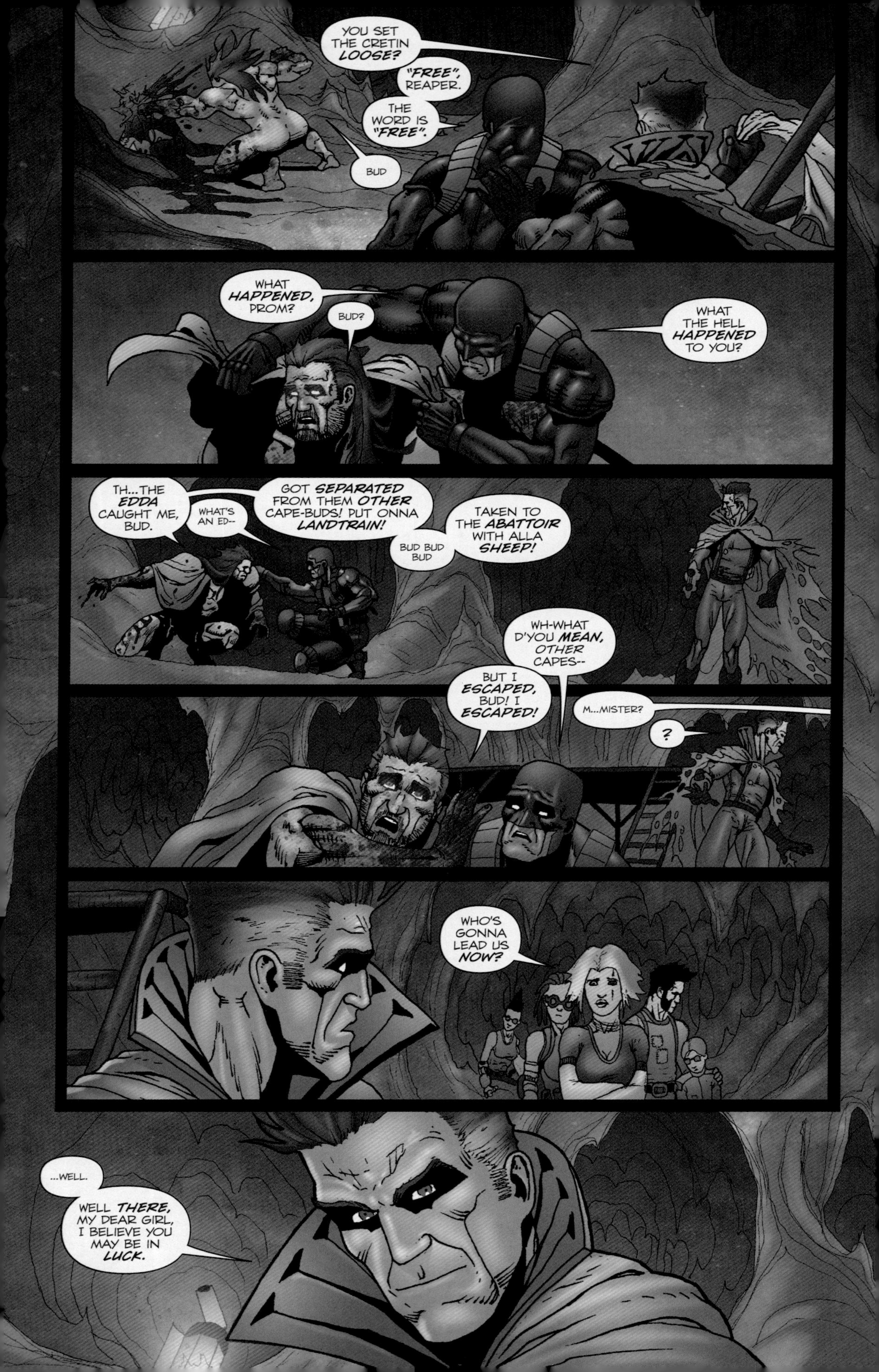
YOU SET THE CRETIN LOOSE?
"FREE", REAPER.
THE WORD IS "FREE".
BUD
WHAT HAPPENED, PROM?
BUD?
WHAT THE HELL HAPPENED TO YOU?
TH...THE EDDA CAUGHT ME, BUD.
WHAT'S AN ED--
GOT SEPARATED FROM THEM OTHER CAPE-BUDS! PUT ONNA LANDTRAIN!
BUD BUD BUD
TAKEN TO THE ABATTOIR WITH ALLA SHEEP!
WH-WHAT D'YOU MEAN, OTHER CAPES--
BUT I ESCAPED, BUD! I ESCAPED!
M...MISTER?
?
WHO'S GONNA LEAD US NOW?
...WELL.
WELL THERE, MY DEAR GIRL, I BELIEVE YOU MAY BE IN LUCK.

ÜBERVILLE PENITENTIARY
FOR EXTRAHUMAN/COSTUMED CRIMINALS

THIS IS A RECORDED MESSAGE ≥ZZZZK≤

FROM THE MECHAWARDEN

PRISONERS ARE TO REMAIN IN THEIR CELLS ≥ZZZZK≤

FOR THEIR *OWN* SAFETY ≥ZZZZK≤

UNTIL THE PRESENT EMERGENCY IS OV-- ≥ZZZzk--*≤

WELL, NOW...

...THIS *IS* A TURN-UP FOR THE BOOKS.

ABSOLUTE
THE PEOPLE IN GRATITUDE FOR HIS VIRTUE AND VALOR
HE DESERTED US

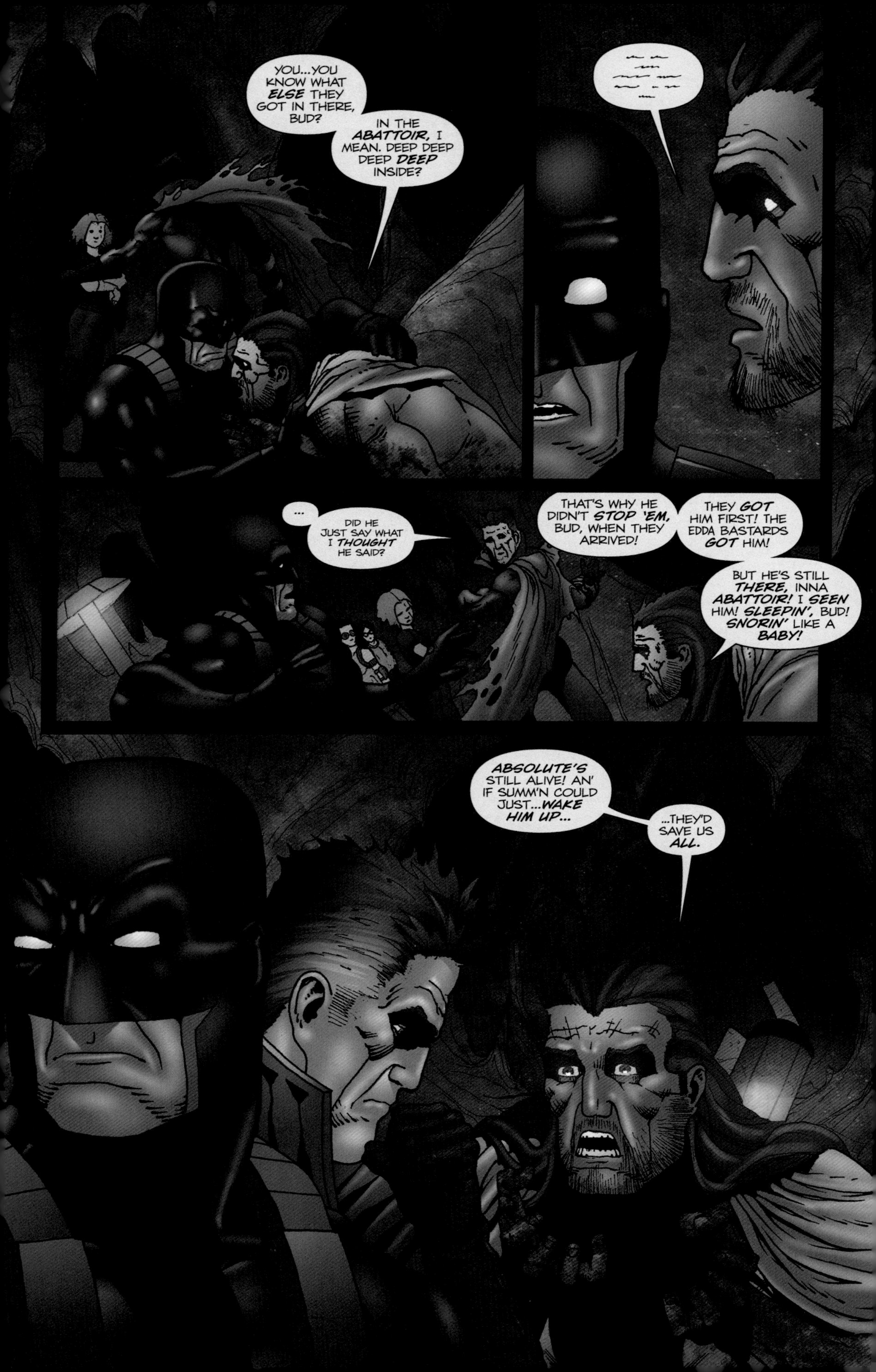
YOU...YOU KNOW WHAT ELSE THEY GOT IN THERE, BUD?
IN THE ABATTOIR, I MEAN. DEEP DEEP DEEP DEEP INSIDE?
...
DID HE JUST SAY WHAT I THOUGHT HE SAID?
THAT'S WHY HE DIDN'T STOP 'EM, BUD, WHEN THEY ARRIVED!
THEY GOT HIM FIRST! THE EDDA BASTARDS GOT HIM!
BUT HE'S STILL THERE, INNA ABATTOIR! I SEEN HIM! SLEEPIN', BUD! SNORIN' LIKE A BABY!
ABSOLUTE'S STILL ALIVE! AN' IF SUMM'N COULD JUST...WAKE HIM UP...
...THEY'D SAVE US ALL.

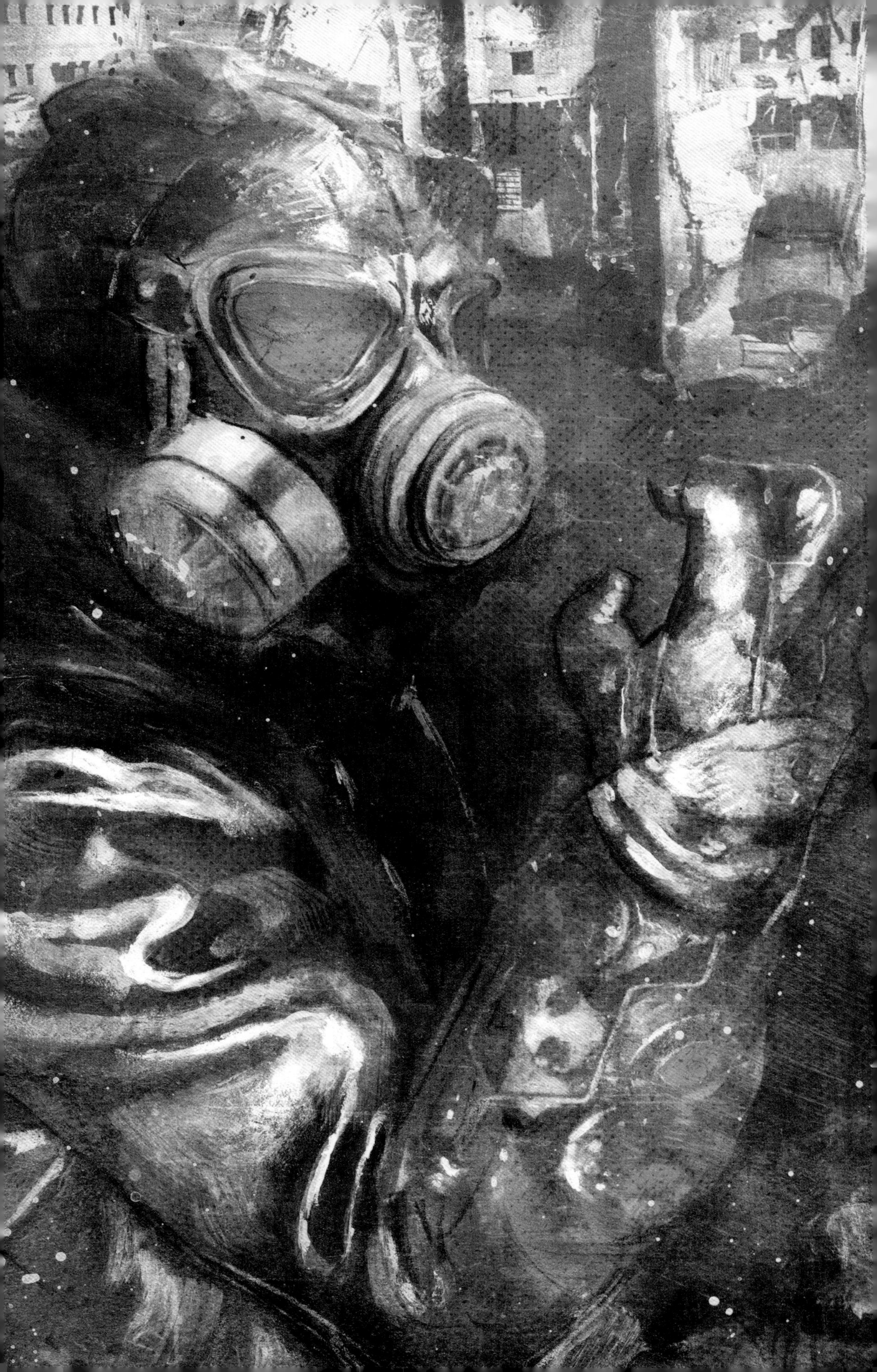

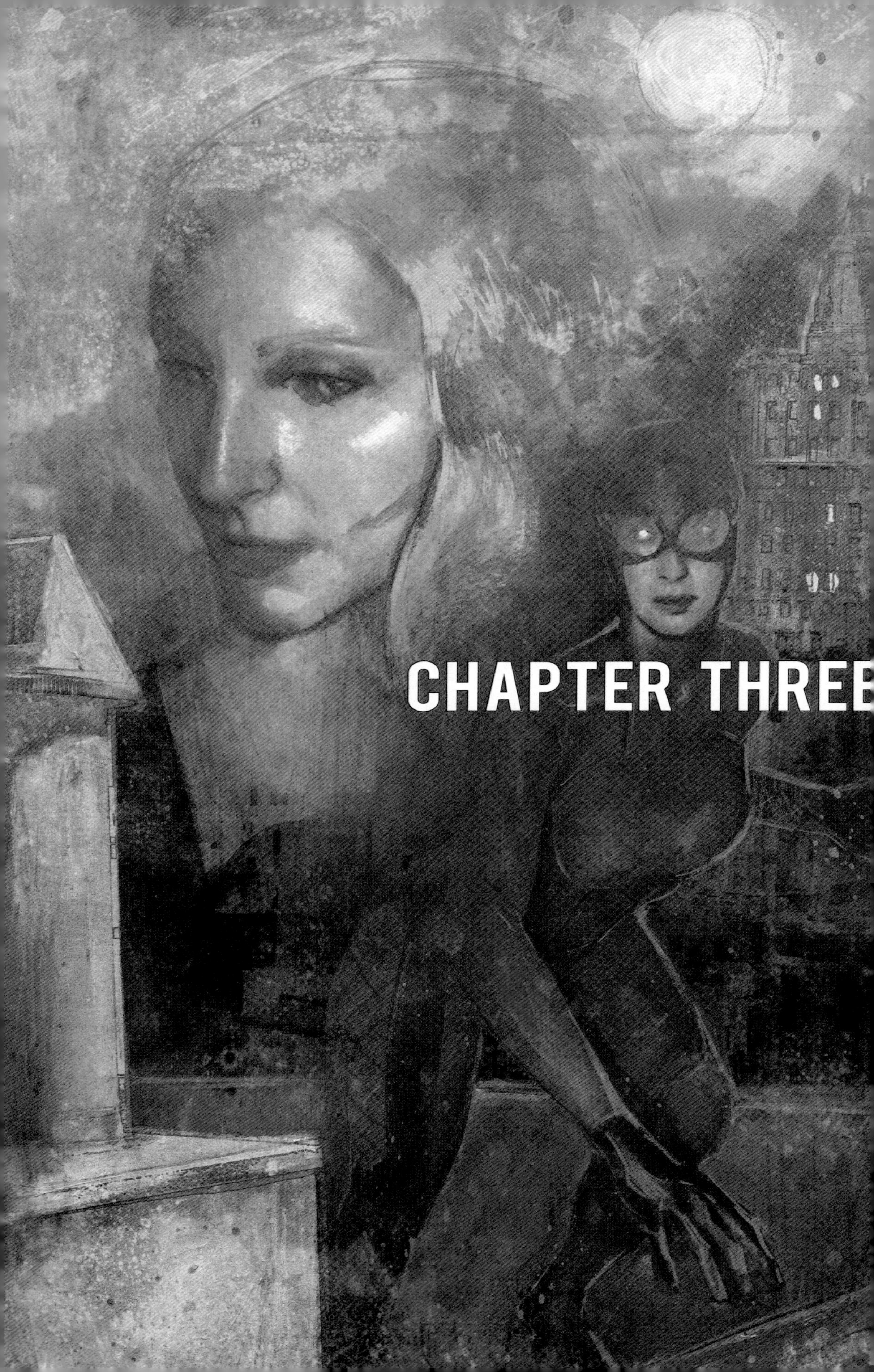

# CHAPTER THREE

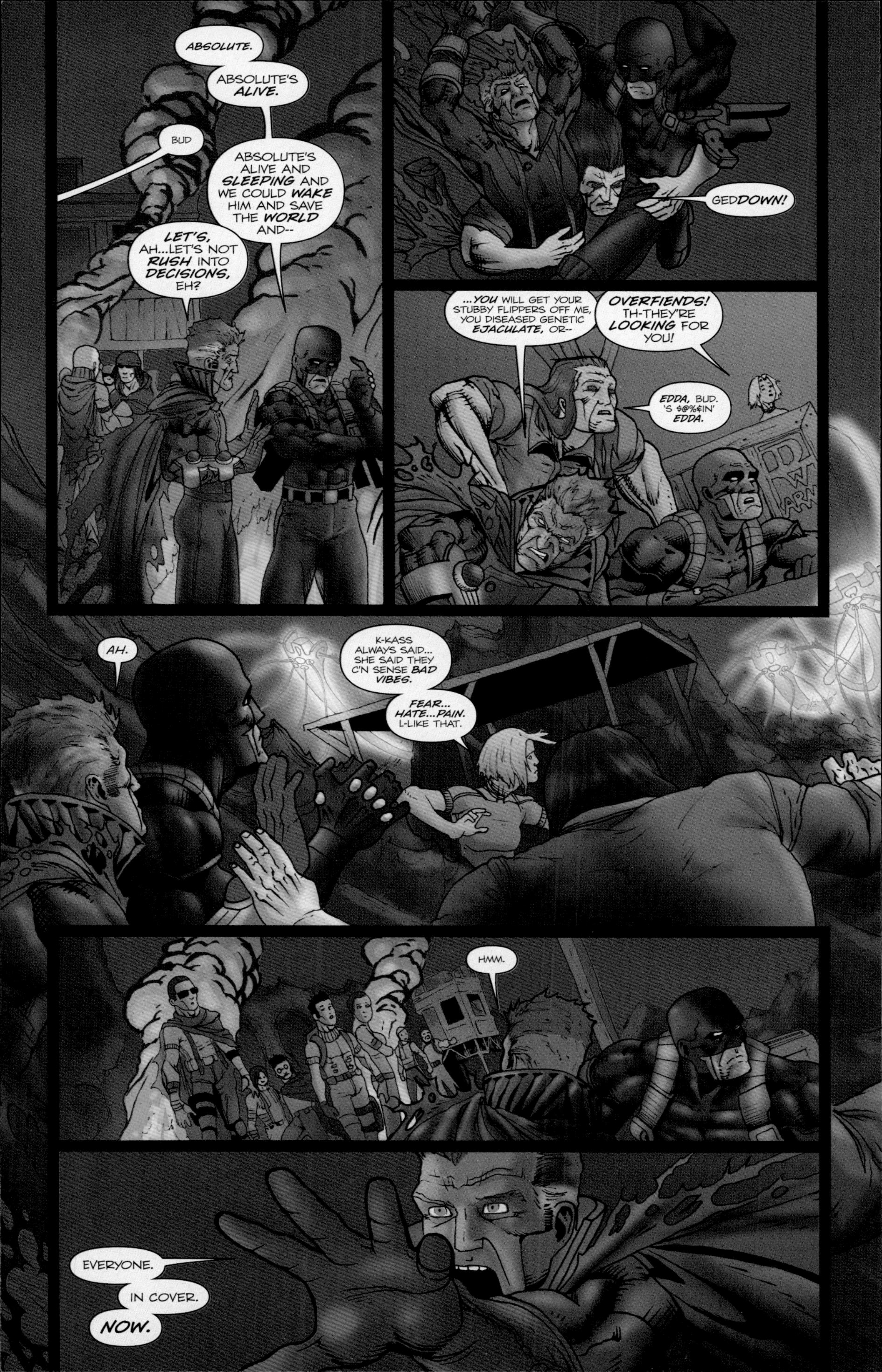

ABSOLUTE.
ABSOLUTE'S ALIVE.
BUD
ABSOLUTE'S ALIVE AND SLEEPING AND WE COULD WAKE HIM AND SAVE THE WORLD AND--
LET'S, AH...LET'S NOT RUSH INTO DECISIONS, EH?
GEDDOWN!
...YOU WILL GET YOUR STUBBY FLIPPERS OFF ME, YOU DISEASED GENETIC EJACULATE, OR--
OVERFIENDS! TH-THEY'RE LOOKING FOR YOU!
EDDA, BUD. 'S $@%$IN' EDDA.
AH.
K-KASS ALWAYS SAID... SHE SAID THEY C'N SENSE BAD VIBES.
FEAR... HATE...PAIN. L-LIKE THAT.
HMM.
EVERYONE.
IN COVER.
NOW.

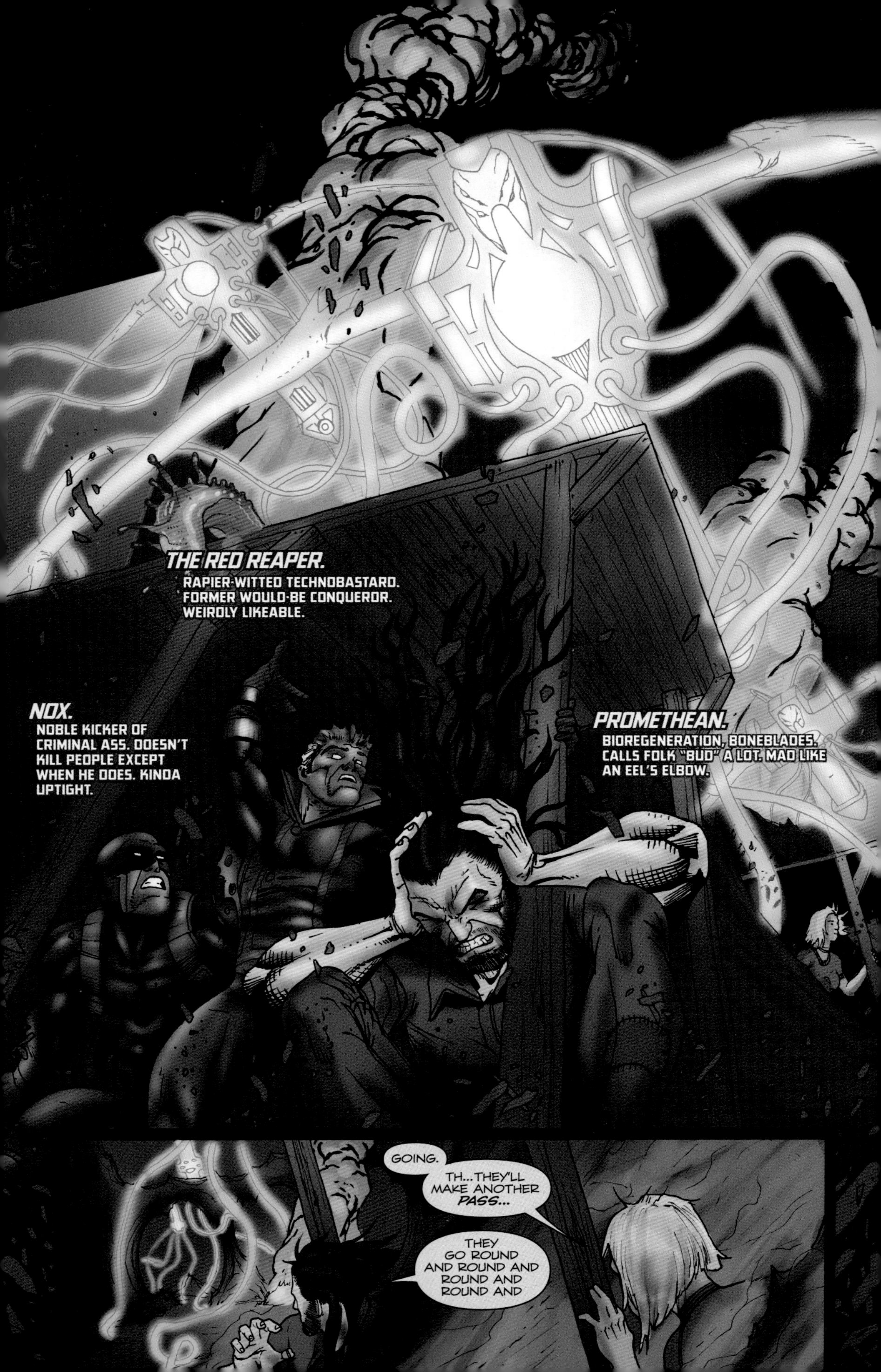
THE RED REAPER.
RAPIER-WITTED TECHNOBASTARD. FORMER WOULD-BE CONQUEROR. WEIRDLY LIKEABLE.
NOX.
NOBLE KICKER OF CRIMINAL ASS. DOESN'T KILL PEOPLE EXCEPT WHEN HE DOES. KINDA UPTIGHT.
PROMETHEAN.
BIOREGENERATION, BONEBLADES. CALLS FOLK "BUD" A LOT. MAD LIKE AN EEL'S ELBOW.
GOING.
TH...THEY'LL MAKE ANOTHER PASS...
THEY GO ROUND AND ROUND AND ROUND AND ROUND AND

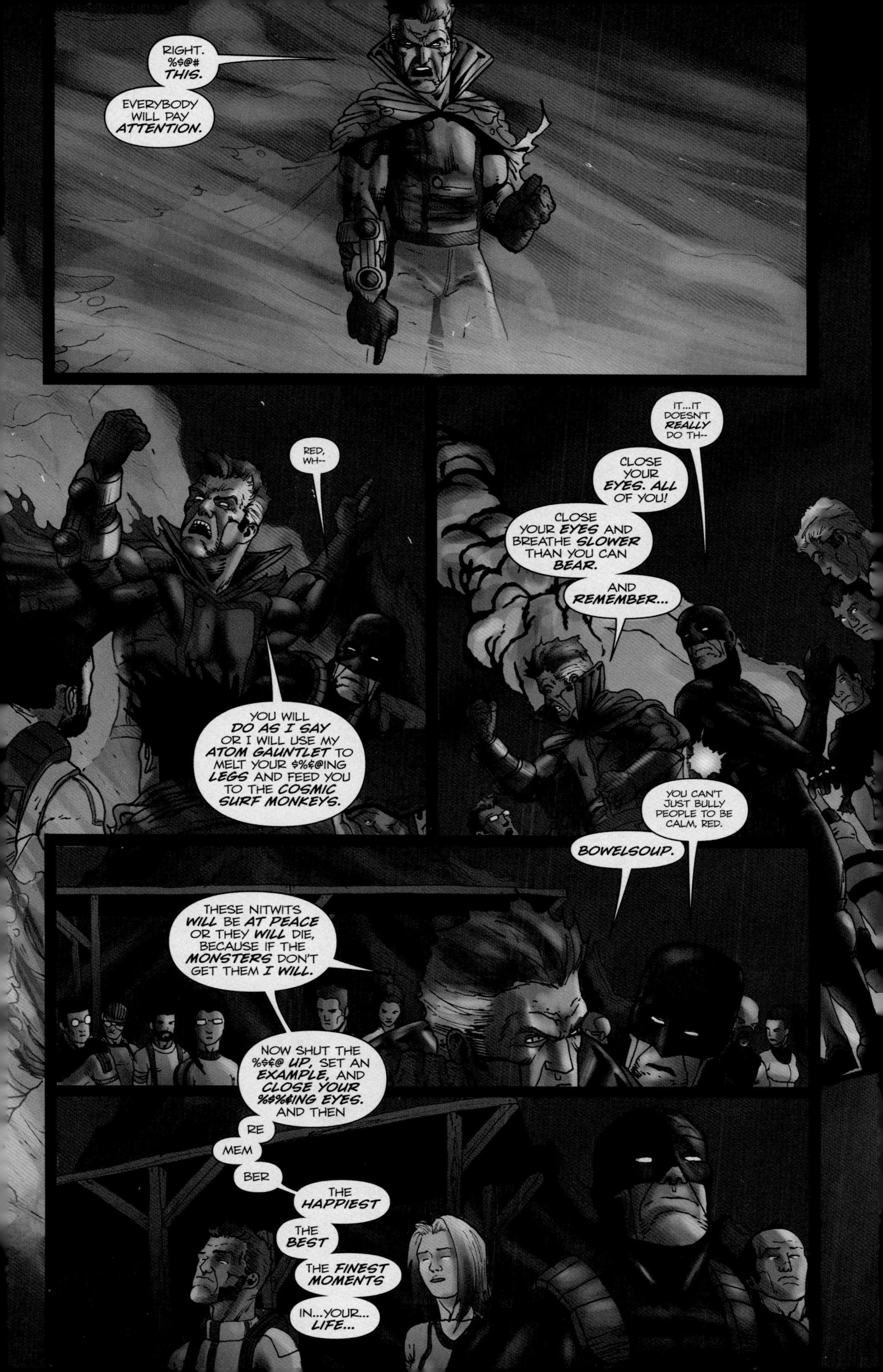
RIGHT. %$@# THIS.
EVERYBODY WILL PAY ATTENTION.
RED, WH--
YOU WILL DO AS I SAY OR I WILL USE MY ATOM GAUNTLET TO MELT YOUR $%$@ING LEGS AND FEED YOU TO THE COSMIC SURF MONKEYS.
IT...IT DOESN'T REALLY DO TH--
CLOSE YOUR EYES. ALL OF YOU!
CLOSE YOUR EYES AND BREATHE SLOWER THAN YOU CAN BEAR.
AND REMEMBER...
YOU CAN'T JUST BULLY PEOPLE TO BE CALM, RED.
BOWELSOUP.
THESE NITWITS WILL BE AT PEACE OR THEY WILL DIE, BECAUSE IF THE MONSTERS DON'T GET THEM I WILL.
NOW SHUT THE %$$@ UP, SET AN EXAMPLE, AND CLOSE YOUR %$%$ING EYES. AND THEN
RE
MEM
BER
THE HAPPIEST
THE BEST
THE FINEST MOMENTS
IN...YOUR... LIFE...

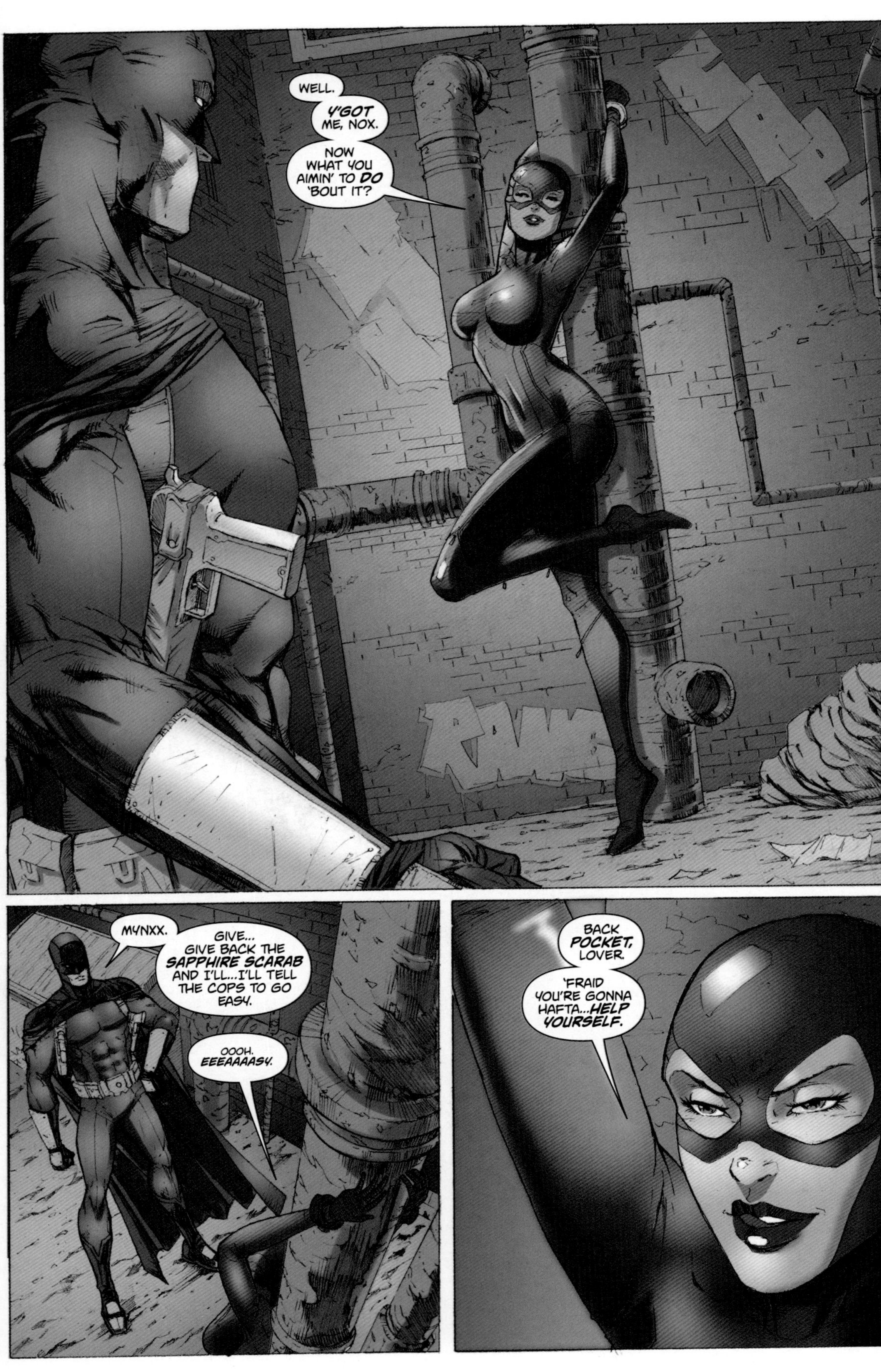
WELL.
Y'GOT ME, NOX.
NOW WHAT YOU AIMIN' TO DO 'BOUT IT?
MYNXX.
GIVE... GIVE BACK THE SAPPHIRE SCARAB AND I'LL...I'LL TELL THE COPS TO GO EASY.
OOOH. EEEAAAAASY.
BACK POCKET, LOVER.
'FRAID YOU'RE GONNA HAFTA...HELP YOURSELF.

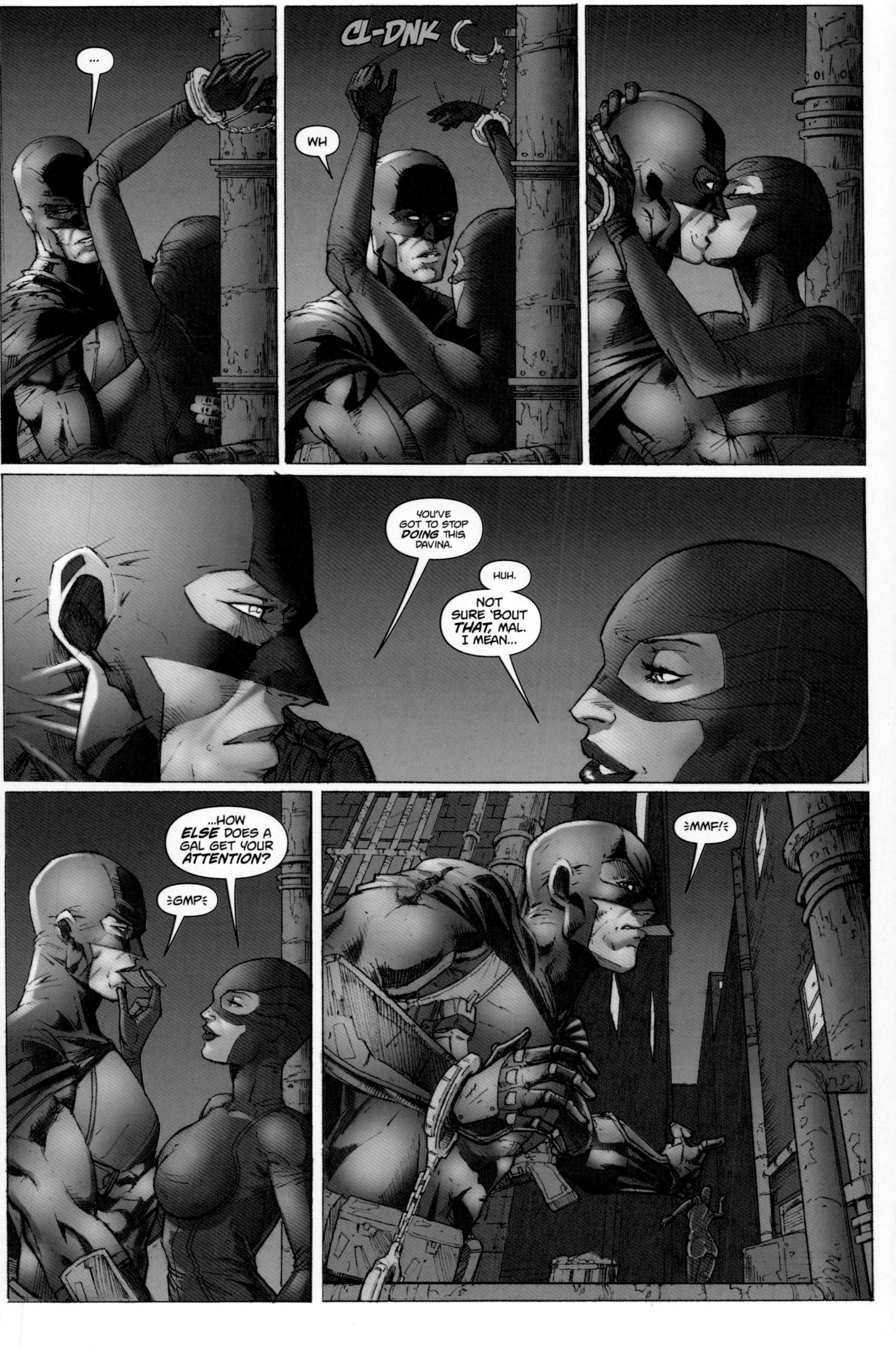
...
CL-DNK
WH
YOU'VE GOT TO STOP DOING THIS, DAVINA.
HUH.
NOT SURE 'BOUT THAT, MAL. I MEAN...
...HOW ELSE DOES A GAL GET YOUR ATTENTION?
GMP
MMF!

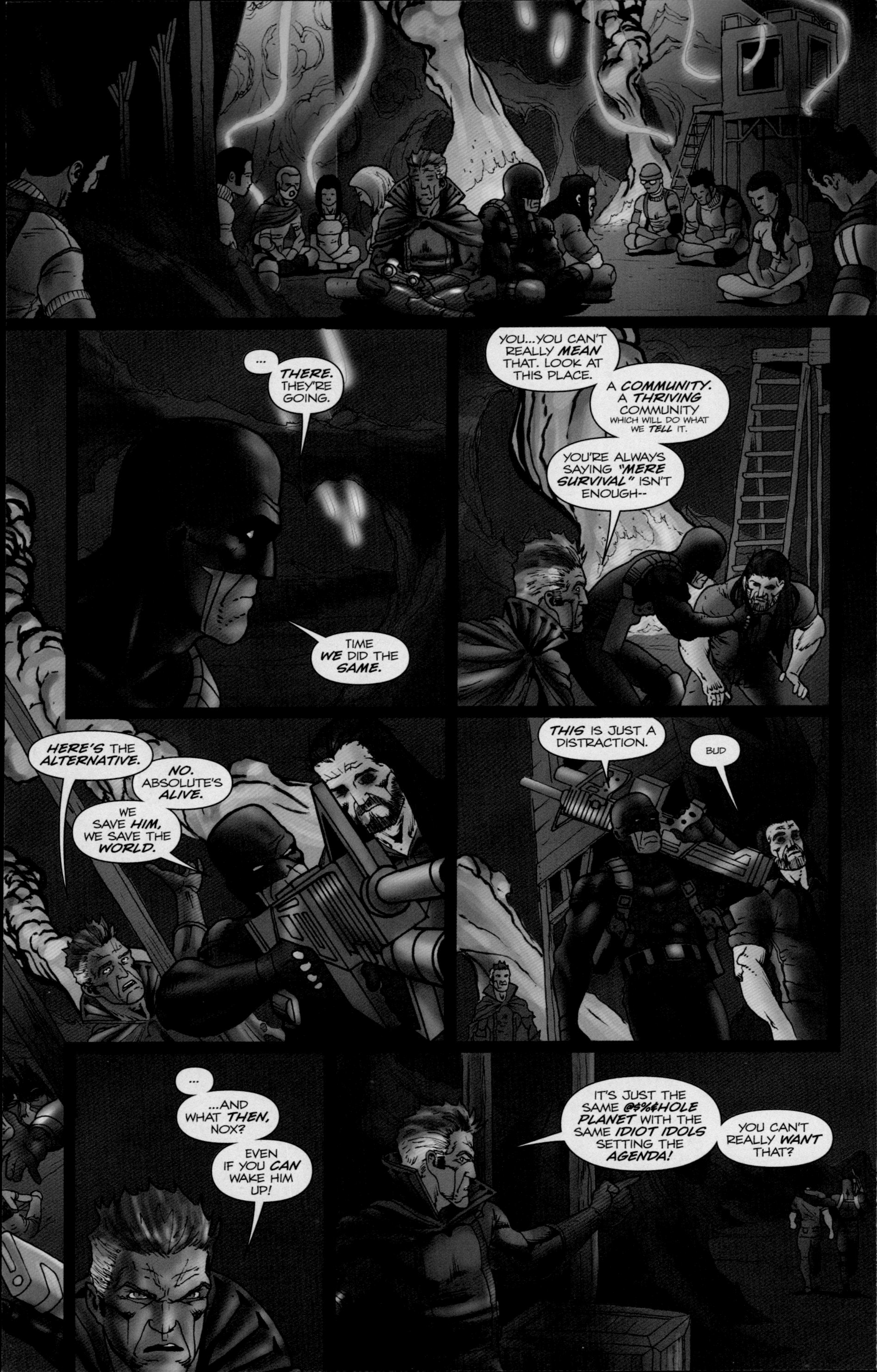
...
THERE. THEY'RE GOING.
TIME WE DID THE SAME.
YOU...YOU CAN'T REALLY MEAN THAT. LOOK AT THIS PLACE.
A COMMUNITY. A THRIVING COMMUNITY WHICH WILL DO WHAT WE TELL IT.
YOU'RE ALWAYS SAYING "MERE SURVIVAL" ISN'T ENOUGH--
HERE'S THE ALTERNATIVE.
NO. ABSOLUTE'S ALIVE.
WE SAVE HIM, WE SAVE THE WORLD.
THIS IS JUST A DISTRACTION.
BUD
...
...AND WHAT THEN, NOX?
EVEN IF YOU CAN WAKE HIM UP!
IT'S JUST THE SAME @$%¢HOLE PLANET WITH THE SAME IDIOT IDOLS SETTING THE AGENDA!
YOU CAN'T REALLY WANT THAT?

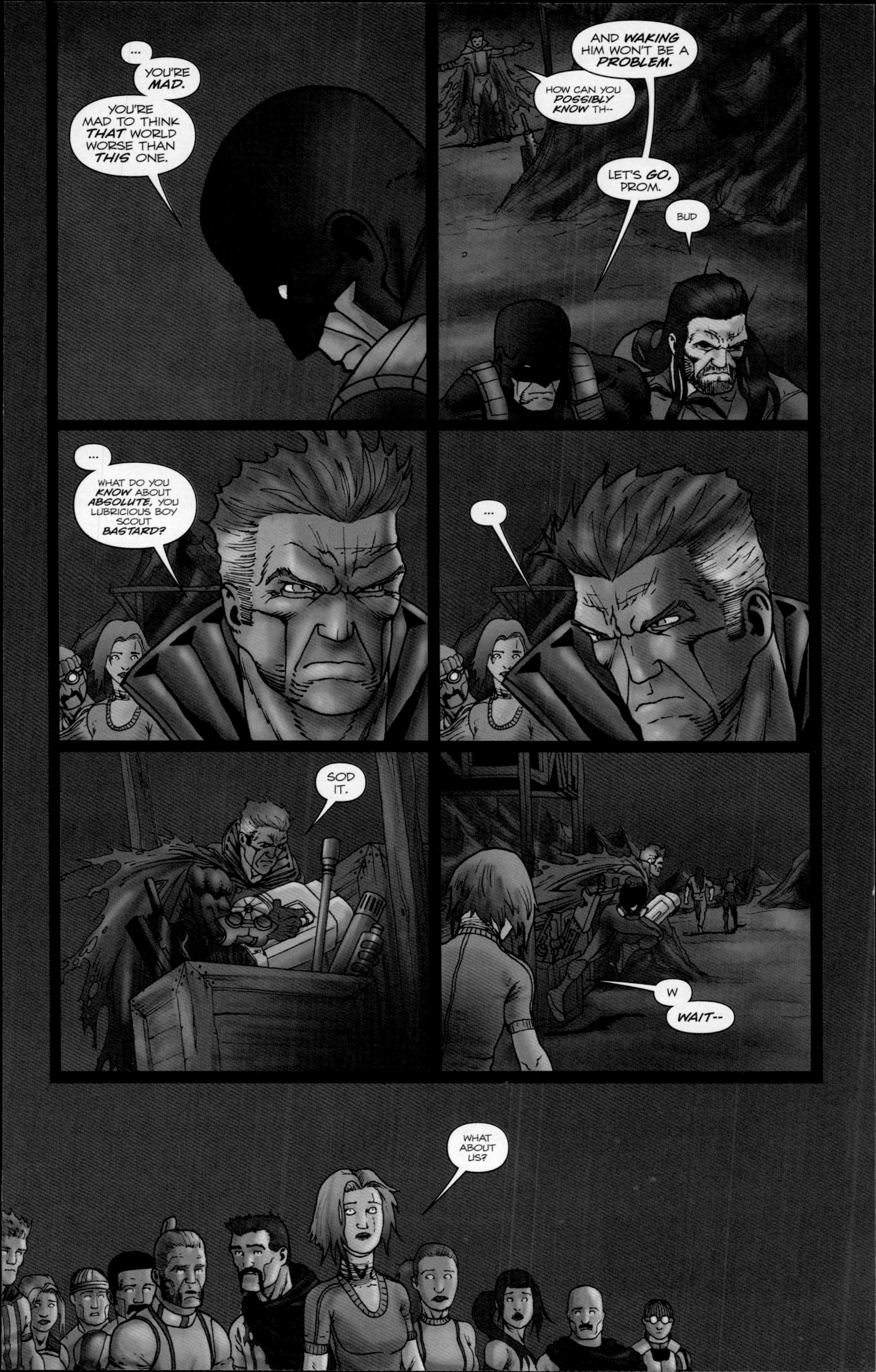
...
YOU'RE MAD.
YOU'RE MAD TO THINK THAT WORLD WORSE THAN THIS ONE.
AND WAKING HIM WON'T BE A PROBLEM.
HOW CAN YOU POSSIBLY KNOW TH--
LET'S GO, PROM.
BUD
...
WHAT DO YOU KNOW ABOUT ABSOLUTE, YOU LUBRICIOUS BOY SCOUT BASTARD?
...
SOD IT.
W
WAIT--
WHAT ABOUT US?

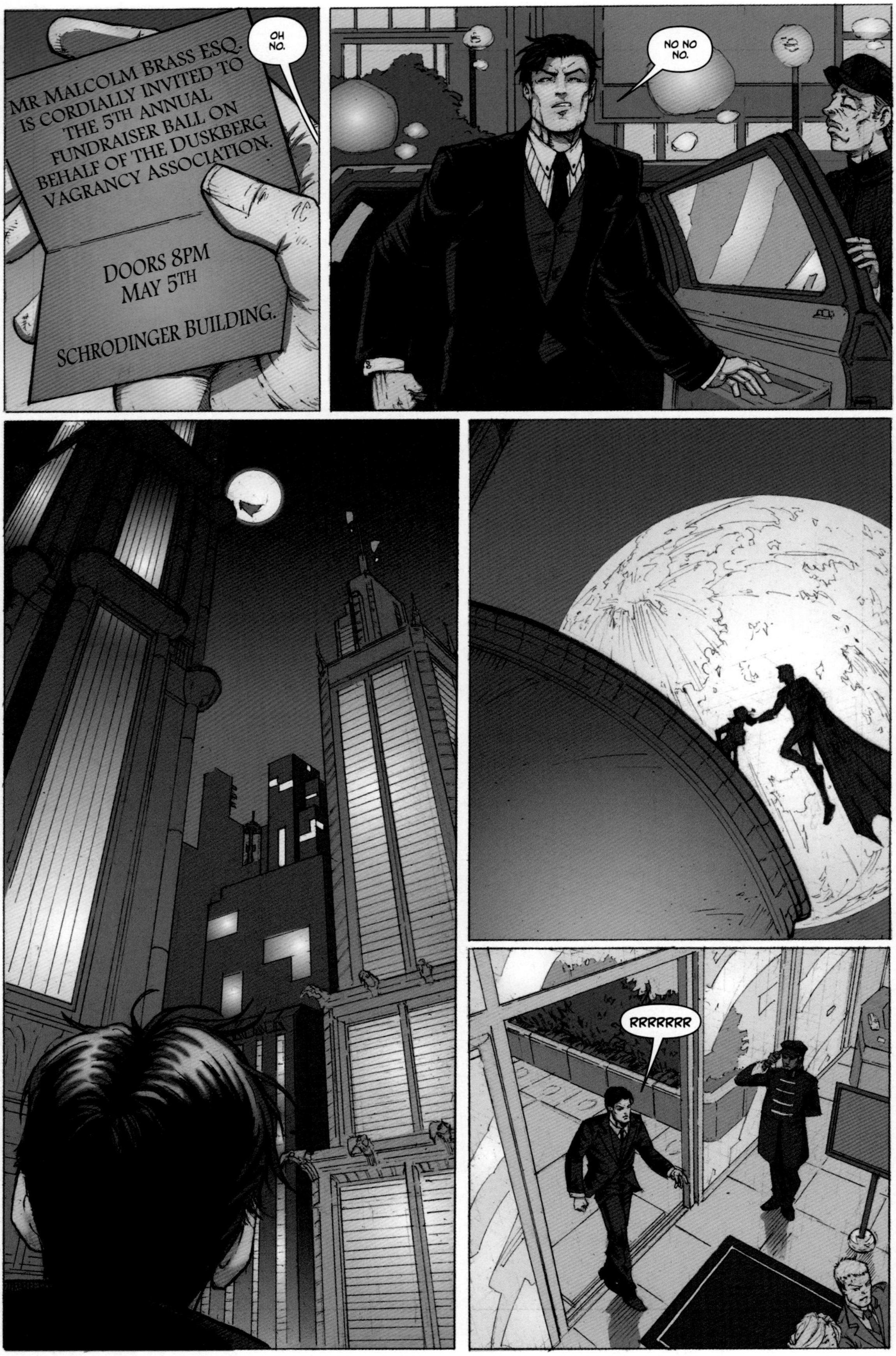
Mr Malcolm Brass Esq.
is cordially invited to
the 5th annual
fundraiser ball on
behalf of the Duskberg
Vagrancy Association.
Doors 8PM
May 5th
Schrodinger Building.
OH NO.
NO NO NO.
RRRRRRR

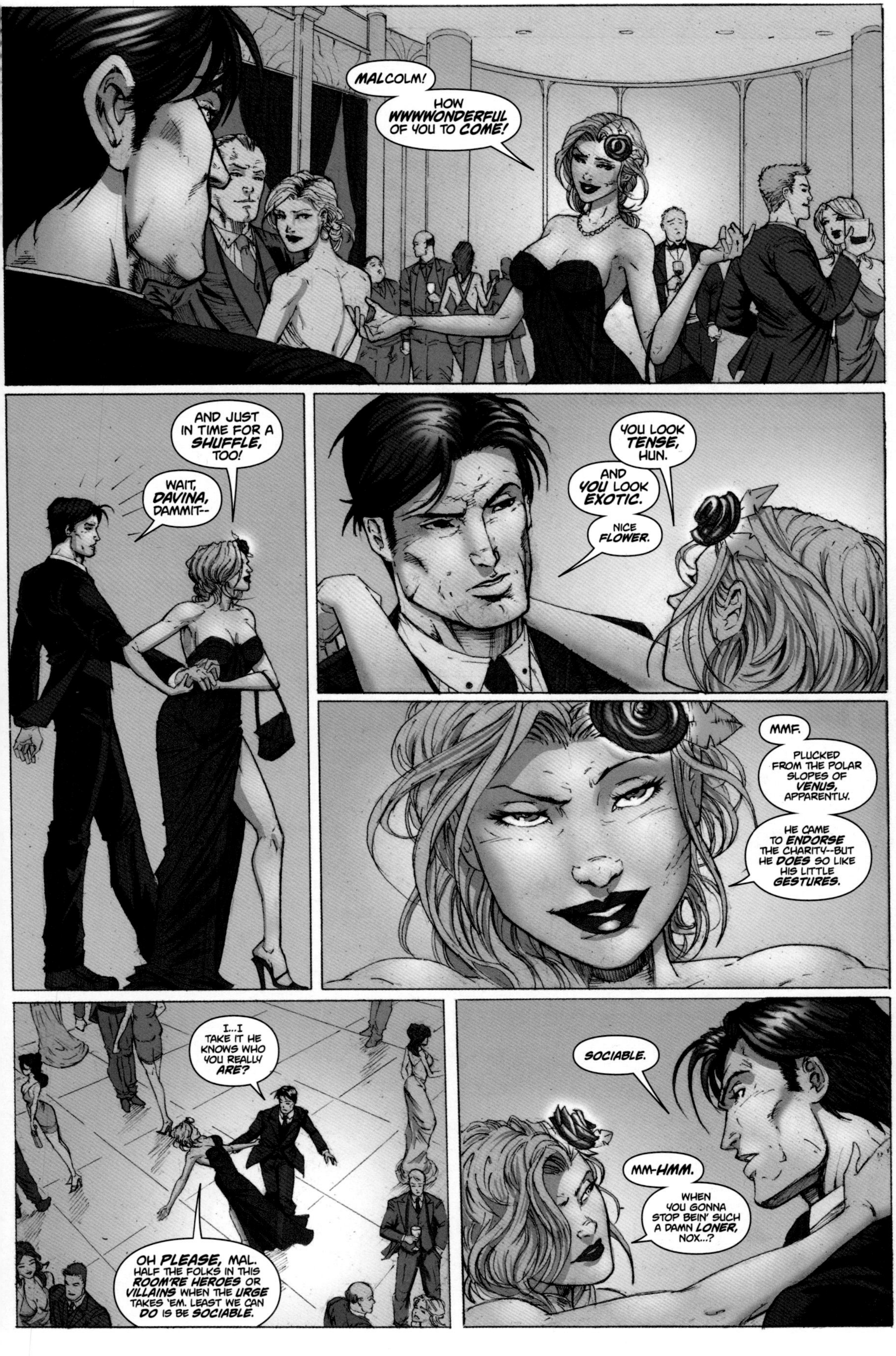
MALCOLM!
HOW WWWWONDERFUL OF YOU TO COME!
AND JUST IN TIME FOR A SHUFFLE, TOO!
WAIT, DAVINA, DAMMIT--
YOU LOOK TENSE, HUN.
AND YOU LOOK EXOTIC.
NICE FLOWER.
MMF.
PLUCKED FROM THE POLAR SLOPES OF VENUS, APPARENTLY.
HE CAME TO ENDORSE THE CHARITY--BUT HE DOES SO LIKE HIS LITTLE GESTURES.
I...I TAKE IT HE KNOWS WHO YOU REALLY ARE?
OH PLEASE, MAL. HALF THE FOLKS IN THIS ROOM'RE HEROES OR VILLAINS WHEN THE URGE TAKES 'EM. LEAST WE CAN DO IS BE SOCIABLE.
SOCIABLE.
MM-HMM.
WHEN YOU GONNA STOP BEIN' SUCH A DAMN LONER, NOX...?

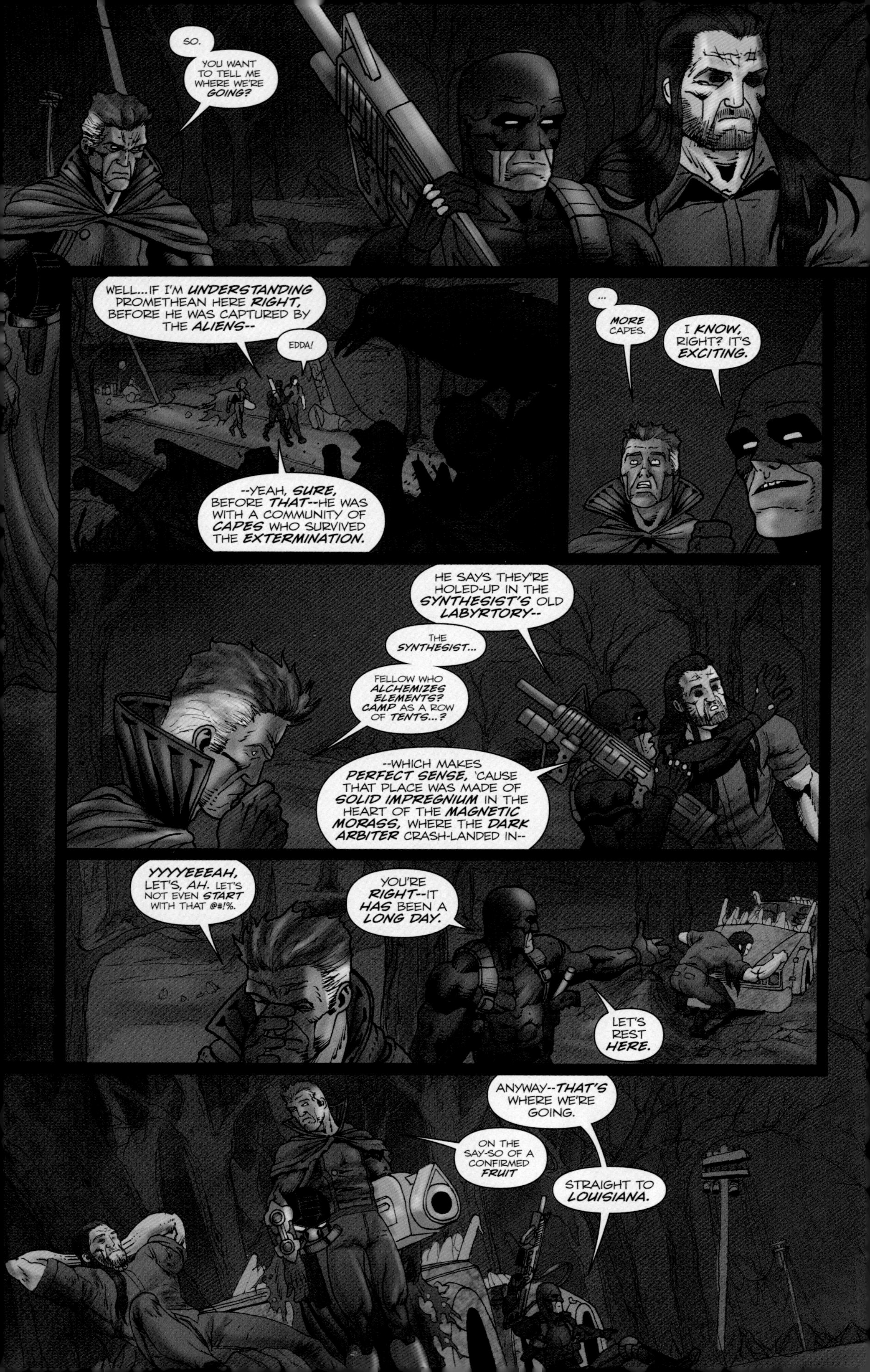
SO.
YOU WANT TO TELL ME WHERE WE'RE GOING?
WELL...IF I'M UNDERSTANDING PROMETHEAN HERE RIGHT, BEFORE HE WAS CAPTURED BY THE ALIENS--
EDDA!
--YEAH, SURE, BEFORE THAT--HE WAS WITH A COMMUNITY OF CAPES WHO SURVIVED THE EXTERMINATION.
...
MORE CAPES.
I KNOW, RIGHT? IT'S EXCITING.
HE SAYS THEY'RE HOLED-UP IN THE SYNTHESIST'S OLD LABYRTORY--
THE SYNTHESIST...
FELLOW WHO ALCHEMIZES ELEMENTS? CAMP AS A ROW OF TENTS...?
--WHICH MAKES PERFECT SENSE, 'CAUSE THAT PLACE WAS MADE OF SOLID IMPREGNIUM IN THE HEART OF THE MAGNETIC MORASS, WHERE THE DARK ARBITER CRASH-LANDED IN--
YYYYEEEAH, LET'S, AH. LET'S NOT EVEN START WITH THAT @#!%.
YOU'RE RIGHT--IT HAS BEEN A LONG DAY.
LET'S REST HERE.
ANYWAY--THAT'S WHERE WE'RE GOING.
ON THE SAY-SO OF A CONFIRMED FRUIT
STRAIGHT TO LOUISIANA.

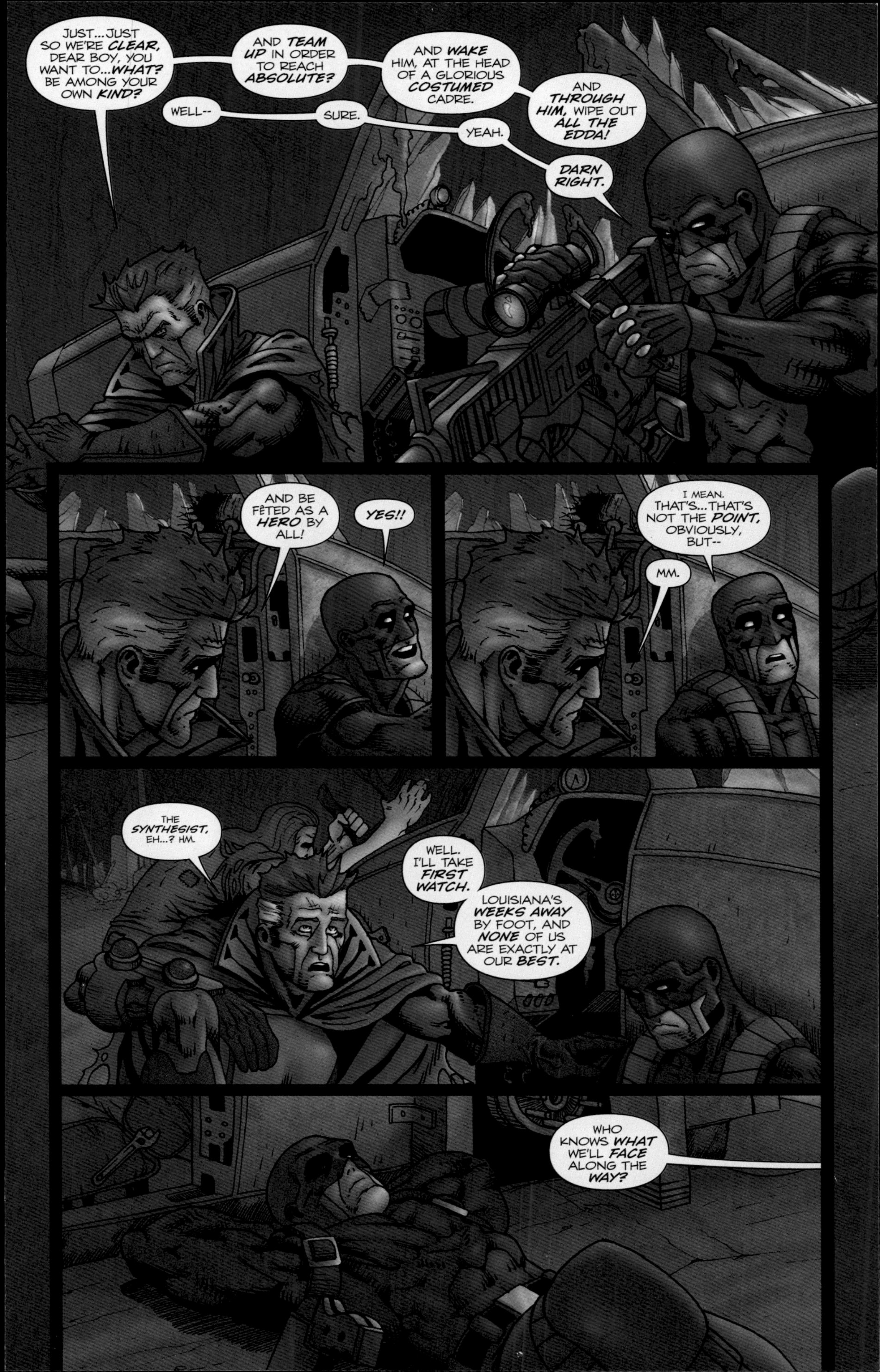
JUST... JUST SO WE'RE CLEAR, DEAR BOY, YOU WANT TO... WHAT? BE AMONG YOUR OWN KIND?
WELL--
AND TEAM UP IN ORDER TO REACH ABSOLUTE?
SURE.
AND WAKE HIM, AT THE HEAD OF A GLORIOUS COSTUMED CADRE.
YEAH.
AND THROUGH HIM, WIPE OUT ALL THE EDDA!
DARN RIGHT.
AND BE FÊTED AS A HERO BY ALL!
YES!!
I MEAN. THAT'S... THAT'S NOT THE POINT, OBVIOUSLY, BUT--
MM.
THE SYNTHESIST, EH...? HM.
WELL. I'LL TAKE FIRST WATCH.
LOUISIANA'S WEEKS AWAY BY FOOT, AND NONE OF US ARE EXACTLY AT OUR BEST.
WHO KNOWS WHAT WE'LL FACE ALONG THE WAY?

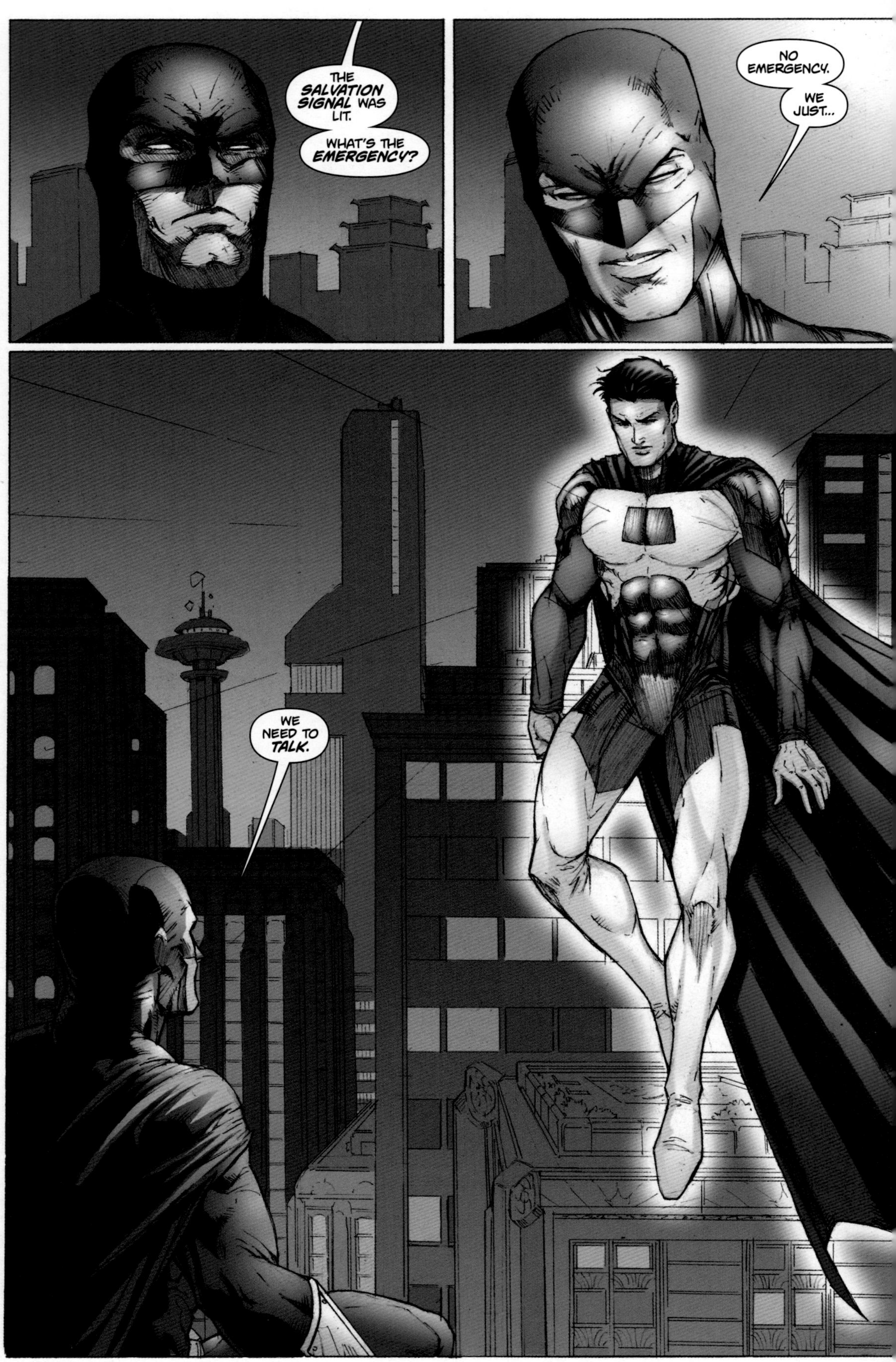
THE SALVATION SIGNAL WAS LIT.
WHAT'S THE EMERGENCY?
NO EMERGENCY.
WE JUST...
WE NEED TO TALK.

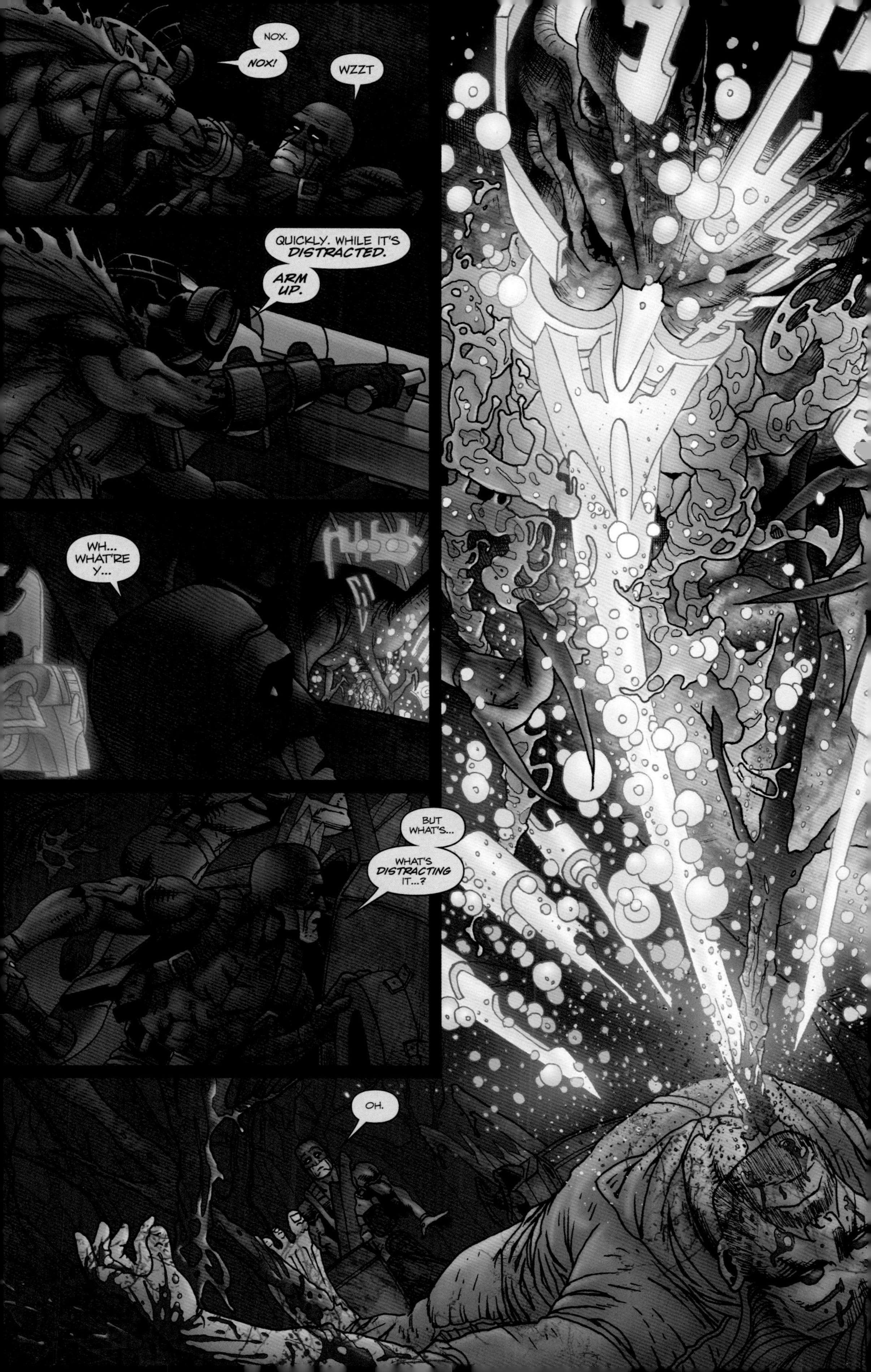
NOX.
NOX!
WZZT
QUICKLY. WHILE IT'S DISTRACTED.
ARM UP.
WH... WHAT'RE Y...
BUT WHAT'S...
WHAT'S DISTRACTING IT...?
OH.

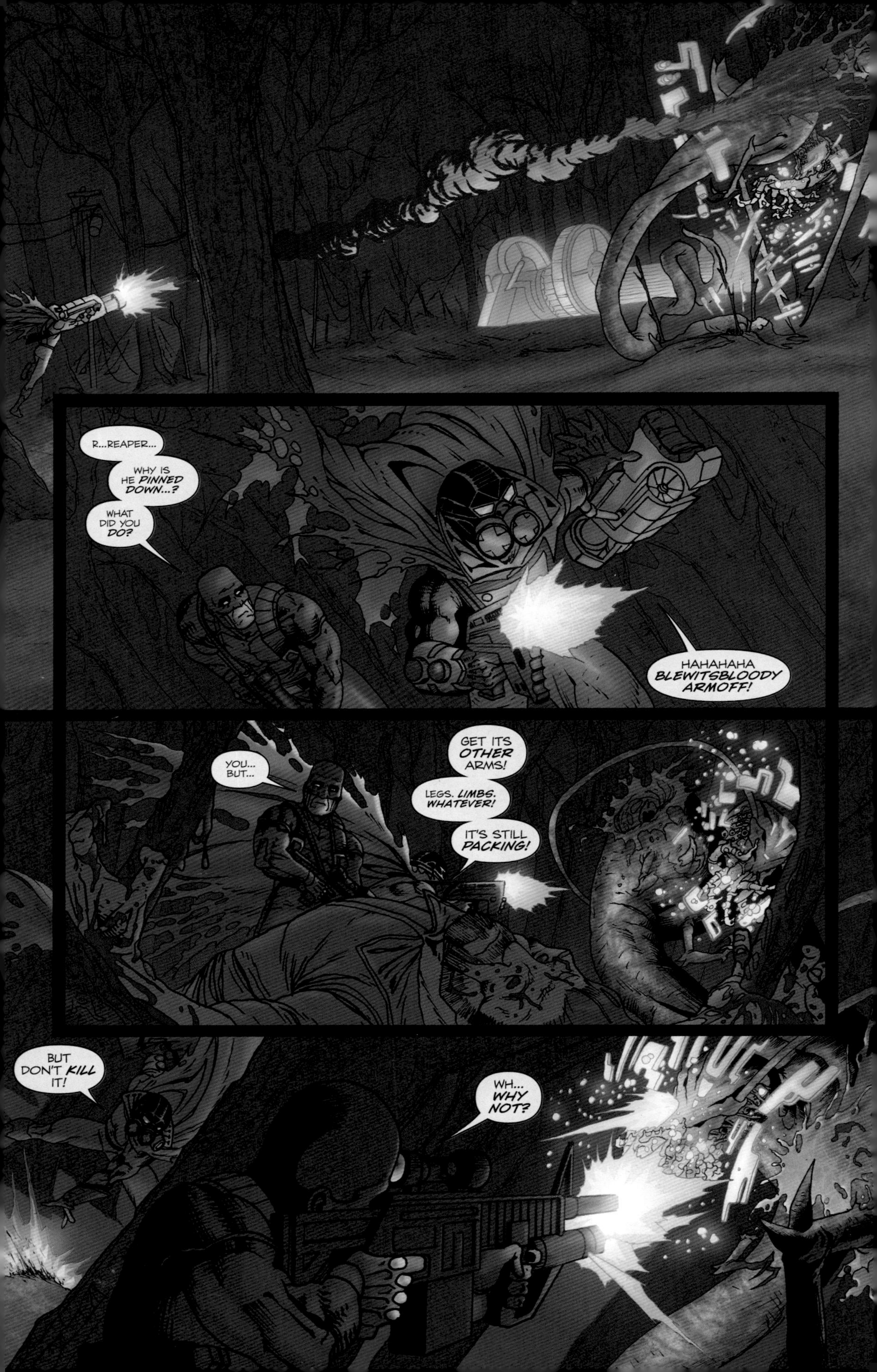
R...REAPER...
WHY IS HE PINNED DOWN...?
WHAT DID YOU DO?
HAHAHAHA BLEWITSBLOODY ARMOFF!
YOU... BUT...
GET ITS OTHER ARMS!
LEGS. LIMBS. WHATEVER!
IT'S STILL PACKING!
BUT DON'T KILL IT!
WH... WHY NOT?

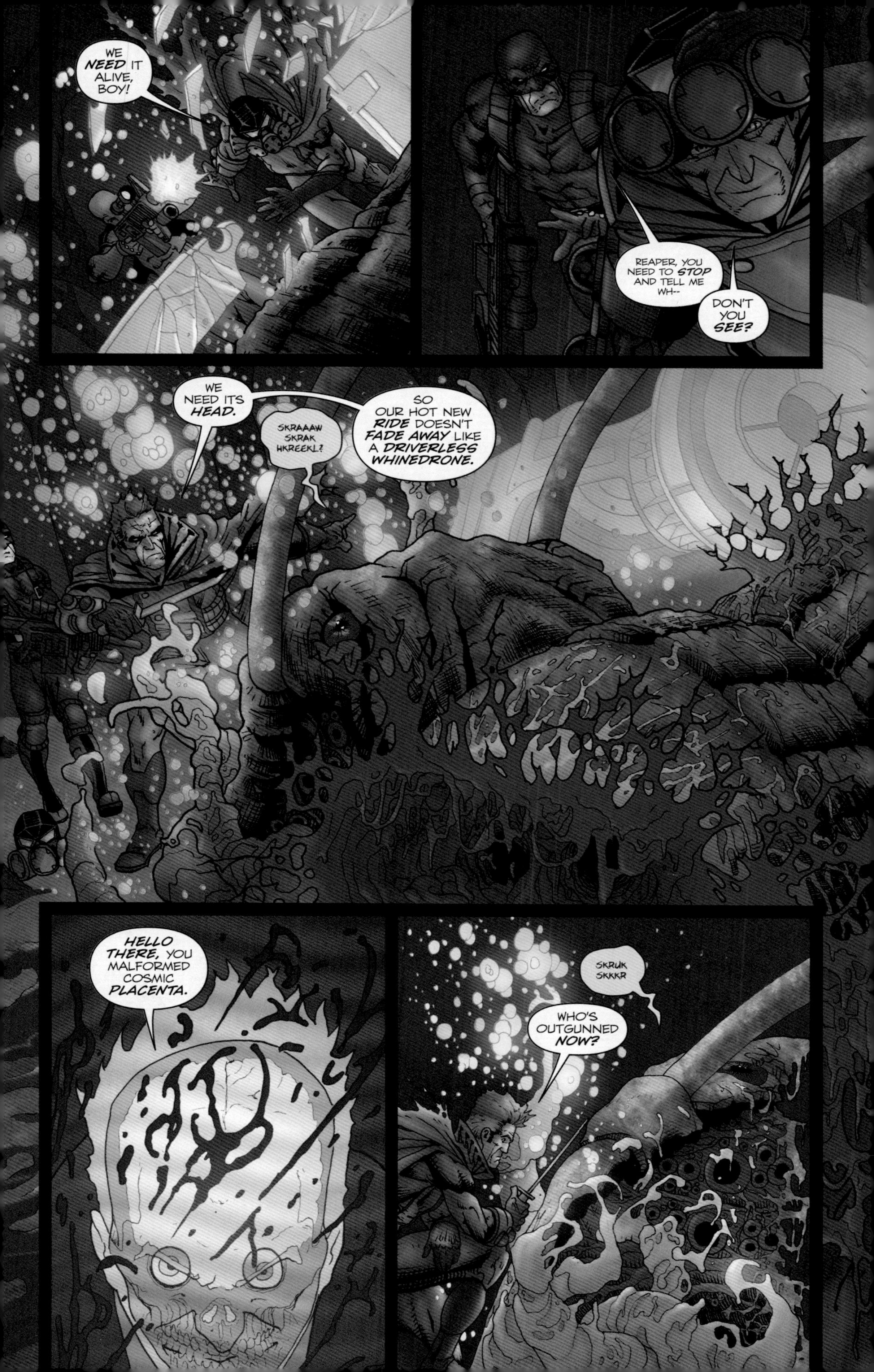
WE NEED IT ALIVE, BOY!
REAPER, YOU NEED TO STOP AND TELL ME WH--
DON'T YOU SEE?
WE NEED ITS HEAD.
SO OUR HOT NEW RIDE DOESN'T FADE AWAY LIKE A DRIVERLESS WHINEDRONE.
SKRAAAW SKRAK HKREEKL?
HELLO THERE, YOU MALFORMED COSMIC PLACENTA.
SKRUK SKKKR
WHO'S OUTGUNNED NOW?

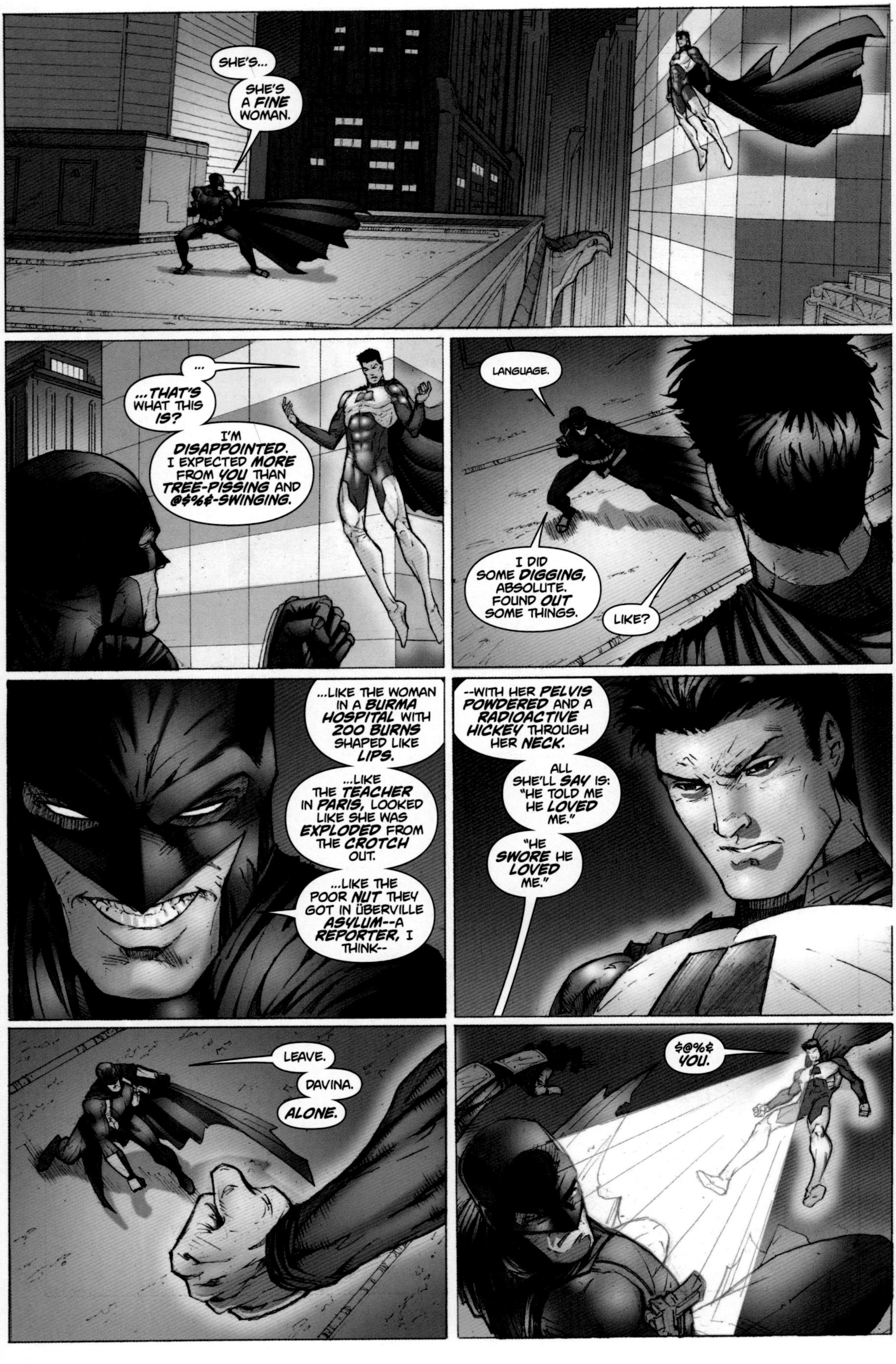
SHE'S...
SHE'S A *FINE* WOMAN.
...
...*THAT'S* WHAT THIS *IS?*
I'M *DISAPPOINTED*. I EXPECTED *MORE* FROM *YOU* THAN *TREE-PISSING* AND *@$%&-SWINGING*.
LANGUAGE.
I DID SOME *DIGGING*, ABSOLUTE. FOUND *OUT* SOME THINGS.
LIKE?
...LIKE THE WOMAN IN A *BURMA HOSPITAL* WITH *200 BURNS* SHAPED LIKE *LIPS*.
...LIKE THE *TEACHER* IN *PARIS*, LOOKED LIKE SHE WAS *EXPLODED* FROM THE *CROTCH* OUT.
...LIKE THE POOR *NUT* THEY GOT IN ÜBERVILLE *ASYLUM*--A *REPORTER*, I THINK--
--WITH HER *PELVIS POWDERED* AND A *RADIOACTIVE HICKEY* THROUGH HER *NECK*.
ALL SHE'LL *SAY* IS: "HE TOLD ME HE *LOVED* ME."
"HE *SWORE* HE *LOVED* ME."
LEAVE.
DAVINA.
*ALONE*.
*$@%& YOU*.

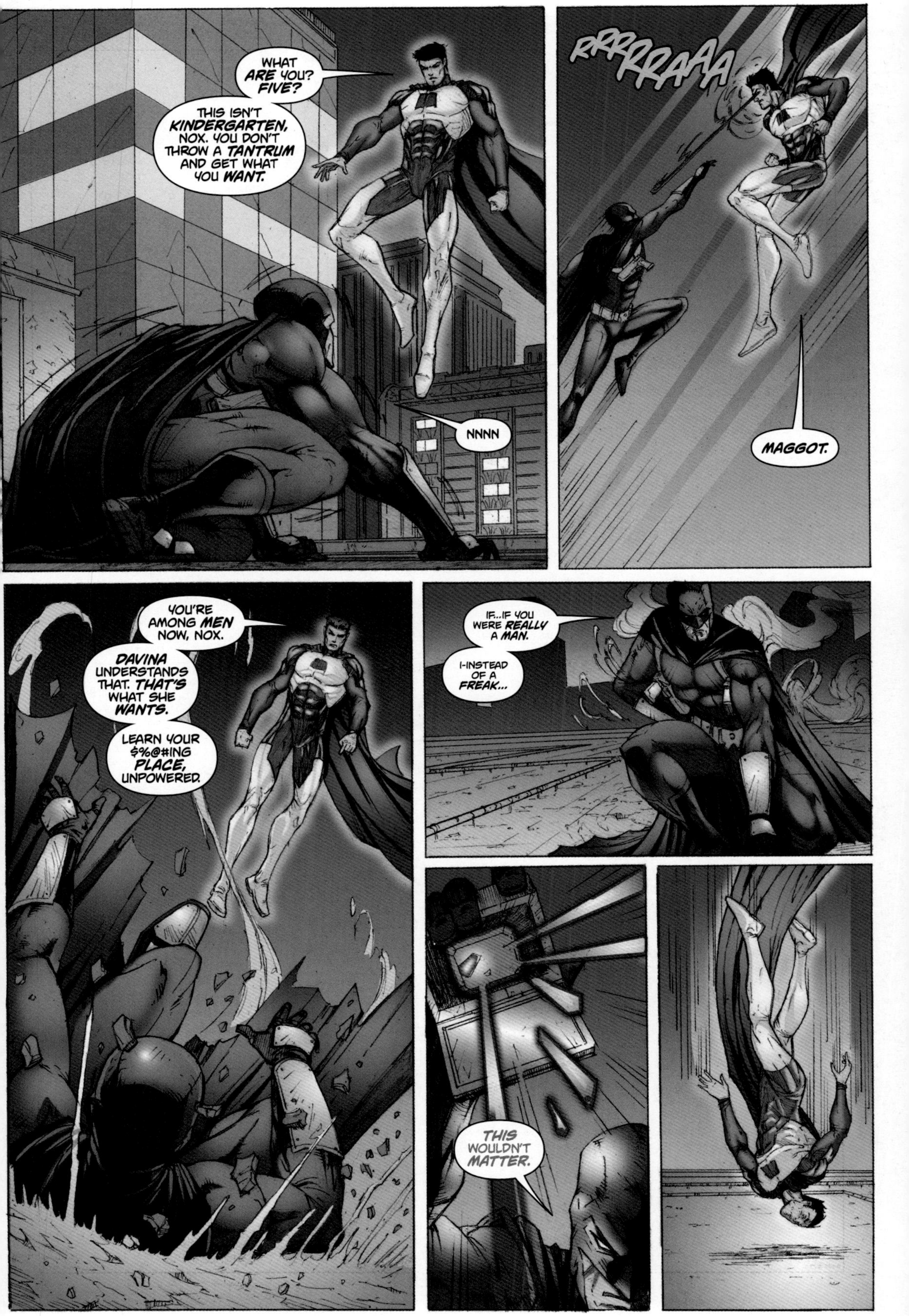
WHAT ARE YOU? FIVE?
THIS ISN'T KINDERGARTEN, NOX. YOU DON'T THROW A TANTRUM AND GET WHAT YOU WANT.
NNNN
RRRRRAAAA
MAGGOT.
YOU'RE AMONG MEN NOW, NOX.
DAVINA UNDERSTANDS THAT. THAT'S WHAT SHE WANTS.
LEARN YOUR $%@#ING PLACE, UNPOWERED.
IF...IF YOU WERE REALLY A MAN.
I-INSTEAD OF A FREAK...
THIS WOULDN'T MATTER.

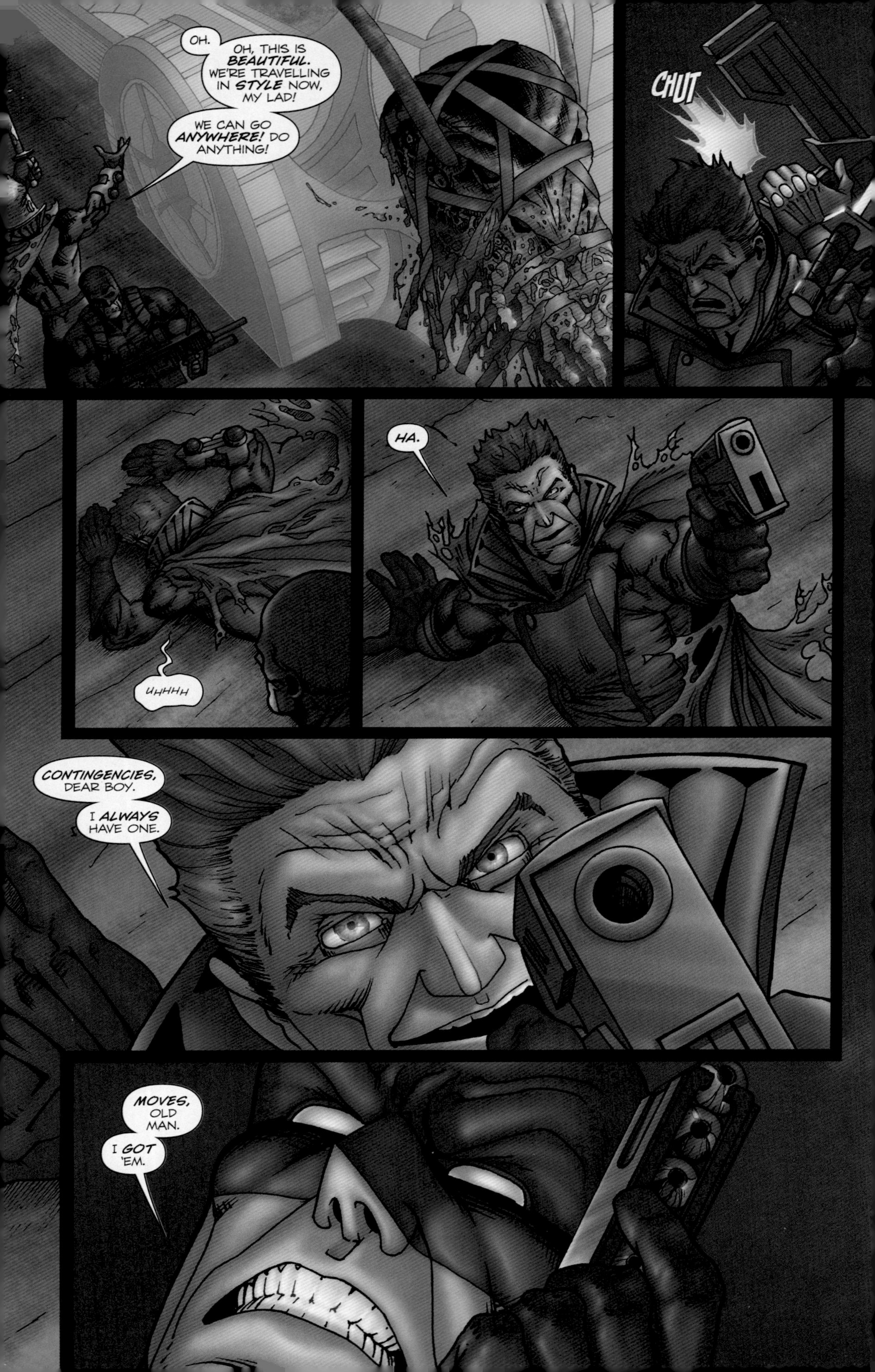
OH.
OH, THIS IS BEAUTIFUL. WE'RE TRAVELLING IN STYLE NOW, MY LAD!
WE CAN GO ANYWHERE! DO ANYTHING!
CHUT
UHHHH
HA.
CONTINGENCIES, DEAR BOY.
I ALWAYS HAVE ONE.
MOVES, OLD MAN.
I GOT 'EM.

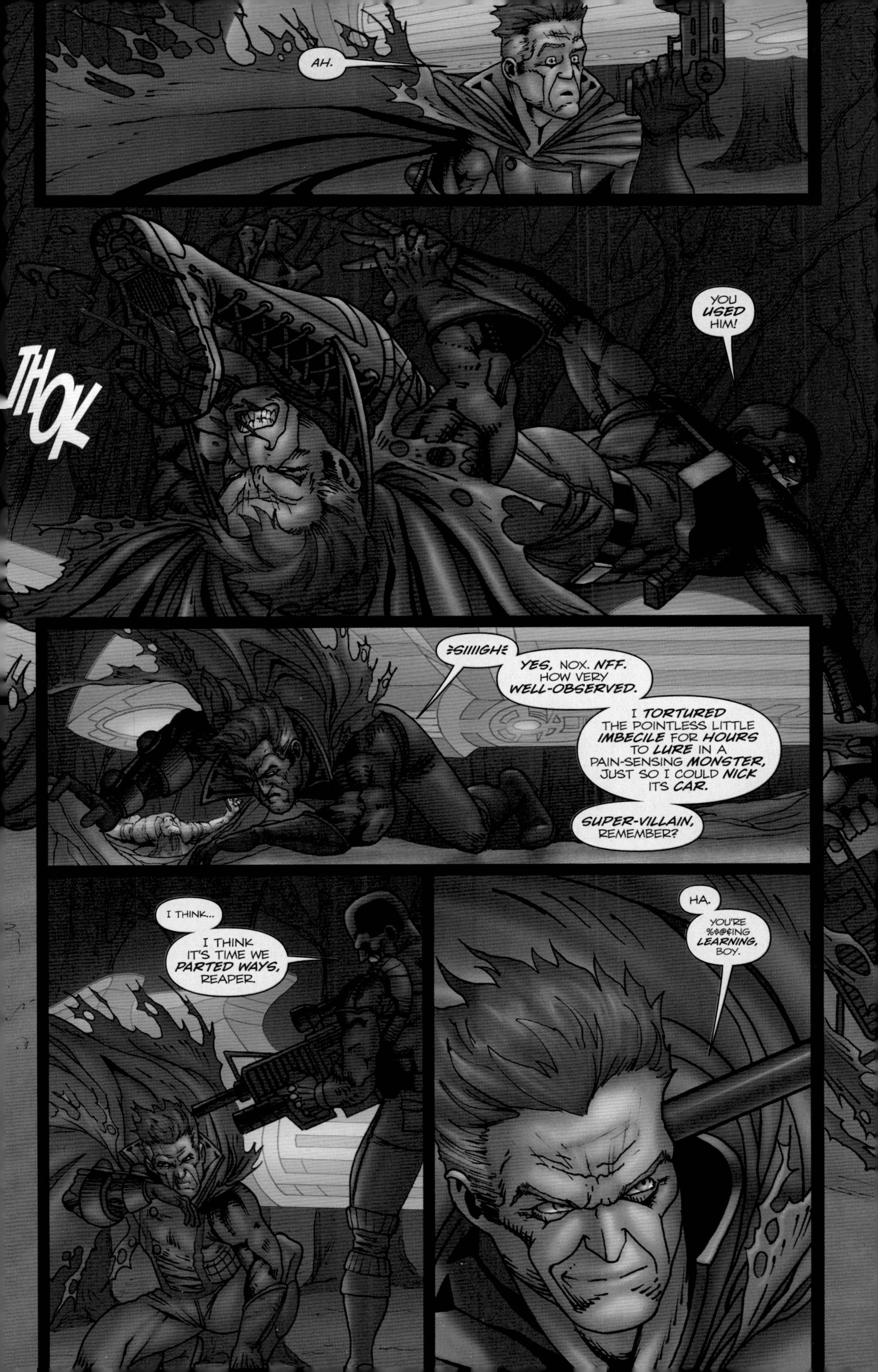
AH.
YOU USED HIM!
THOK
SIIIIGH
YES, NOX. NFF. HOW VERY WELL-OBSERVED.
I TORTURED THE POINTLESS LITTLE IMBECILE FOR HOURS TO LURE IN A PAIN-SENSING MONSTER, JUST SO I COULD NICK ITS CAR.
SUPER-VILLAIN, REMEMBER?
I THINK...
I THINK IT'S TIME WE PARTED WAYS, REAPER.
HA.
YOU'RE %$@¢ING LEARNING, BOY.

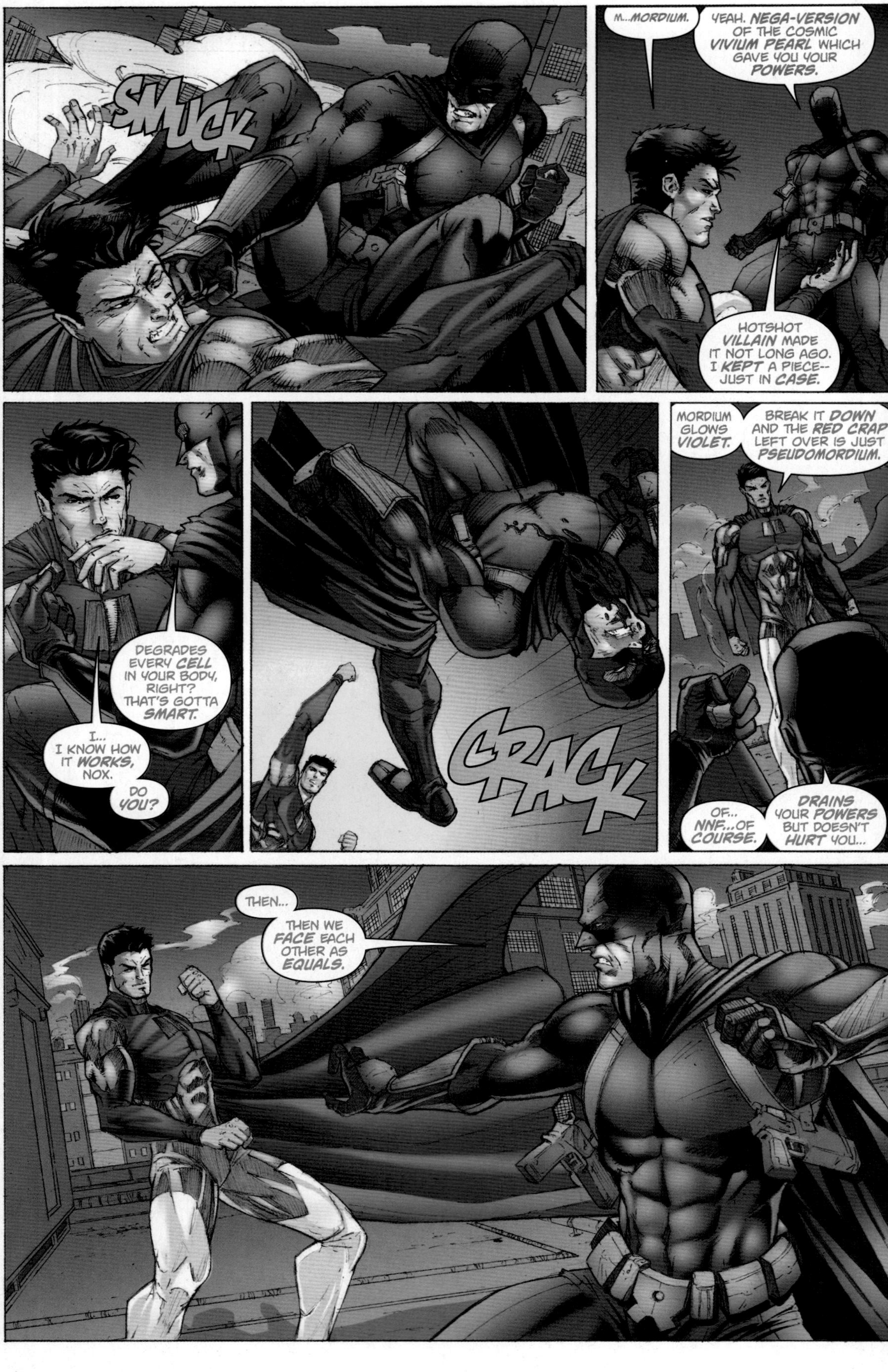
SMUCK
M...MORDIUM.
YEAH. NEGA-VERSION OF THE COSMIC VIVIUM PEARL WHICH GAVE YOU YOUR POWERS.
HOTSHOT VILLAIN MADE IT NOT LONG AGO. I KEPT A PIECE-- JUST IN CASE--
DEGRADES EVERY CELL IN YOUR BODY, RIGHT? THAT'S GOTTA SMART.
I... I KNOW HOW IT WORKS, NOX.
DO YOU?
CRACK
MORDIUM GLOWS VIOLET.
BREAK IT DOWN AND THE RED CRAP LEFT OVER IS JUST PSEUDOMORDIUM.
DRAINS YOUR POWERS BUT DOESN'T HURT YOU...
OF... NNF...OF COURSE.
THEN...
THEN WE FACE EACH OTHER AS EQUALS.

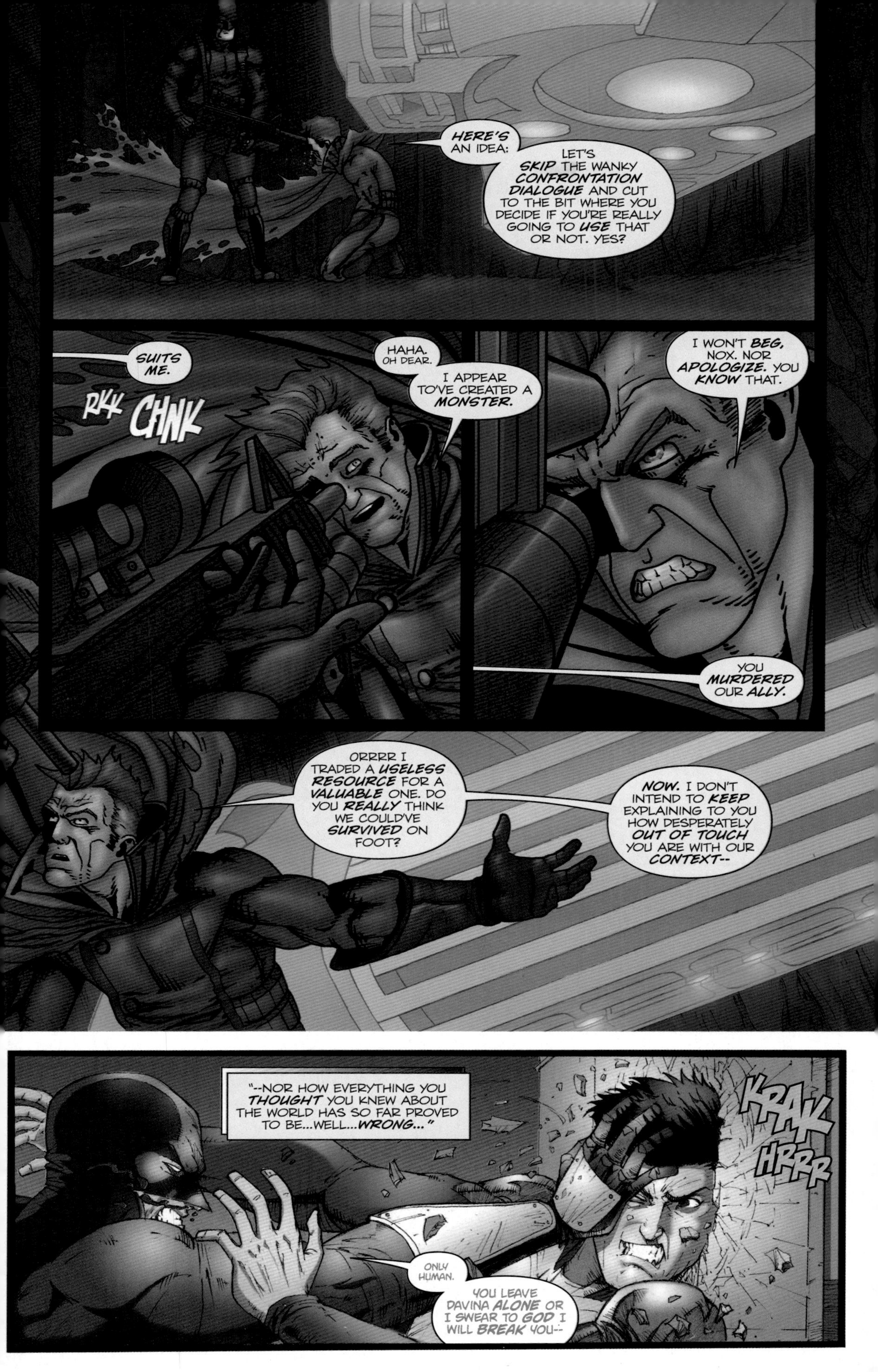
HERE'S AN IDEA:
LET'S SKIP THE WANKY CONFRONTATION DIALOGUE AND CUT TO THE BIT WHERE YOU DECIDE IF YOU'RE REALLY GOING TO USE THAT OR NOT. YES?
SUITS ME.
RKK CHNK
HAHA. OH DEAR.
I APPEAR TO'VE CREATED A MONSTER.
I WON'T BEG, NOX. NOR APOLOGIZE. YOU KNOW THAT.
YOU MURDERED OUR ALLY.
ORRRR I TRADED A USELESS RESOURCE FOR A VALUABLE ONE. DO YOU REALLY THINK WE COULD'VE SURVIVED ON FOOT?
NOW. I DON'T INTEND TO KEEP EXPLAINING TO YOU HOW DESPERATELY OUT OF TOUCH YOU ARE WITH OUR CONTEXT--
"--NOR HOW EVERYTHING YOU THOUGHT YOU KNEW ABOUT THE WORLD HAS SO FAR PROVED TO BE...WELL...WRONG..."
KRAK
HRRR
ONLY HUMAN.
YOU LEAVE DAVINA ALONE OR I SWEAR TO GOD I WILL BREAK YOU--

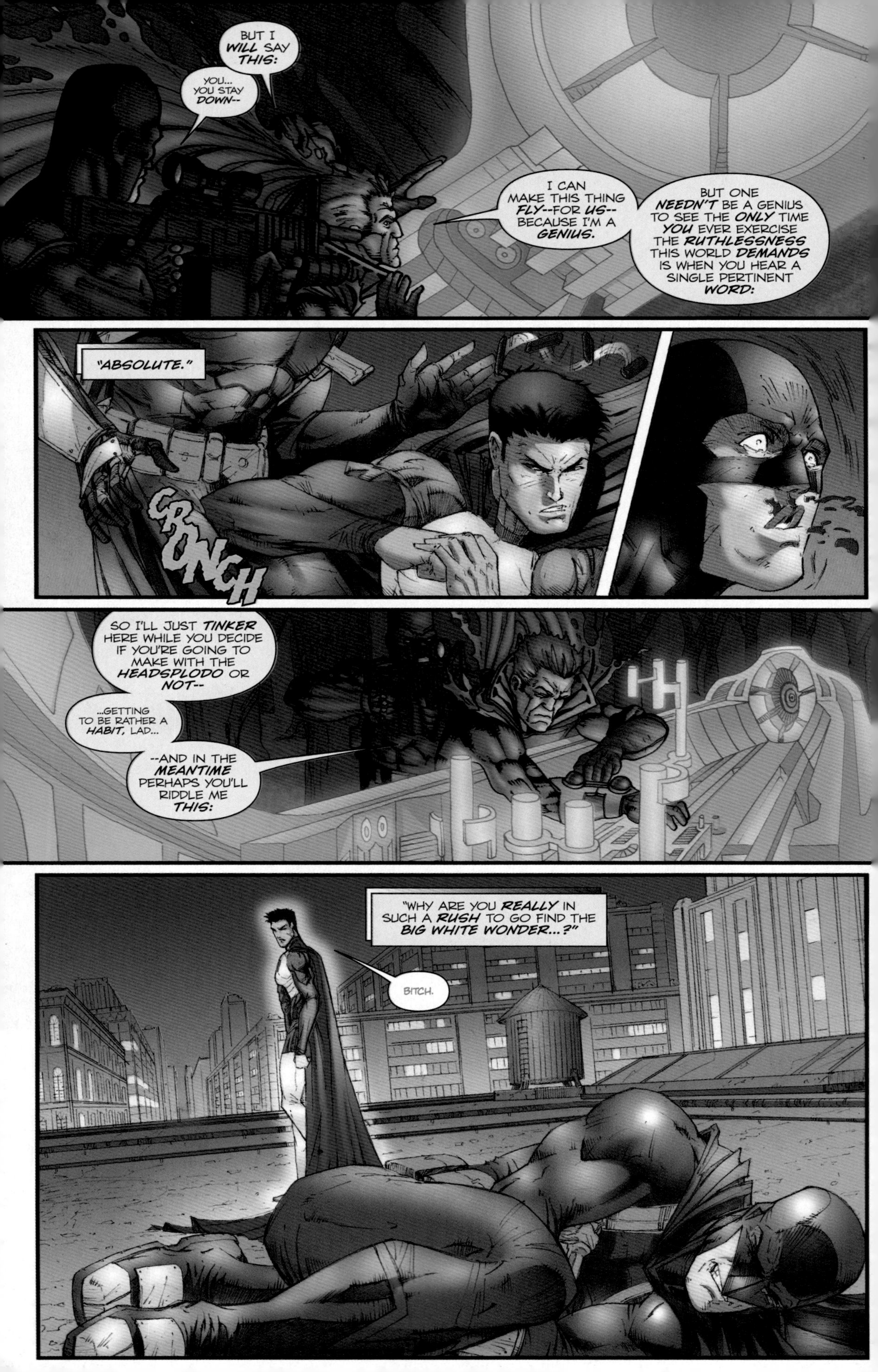
BUT I WILL SAY THIS:
YOU... YOU STAY DOWN--
I CAN MAKE THIS THING FLY--FOR US--BECAUSE I'M A GENIUS.
BUT ONE NEEDN'T BE A GENIUS TO SEE THE ONLY TIME YOU EVER EXERCISE THE RUTHLESSNESS THIS WORLD DEMANDS IS WHEN YOU HEAR A SINGLE PERTINENT WORD:
"ABSOLUTE."
CRONCH
SO I'LL JUST TINKER HERE WHILE YOU DECIDE IF YOU'RE GOING TO MAKE WITH THE HEADSPLODO OR NOT--
...GETTING TO BE RATHER A HABIT, LAD...
--AND IN THE MEANTIME PERHAPS YOU'LL RIDDLE ME THIS:
"WHY ARE YOU REALLY IN SUCH A RUSH TO GO FIND THE BIG WHITE WONDER...?"
BITCH.

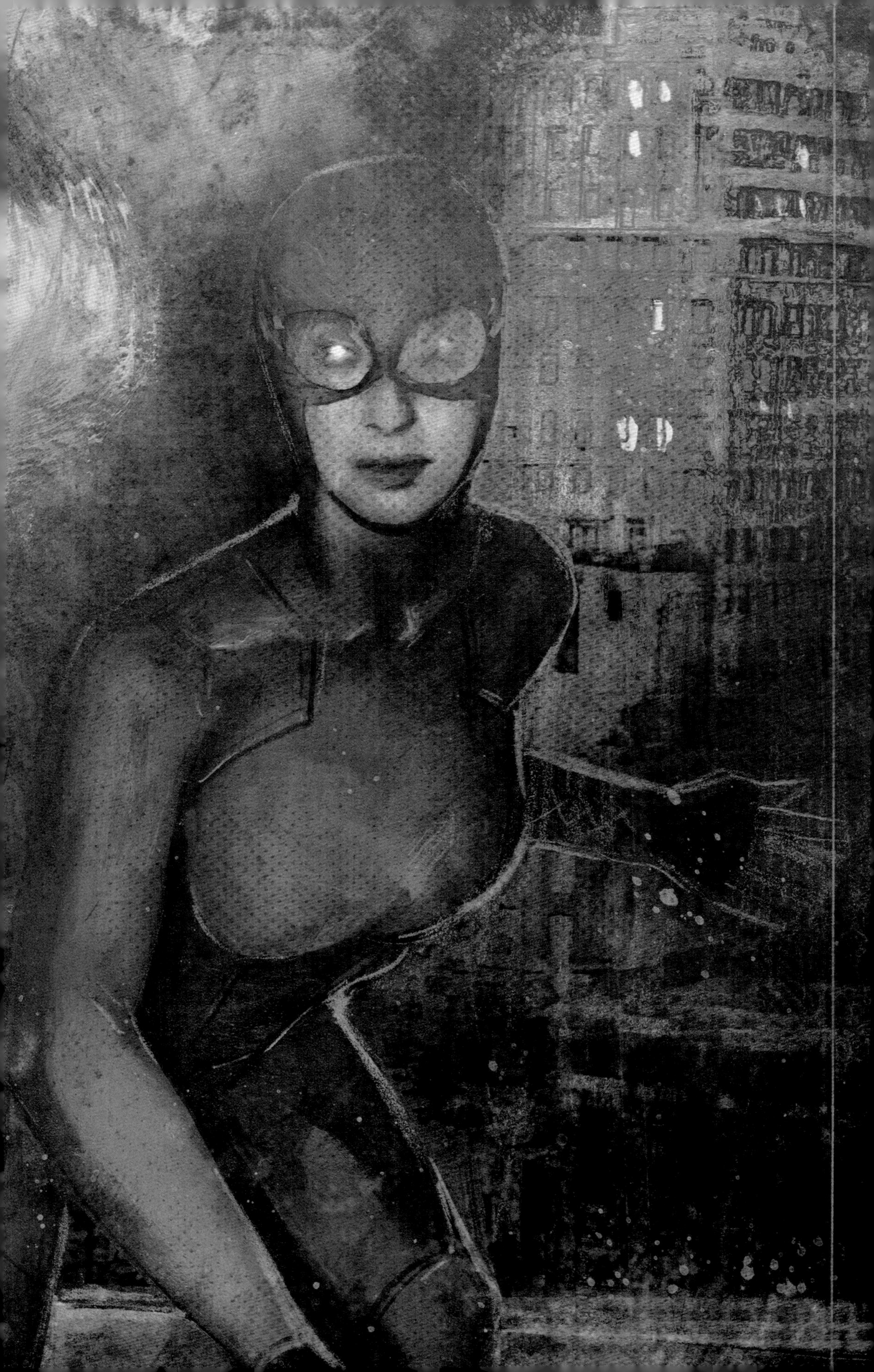

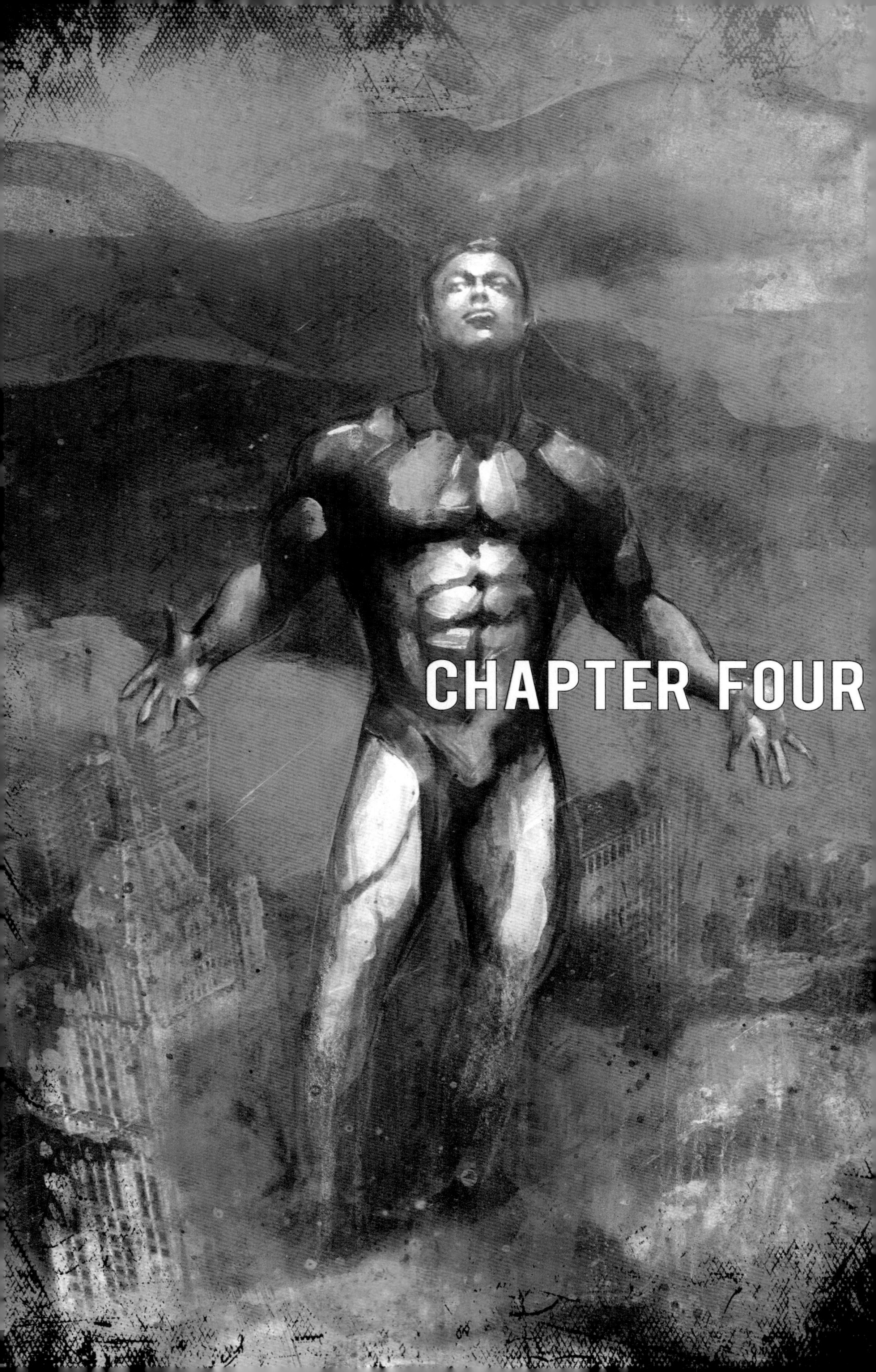

# CHAPTER FOUR

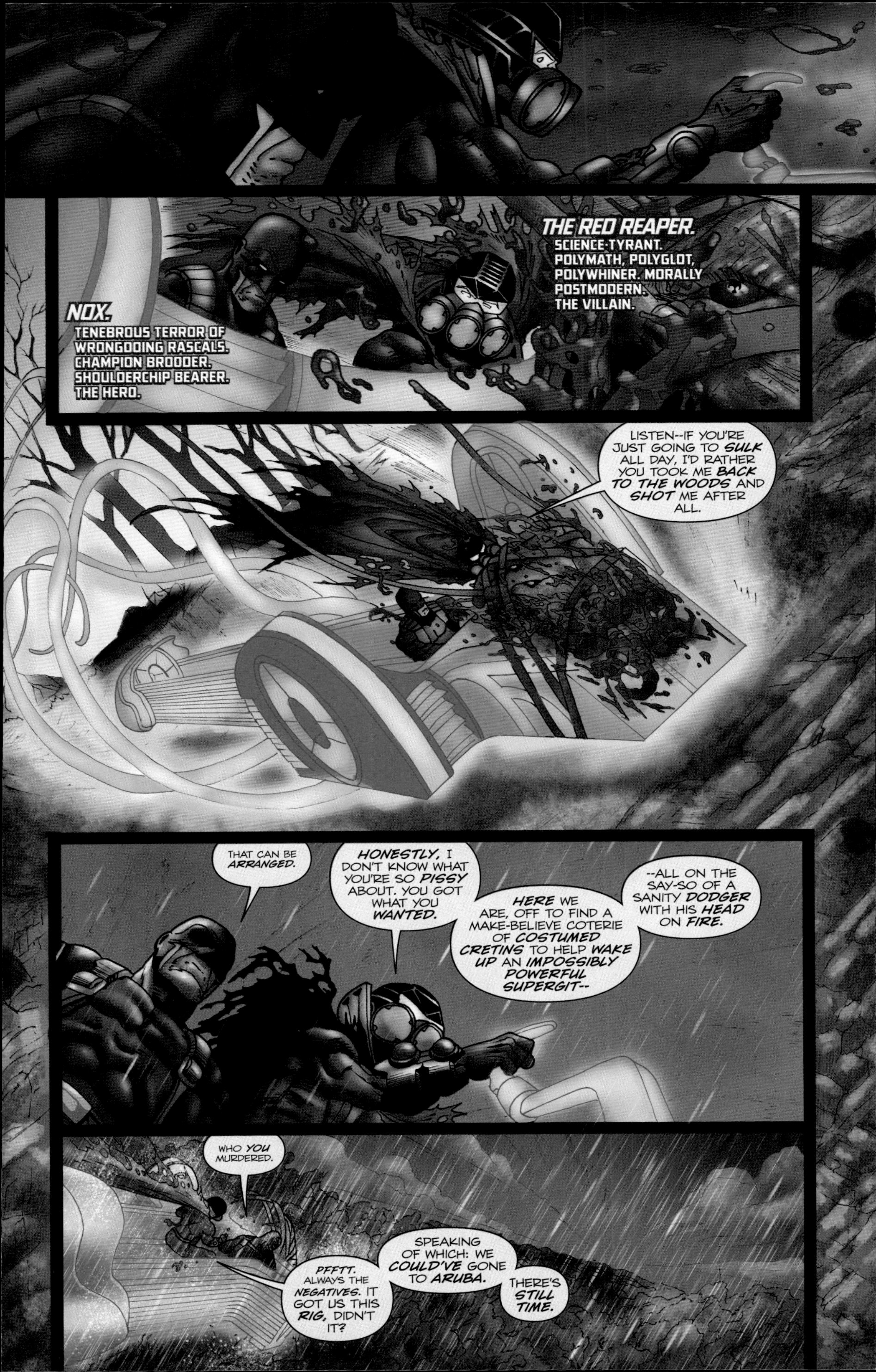

NOX.
TENEBROUS TERROR OF WRONGDOING RASCALS. CHAMPION BROODER. SHOULDERCHIP BEARER. THE HERO.
THE RED REAPER.
SCIENCE-TYRANT. POLYMATH, POLYGLOT, POLYWHINER. MORALLY POSTMODERN. THE VILLAIN.
LISTEN--IF YOU'RE JUST GOING TO SULK ALL DAY, I'D RATHER YOU TOOK ME BACK TO THE WOODS AND SHOT ME AFTER ALL.
THAT CAN BE ARRANGED.
HONESTLY, I DON'T KNOW WHAT YOU'RE SO PISSY ABOUT. YOU GOT WHAT YOU WANTED.
HERE WE ARE, OFF TO FIND A MAKE-BELIEVE COTERIE OF COSTUMED CRETINS TO HELP WAKE UP AN IMPOSSIBLY POWERFUL SUPERGIT--
--ALL ON THE SAY-SO OF A SANITY DODGER WITH HIS HEAD ON FIRE.
WHO YOU MURDERED.
PFFTT. ALWAYS THE NEGATIVES. IT GOT US THIS RIG, DIDN'T IT?
SPEAKING OF WHICH: WE COULD'VE GONE TO ARUBA.
THERE'S STILL TIME.

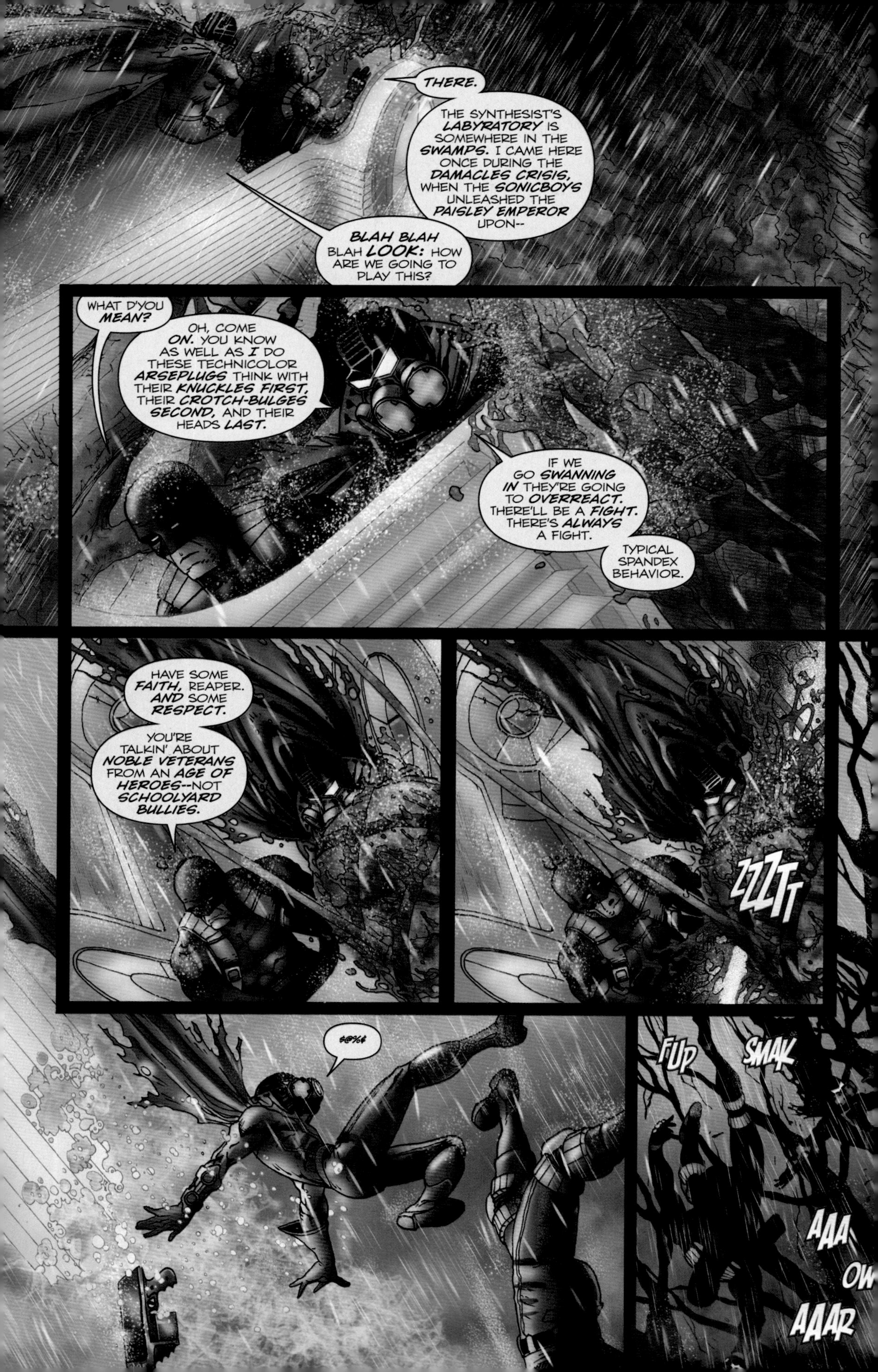
THERE.
THE SYNTHESIST'S LABYRATORY IS SOMEWHERE IN THE SWAMPS. I CAME HERE ONCE DURING THE DAMACLES CRISIS, WHEN THE SONICBOYS UNLEASHED THE PAISLEY EMPEROR UPON--
BLAH BLAH BLAH LOOK: HOW ARE WE GOING TO PLAY THIS?
WHAT D'YOU MEAN?
OH, COME ON. YOU KNOW AS WELL AS I DO THESE TECHNICOLOR ARSEPLUGS THINK WITH THEIR KNUCKLES FIRST, THEIR CROTCH-BULGES SECOND, AND THEIR HEADS LAST.
IF WE GO SWANNING IN THEY'RE GOING TO OVERREACT. THERE'LL BE A FIGHT. THERE'S ALWAYS A FIGHT.
TYPICAL SPANDEX BEHAVIOR.
HAVE SOME FAITH, REAPER. AND SOME RESPECT.
YOU'RE TALKIN' ABOUT NOBLE VETERANS FROM AN AGE OF HEROES--NOT SCHOOLYARD BULLIES.
ZZZTT
$@%$
FUP
SMAK
AAA
OW
AAAR

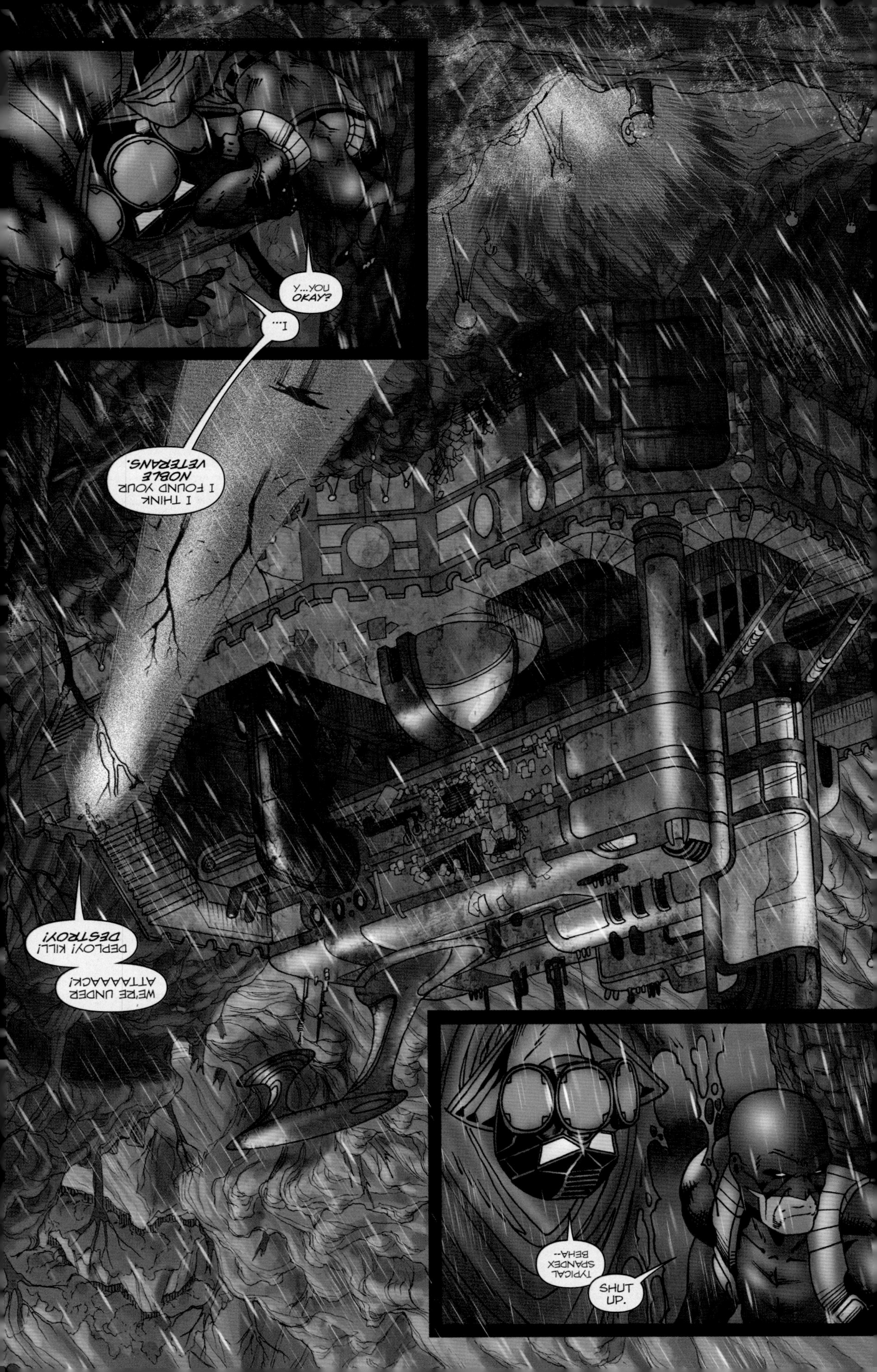
Y...YOU OKAY?
I...
I THINK I FOUND YOUR NOBLE VETERANS.
WE'RE UNDER ATTAAACK!
DEPLOY! KILL! DESTROY!
TYPICAL SPANDEX BEHA--
SHUT UP.

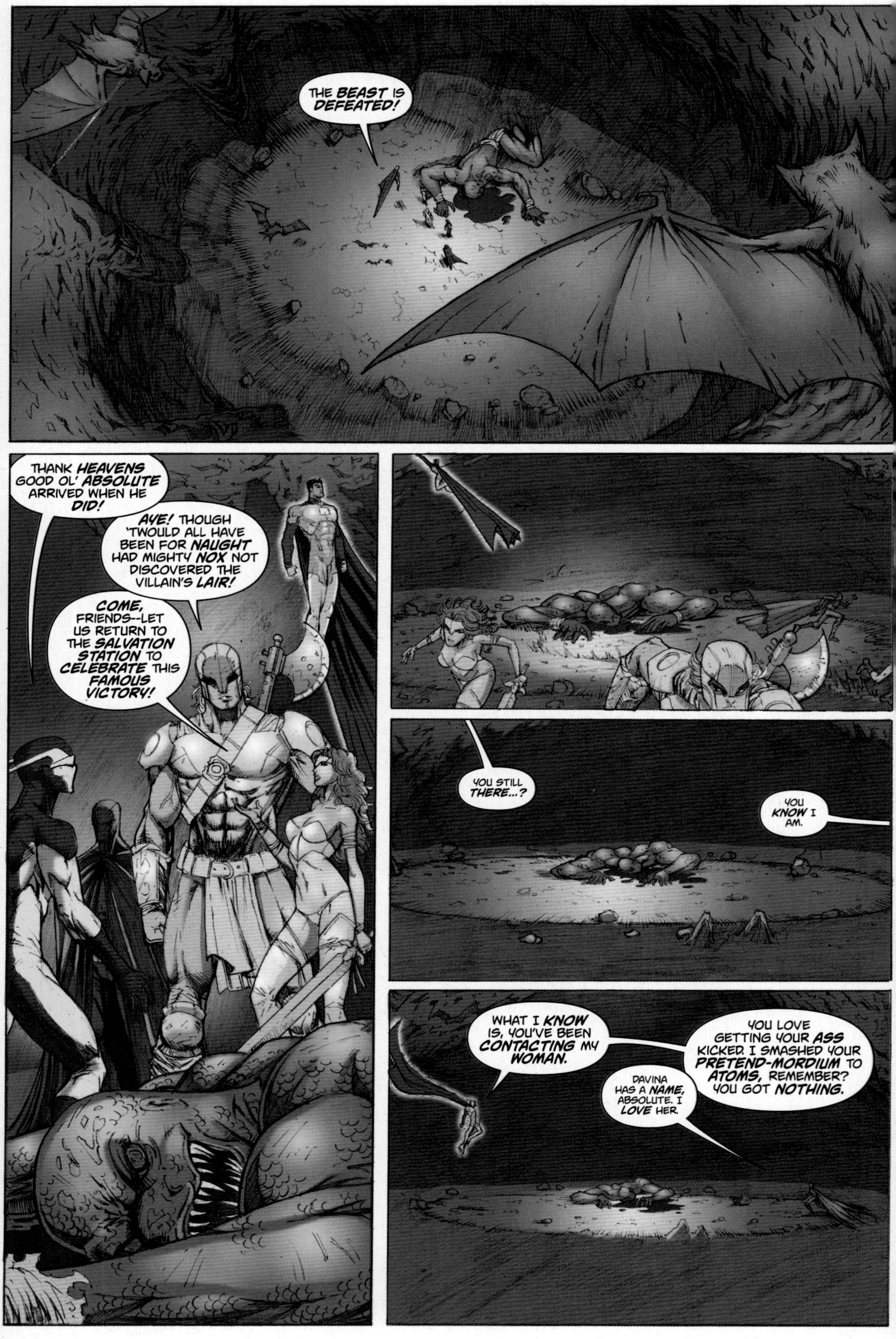
THE BEAST IS DEFEATED!
THANK HEAVENS GOOD OL' ABSOLUTE ARRIVED WHEN HE DID!
AYE! THOUGH 'TWOULD ALL HAVE BEEN FOR NAUGHT HAD MIGHTY NOX NOT DISCOVERED THE VILLAIN'S LAIR!
COME, FRIENDS--LET US RETURN TO THE SALVATION STATION TO CELEBRATE THIS FAMOUS VICTORY!
YOU STILL THERE...?
YOU KNOW I AM.
WHAT I KNOW IS, YOU'VE BEEN CONTACTING MY WOMAN.
YOU LOVE GETTING YOUR ASS KICKED. I SMASHED YOUR PRETEND-MORDIUM TO ATOMS, REMEMBER? YOU GOT NOTHING.
DAVINA HAS A NAME, ABSOLUTE. I LOVE HER.

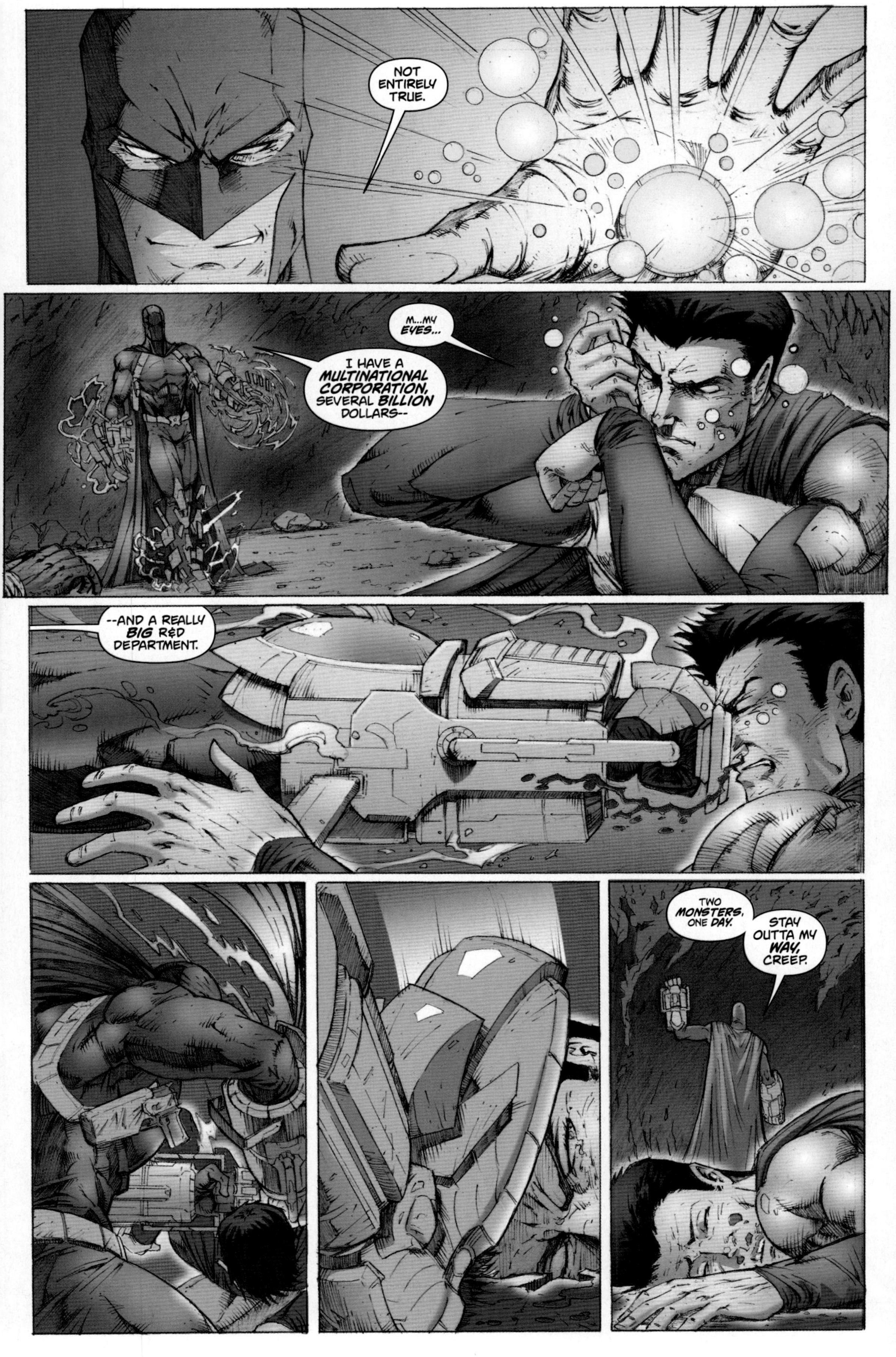
NOT ENTIRELY TRUE.
M...MY EYES...
I HAVE A MULTINATIONAL CORPORATION, SEVERAL BILLION DOLLARS--
--AND A REALLY BIG R&D DEPARTMENT.
TWO MONSTERS, ONE DAY.
STAY OUTTA MY WAY, CREEP.

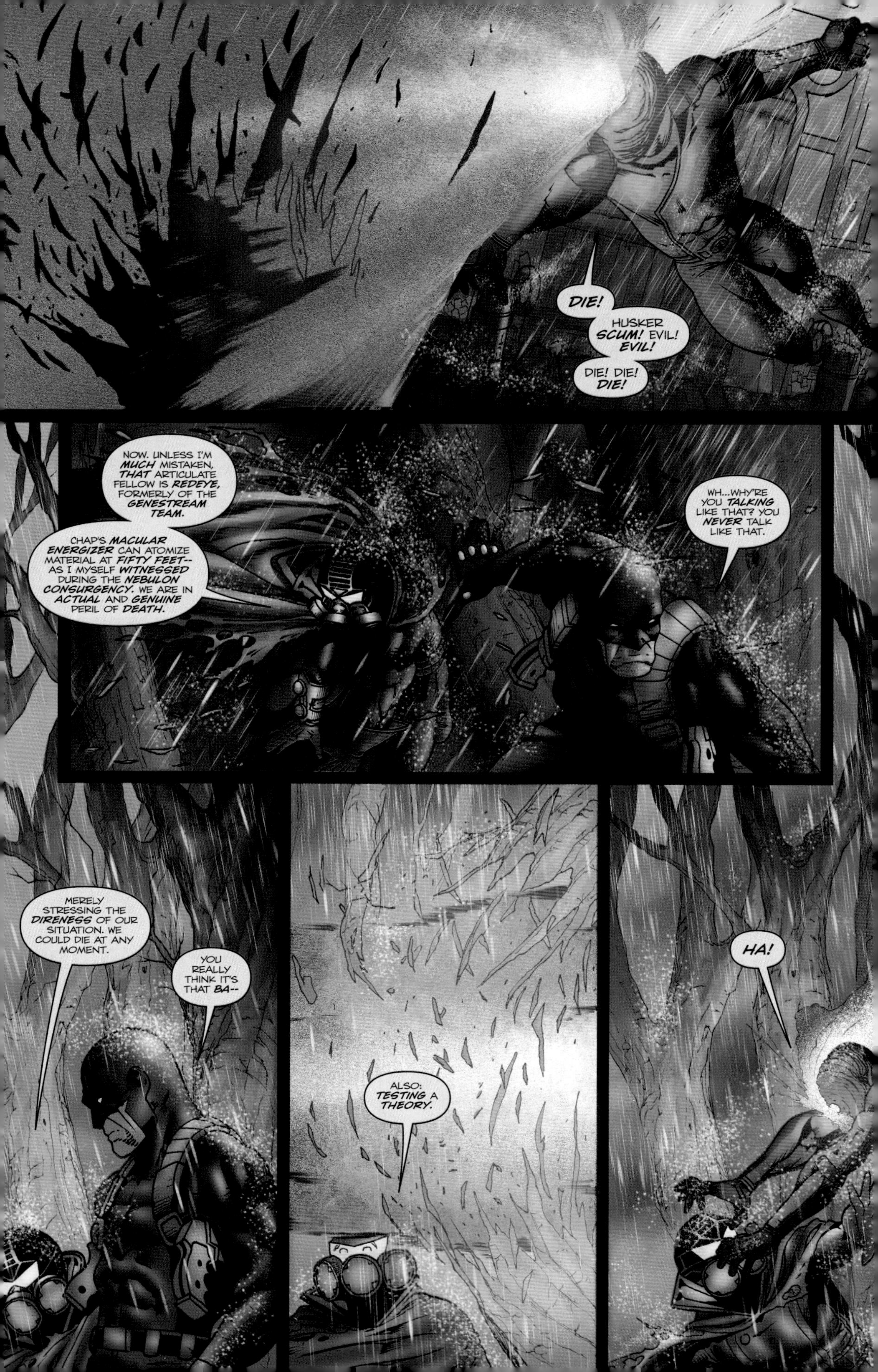
DIE!
HUSKER SCUM! EVIL! EVIL!
DIE! DIE! DIE!
NOW. UNLESS I'M MUCH MISTAKEN, THAT ARTICULATE FELLOW IS REDEYE, FORMERLY OF THE GENESTREAM TEAM.
CHAP'S MACULAR ENERGIZER CAN ATOMIZE MATERIAL AT FIFTY FEET-- AS I MYSELF WITNESSED DURING THE NEBULON CONSURGENCY. WE ARE IN ACTUAL AND GENUINE PERIL OF DEATH.
WH...WHY'RE YOU TALKING LIKE THAT? YOU NEVER TALK LIKE THAT.
MERELY STRESSING THE DIRENESS OF OUR SITUATION. WE COULD DIE AT ANY MOMENT.
YOU REALLY THINK IT'S THAT BA--
ALSO: TESTING A THEORY.
HA!

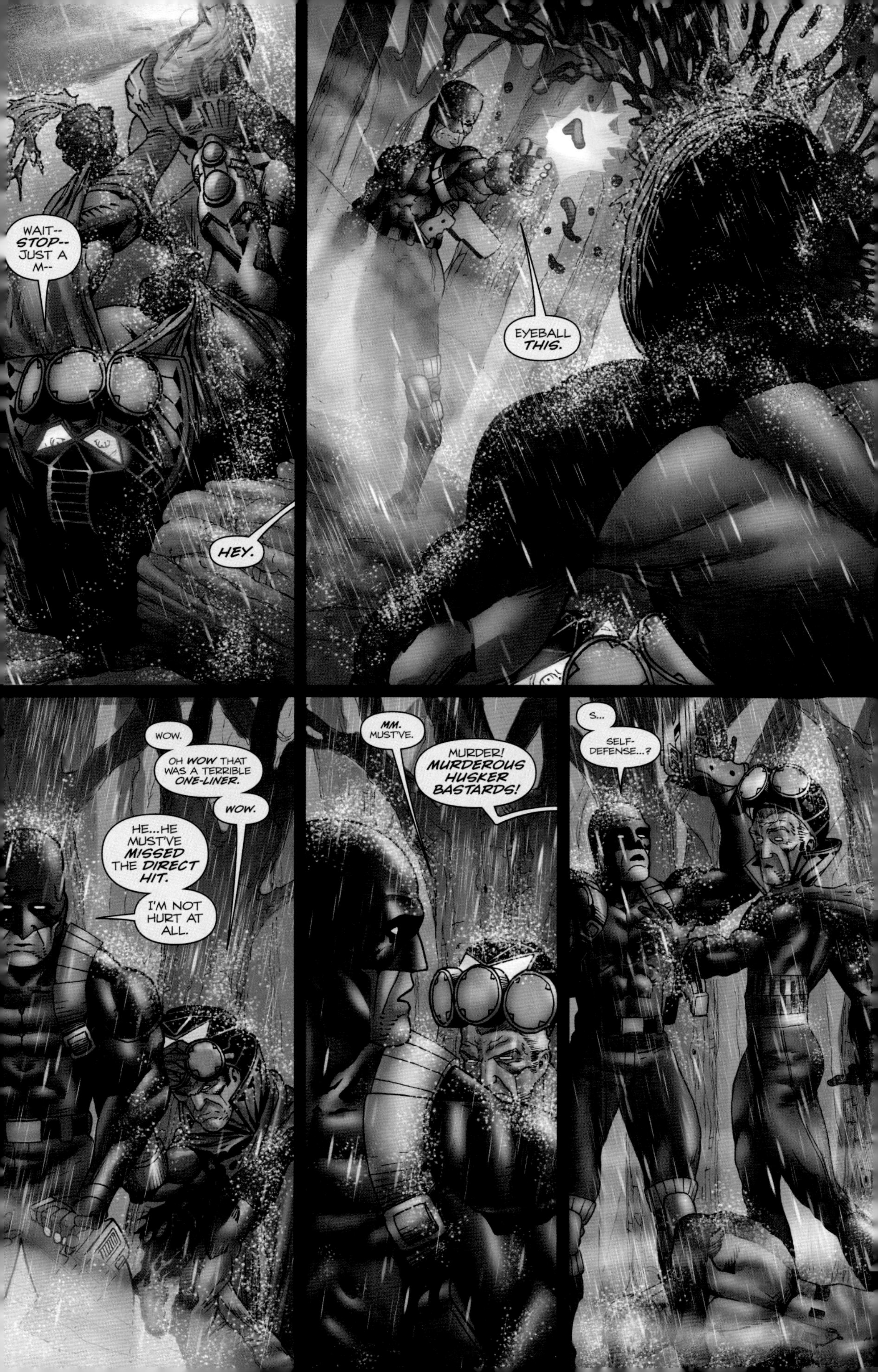
WAIT-- STOP-- JUST A M--
HEY.
EYEBALL THIS.
WOW.
OH WOW THAT WAS A TERRIBLE ONE-LINER.
WOW.
HE...HE MUST'VE MISSED THE DIRECT HIT.
I'M NOT HURT AT ALL.
MM. MUST'VE.
MURDER! MURDEROUS HUSKER BASTARDS!
S...
SELF-DEFENSE...?

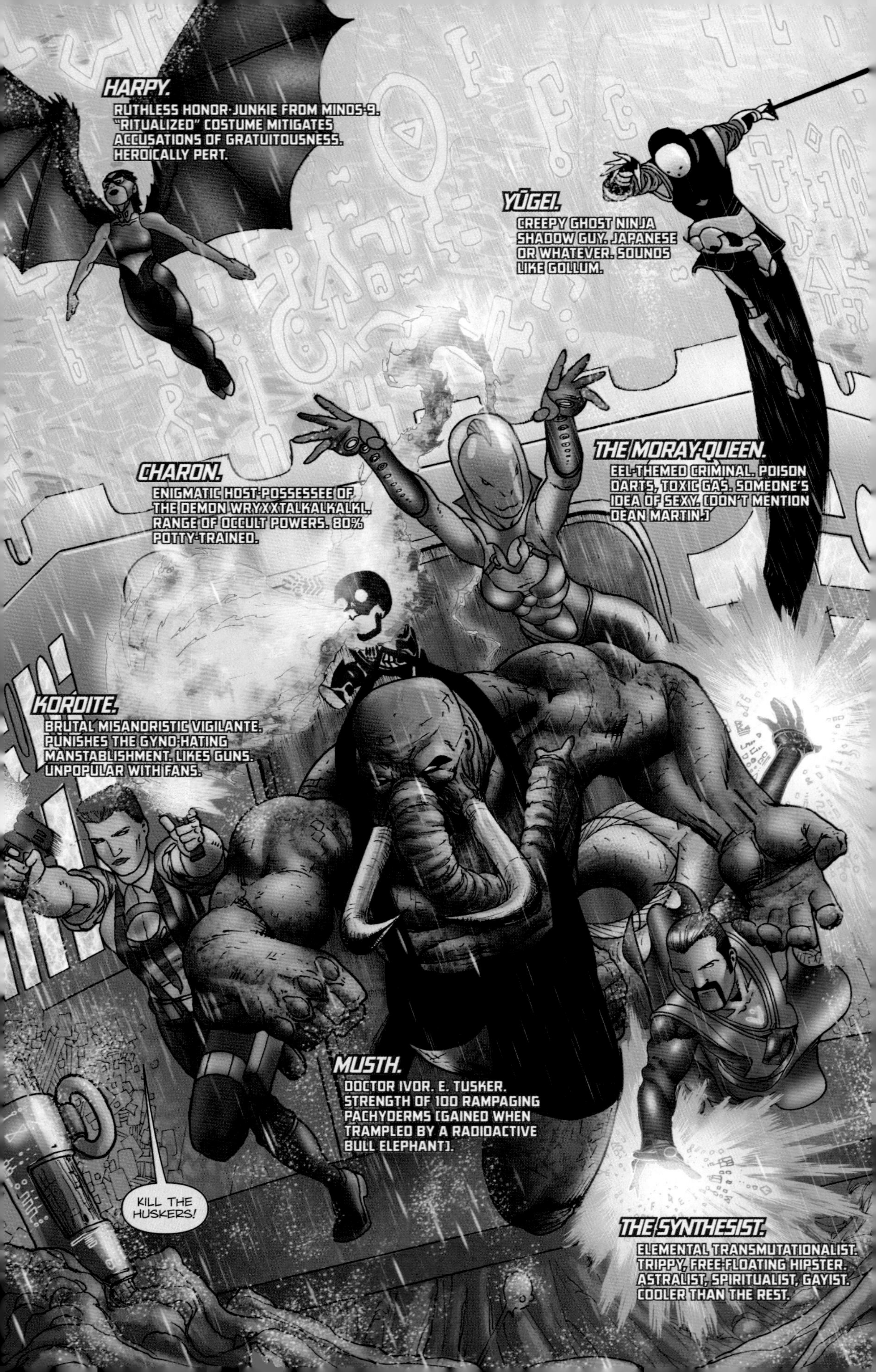
HARPY.
RUTHLESS HONOR-JUNKIE FROM MINOS-9. "RITUALIZED" COSTUME MITIGATES ACCUSATIONS OF GRATUITOUSNESS. HEROICALLY PERT.
YŪGEI.
CREEPY GHOST NINJA SHADOW GUY. JAPANESE OR WHATEVER. SOUNDS LIKE GOLLUM.
CHARON.
ENIGMATIC HOST-POSSESSEE OF THE DEMON WRYXXTALKALKALKL. RANGE OF OCCULT POWERS. 80% POTTY-TRAINED.
THE MORAY-QUEEN.
EEL-THEMED CRIMINAL. POISON DARTS, TOXIC GAS. SOMEONE'S IDEA OF SEXY. (DON'T MENTION DEAN MARTIN.)
KORDITE.
BRUTAL MISANDRISTIC VIGILANTE. PUNISHES THE GYNO-HATING MANSTABLISHMENT. LIKES GUNS. UNPOPULAR WITH FANS.
MUSTH.
DOCTOR IVOR. E. TUSKER. STRENGTH OF 100 RAMPAGING PACHYDERMS (GAINED WHEN TRAMPLED BY A RADIOACTIVE BULL ELEPHANT).
KILL THE HUSKERS!
THE SYNTHESIST.
ELEMENTAL TRANSMUTATIONALIST. TRIPPY, FREE-FLOATING HIPSTER. ASTRALIST, SPIRITUALIST, GAYIST. COOLER THAN THE REST.

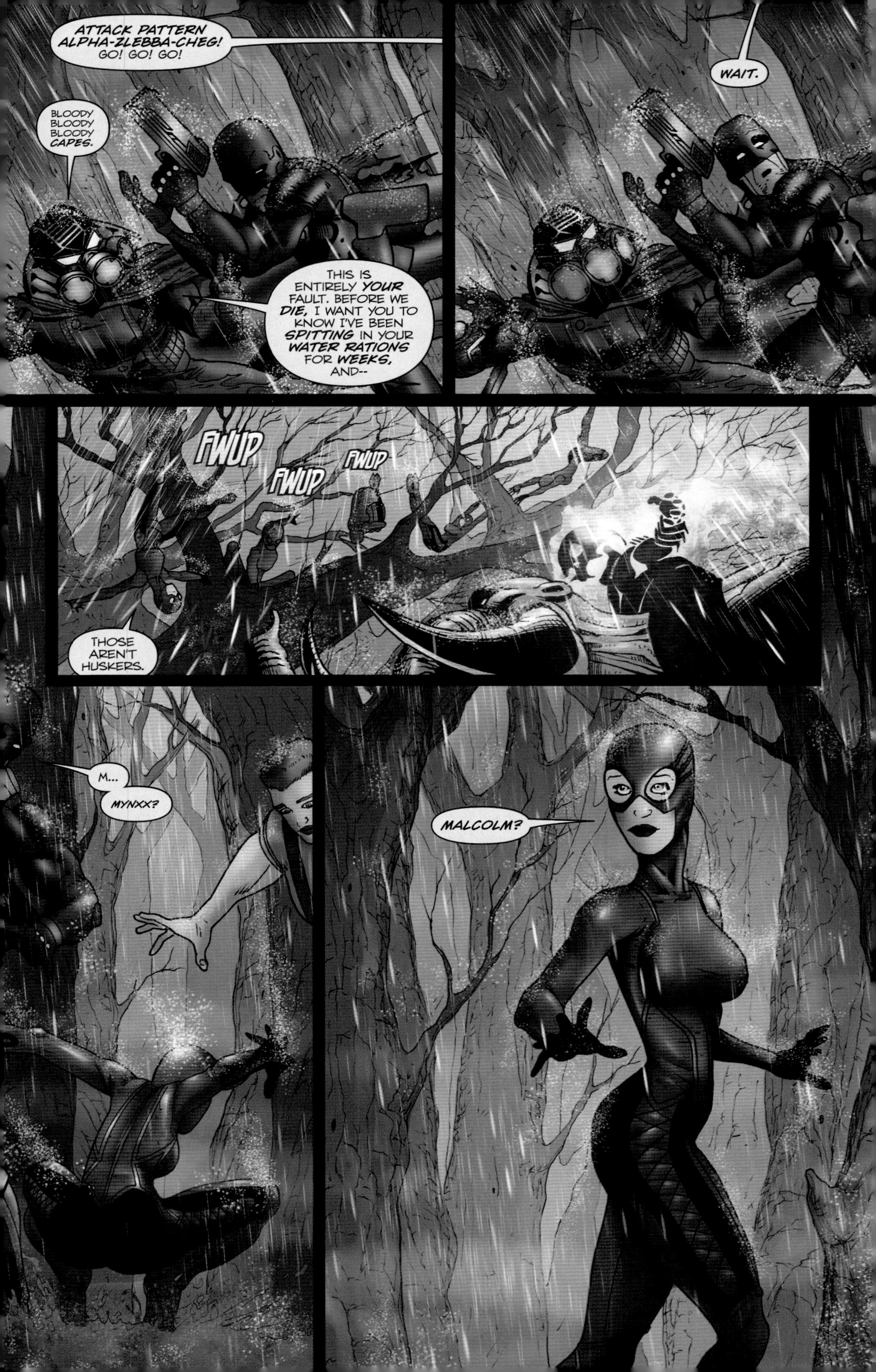
ATTACK PATTERN ALPHA-ZLEBBA-CHEG! GO! GO! GO!
BLOODY BLOODY BLOODY CAPES.
THIS IS ENTIRELY YOUR FAULT. BEFORE WE DIE, I WANT YOU TO KNOW I'VE BEEN SPITTING IN YOUR WATER RATIONS FOR WEEKS, AND--
WAIT.
FWUP
FWUP
FWUP
THOSE AREN'T HUSKERS.
M... MYNXX?
MALCOLM?

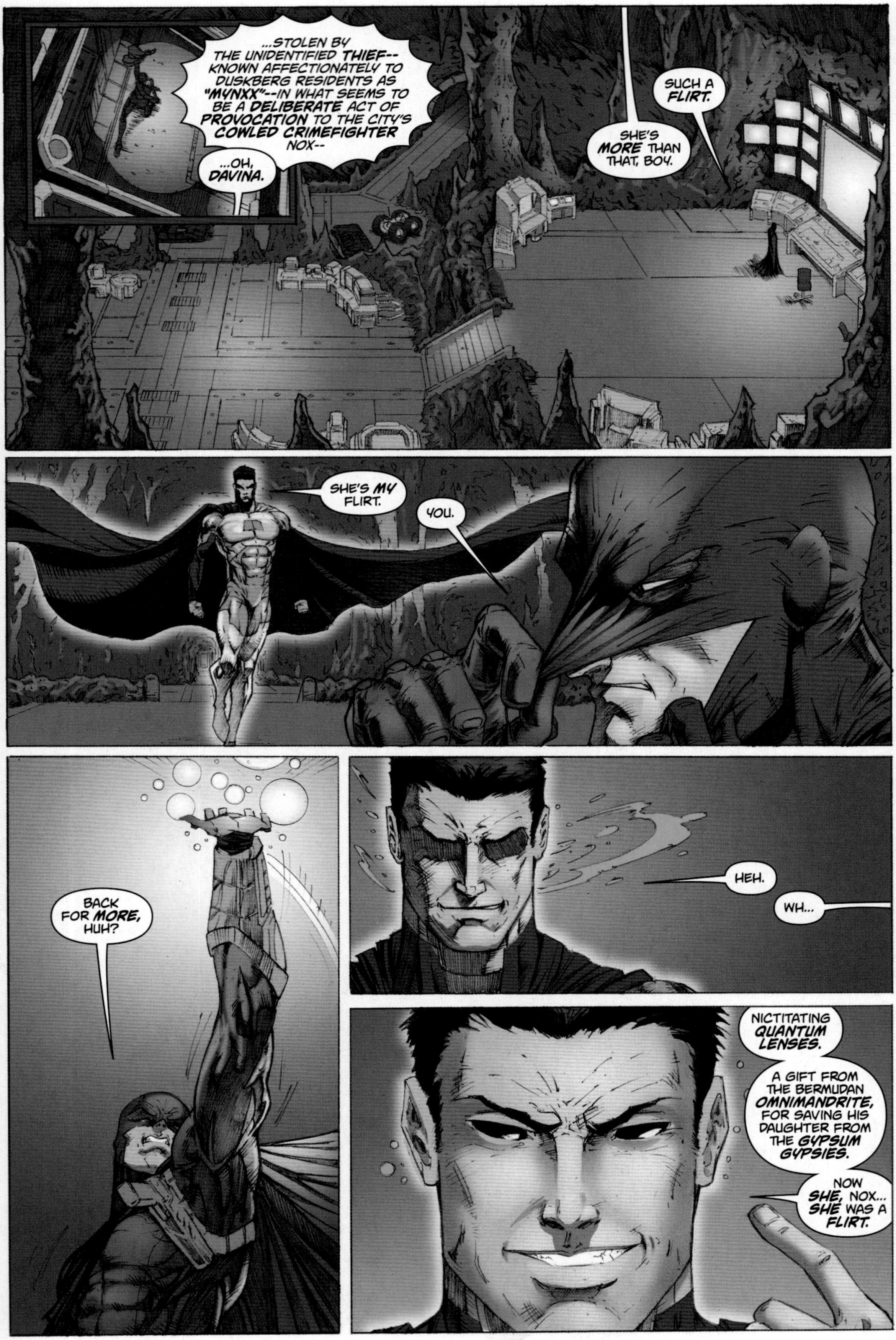
...STOLEN BY THE UNIDENTIFIED THIEF--KNOWN AFFECTIONATELY TO DUSKBERG RESIDENTS AS "MYNXX"--IN WHAT SEEMS TO BE A DELIBERATE ACT OF PROVOCATION TO THE CITY'S COWLED CRIMEFIGHTER NOX--
...OH, DAVINA.
SUCH A FLIRT.
SHE'S MORE THAN THAT, BOY.
SHE'S MY FLIRT.
YOU.
BACK FOR MORE, HUH?
HEH.
WH...
NICTITATING QUANTUM LENSES.
A GIFT FROM THE BERMUDAN OMNIMANDRITE, FOR SAVING HIS DAUGHTER FROM THE GYPSUM GYPSIES.
NOW SHE, NOX... SHE WAS A FLIRT.

BRIEFLY.

FLCK

{WHEEEEEF} {WHEEEEEEEEEF}

YOU HAVE TWO BROKEN RIBS, MALCOLM.

AND--AH--A PUNCTURED LUNG.

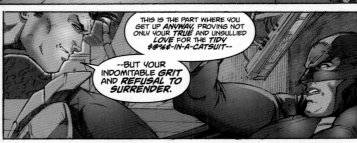

THIS IS THE PART WHERE YOU GET UP *ANYWAY*, PROVING NOT ONLY YOUR *TRUE* AND UNSULLIED *LOVE* FOR THE *TIDY $@%¢-IN-A-CATSUIT*--

--BUT YOUR INDOMITABLE *GRIT* AND *REFUSAL TO SURRENDER.*

EXCEPT...AW... YOU *CAN'T.* CAN YOU? BECAUSE YOU'RE NOT ONE OF *US,* NOXXY.

*UN. POWERED.*

FFFT

YOU *CAN'T*--

AHHHH

--YOU CAN'T EVEN *BEG* ME TO STOP.

SO: YOU SO MUCH AS *TOUCH* HER, YOU POMPOUS LITTLE *ESCAPEE* FROM YOUR *DAD'S KLEENEX*--

--AND I WILL SHATTER EVERYTHING YOU LOVE.

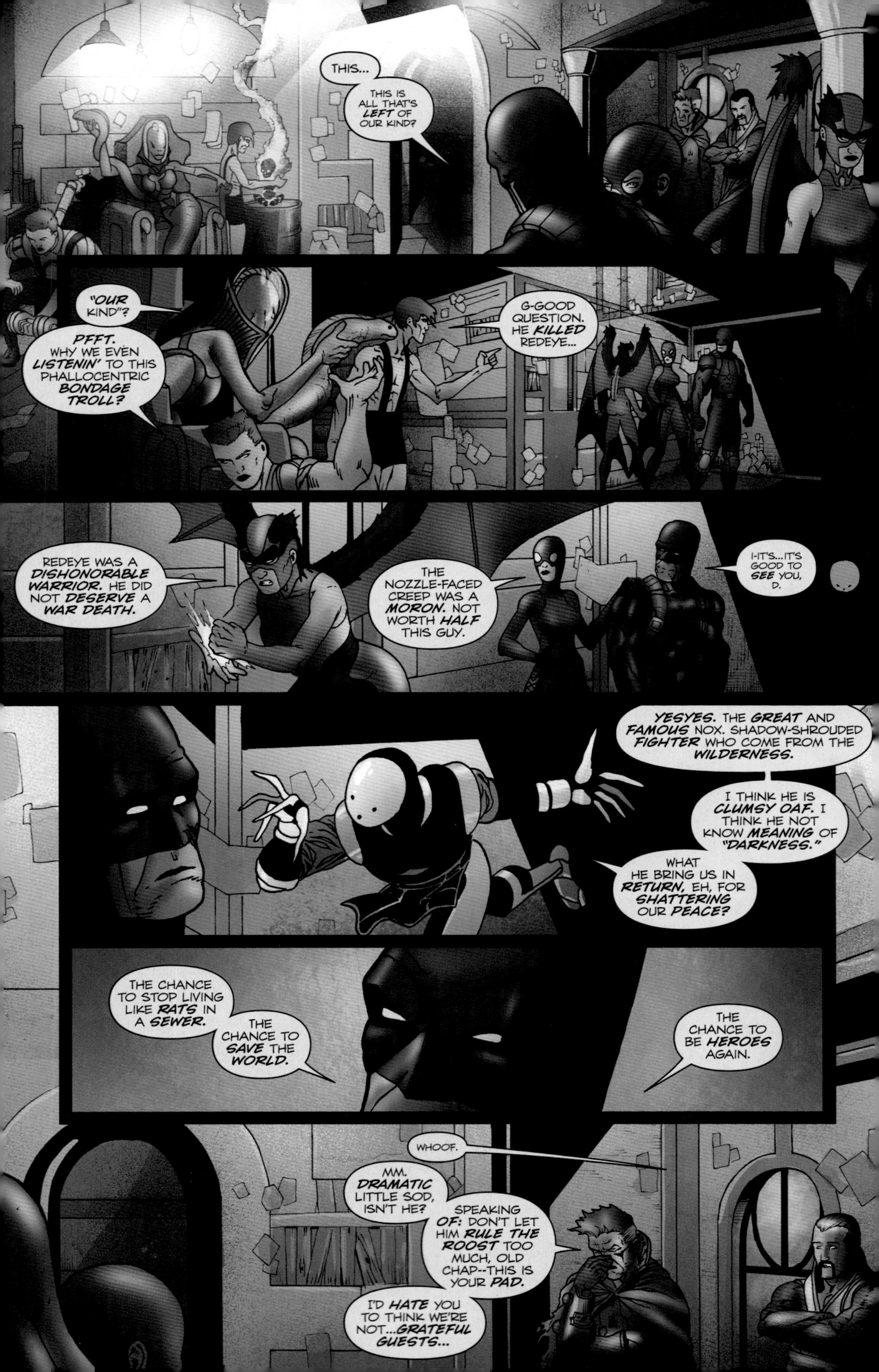
THIS...
THIS IS ALL THAT'S LEFT OF OUR KIND?
"OUR KIND"?
PFFT. WHY WE EVEN LISTENIN' TO THIS PHALLOCENTRIC BONDAGE TROLL?
G-GOOD QUESTION. HE KILLED REDEYE...
REDEYE WAS A DISHONORABLE WARRIOR. HE DID NOT DESERVE A WAR DEATH.
THE NOZZLE-FACED CREEP WAS A MORON. NOT WORTH HALF THIS GUY.
I-IT'S...IT'S GOOD TO SEE YOU, D.
YESYES. THE GREAT AND FAMOUS NOX. SHADOW-SHROUDED FIGHTER WHO COME FROM THE WILDERNESS.
I THINK HE IS CLUMSY OAF. I THINK HE NOT KNOW MEANING OF "DARKNESS."
WHAT HE BRING US IN RETURN, EH, FOR SHATTERING OUR PEACE?
THE CHANCE TO STOP LIVING LIKE RATS IN A SEWER.
THE CHANCE TO SAVE THE WORLD.
THE CHANCE TO BE HEROES AGAIN.
WHOOF.
MM. DRAMATIC LITTLE SOD, ISN'T HE?
SPEAKING OF: DON'T LET HIM RULE THE ROOST TOO MUCH, OLD CHAP--THIS IS YOUR PAD.
I'D HATE YOU TO THINK WE'RE NOT...GRATEFUL GUESTS...

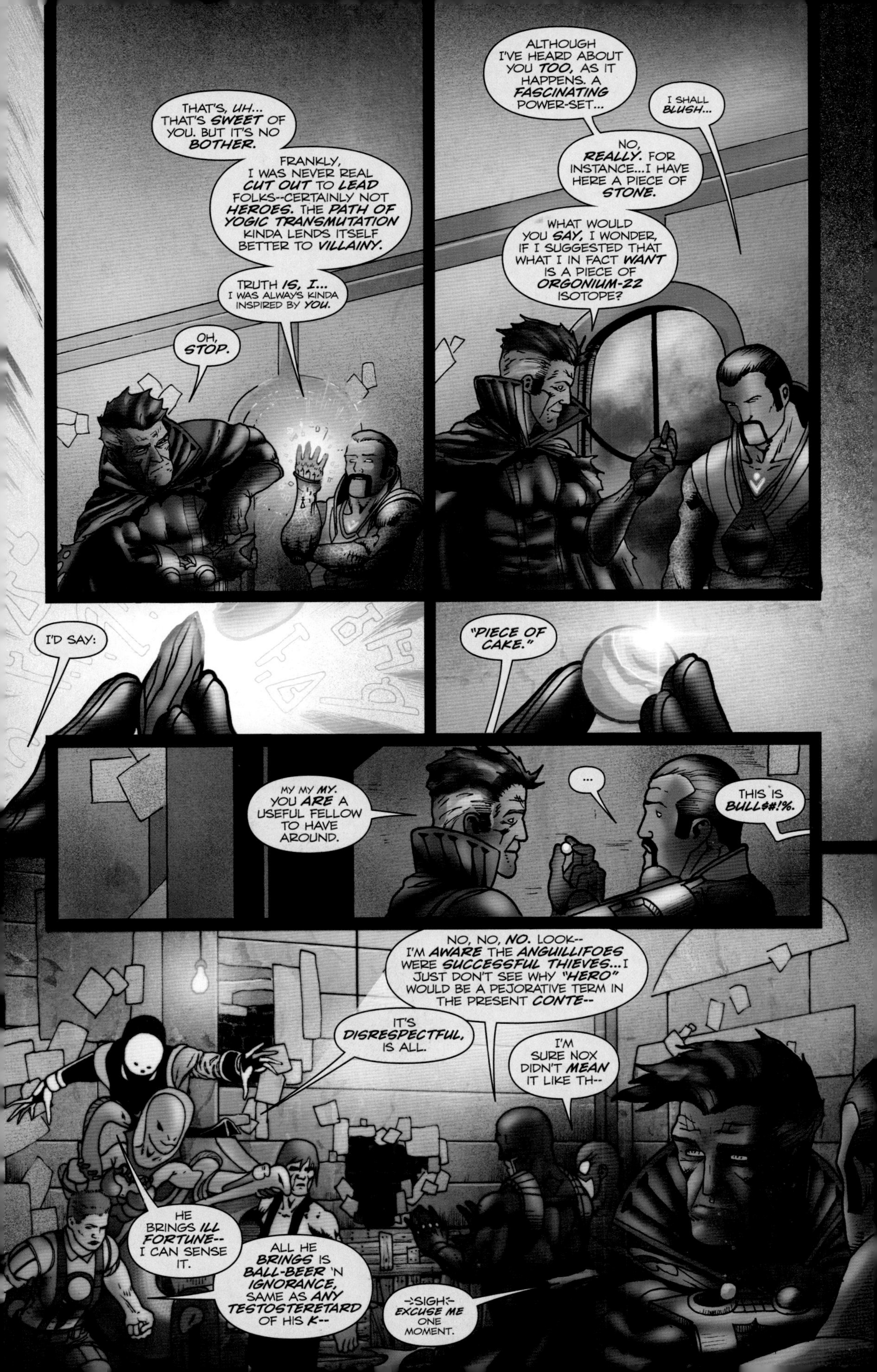
THAT'S, UH... THAT'S SWEET OF YOU. BUT IT'S NO BOTHER.
FRANKLY, I WAS NEVER REAL CUT OUT TO LEAD FOLKS--CERTAINLY NOT HEROES. THE PATH OF YOGIC TRANSMUTATION KINDA LENDS ITSELF BETTER TO VILLAINY.
TRUTH IS, I... I WAS ALWAYS KINDA INSPIRED BY YOU.
OH, STOP.
ALTHOUGH I'VE HEARD ABOUT YOU TOO, AS IT HAPPENS. A FASCINATING POWER-SET...
I SHALL BLUSH...
NO, REALLY. FOR INSTANCE...I HAVE HERE A PIECE OF STONE.
WHAT WOULD YOU SAY, I WONDER, IF I SUGGESTED THAT WHAT I IN FACT WANT IS A PIECE OF ORGONIUM-22 ISOTOPE?
I'D SAY:
"PIECE OF CAKE."
MY MY MY. YOU ARE A USEFUL FELLOW TO HAVE AROUND.
...
THIS IS BULL$#!%.
NO, NO, NO. LOOK-- I'M AWARE THE ANGUILLIFOES WERE SUCCESSFUL THIEVES...I JUST DON'T SEE WHY "HERO" WOULD BE A PEJORATIVE TERM IN THE PRESENT CONTE--
IT'S DISRESPECTFUL, IS ALL.
I'M SURE NOX DIDN'T MEAN IT LIKE TH--
HE BRINGS ILL FORTUNE-- I CAN SENSE IT.
ALL HE BRINGS IS BALL-BEER 'N IGNORANCE, SAME AS ANY TESTOSTERETARD OF HIS K--
-SIGH- EXCUSE ME ONE MOMENT.

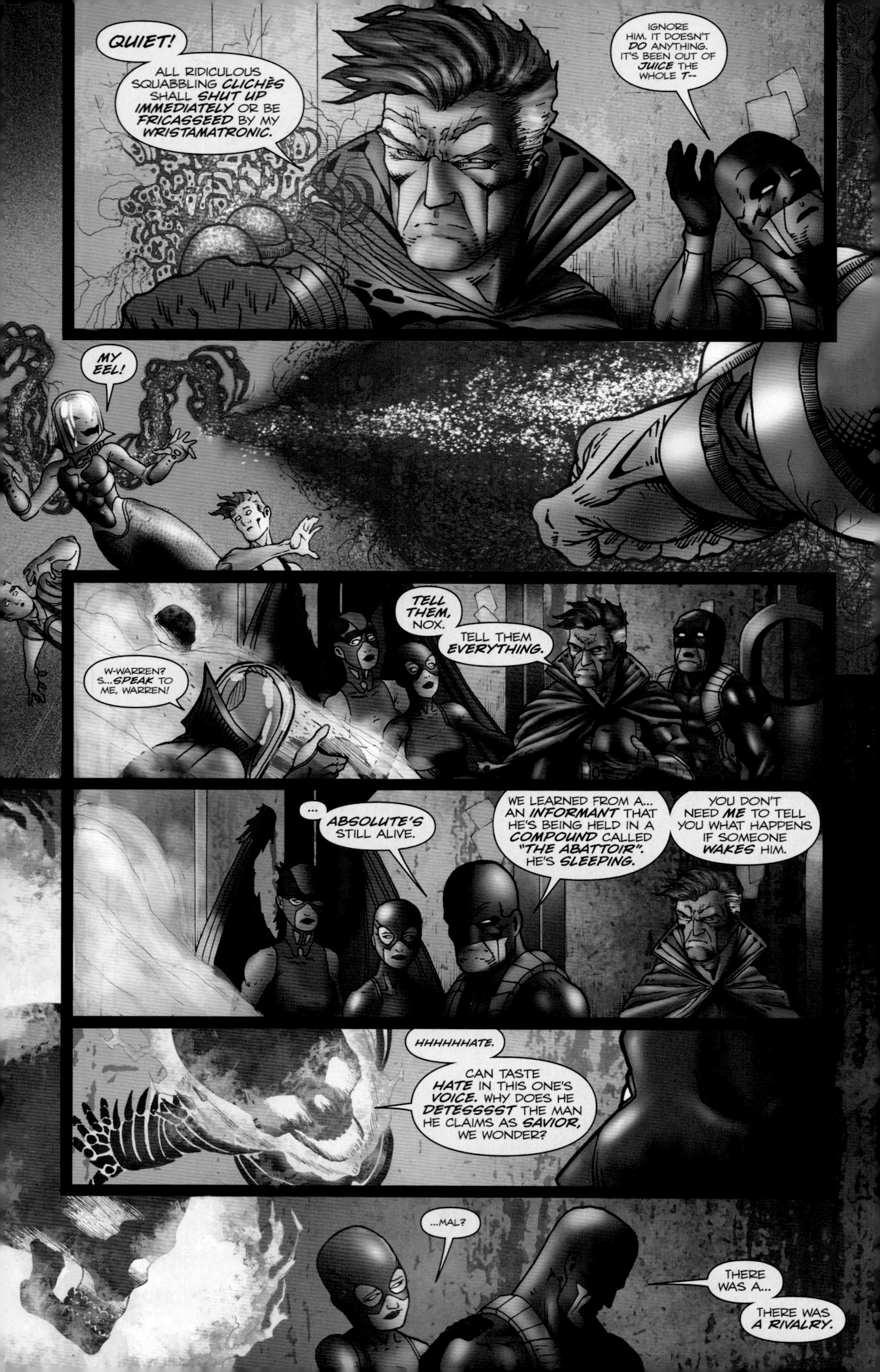
QUIET!
ALL RIDICULOUS SQUABBLING CLICHÉS SHALL SHUT UP IMMEDIATELY OR BE FRICASSEED BY MY WRISTAMATRONIC.
IGNORE HIM. IT DOESN'T DO ANYTHING. IT'S BEEN OUT OF JUICE THE WHOLE T--
MY EEL!
TELL THEM, NOX.
TELL THEM EVERYTHING.
W-WARREN? S...SPEAK TO ME, WARREN!
...ABSOLUTE'S STILL ALIVE.
WE LEARNED FROM A... AN INFORMANT THAT HE'S BEING HELD IN A COMPOUND CALLED "THE ABATTOIR". HE'S SLEEPING.
YOU DON'T NEED ME TO TELL YOU WHAT HAPPENS IF SOMEONE WAKES HIM.
HHHHHHATE.
CAN TASTE HATE IN THIS ONE'S VOICE. WHY DOES HE DETESSSST THE MAN HE CLAIMS AS SAVIOR, WE WONDER?
...MAL?
THERE WAS A...
THERE WAS A RIVALRY.

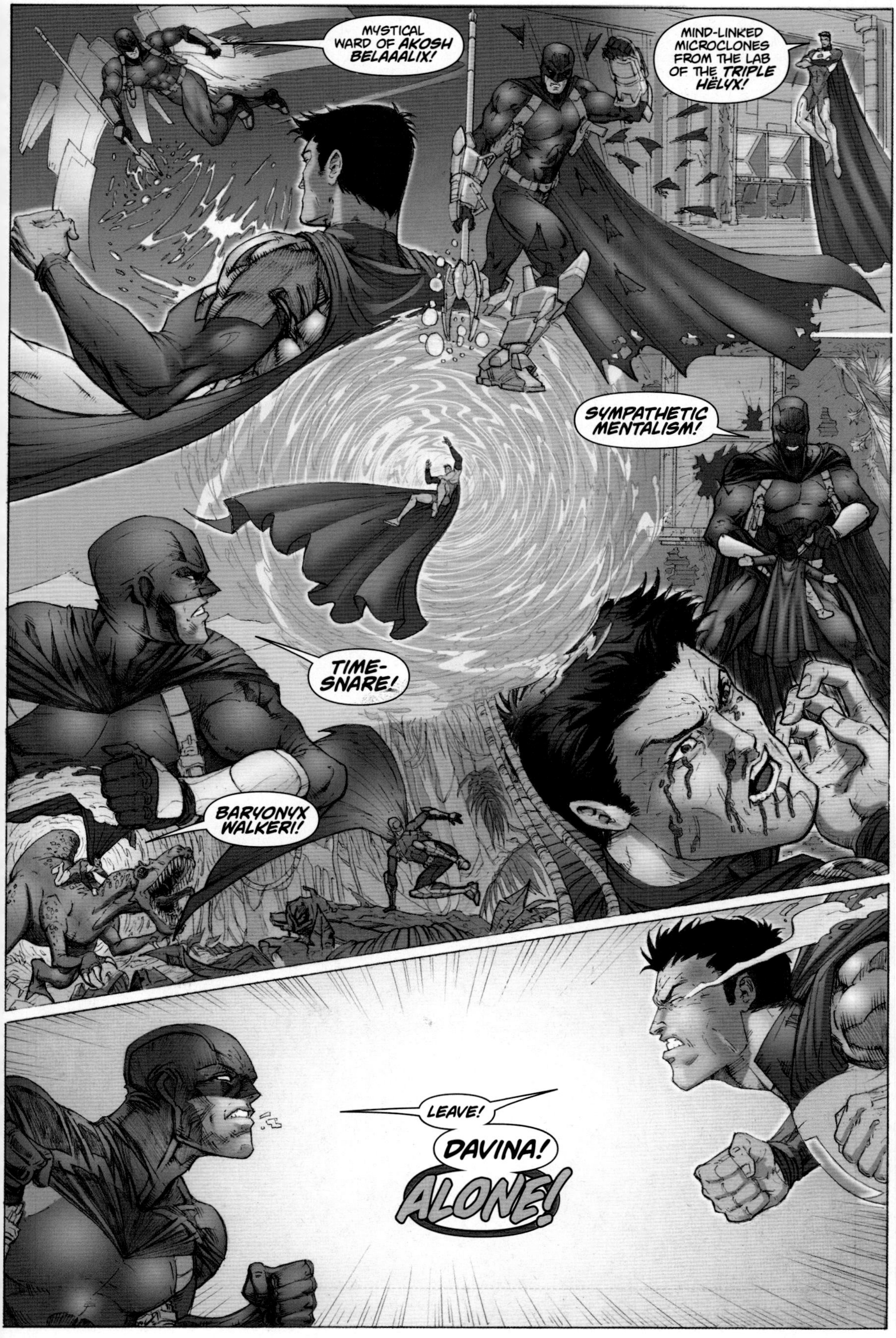
MYSTICAL WARD OF AKOSH BELAAALIX!
MIND-LINKED MICROCLONES FROM THE LAB OF THE TRIPLE HELYX!
SYMPATHETIC MENTALISM!
TIME-SNARE!
BARYONYX WALKERI!
LEAVE!
DAVINA!
ALONE!

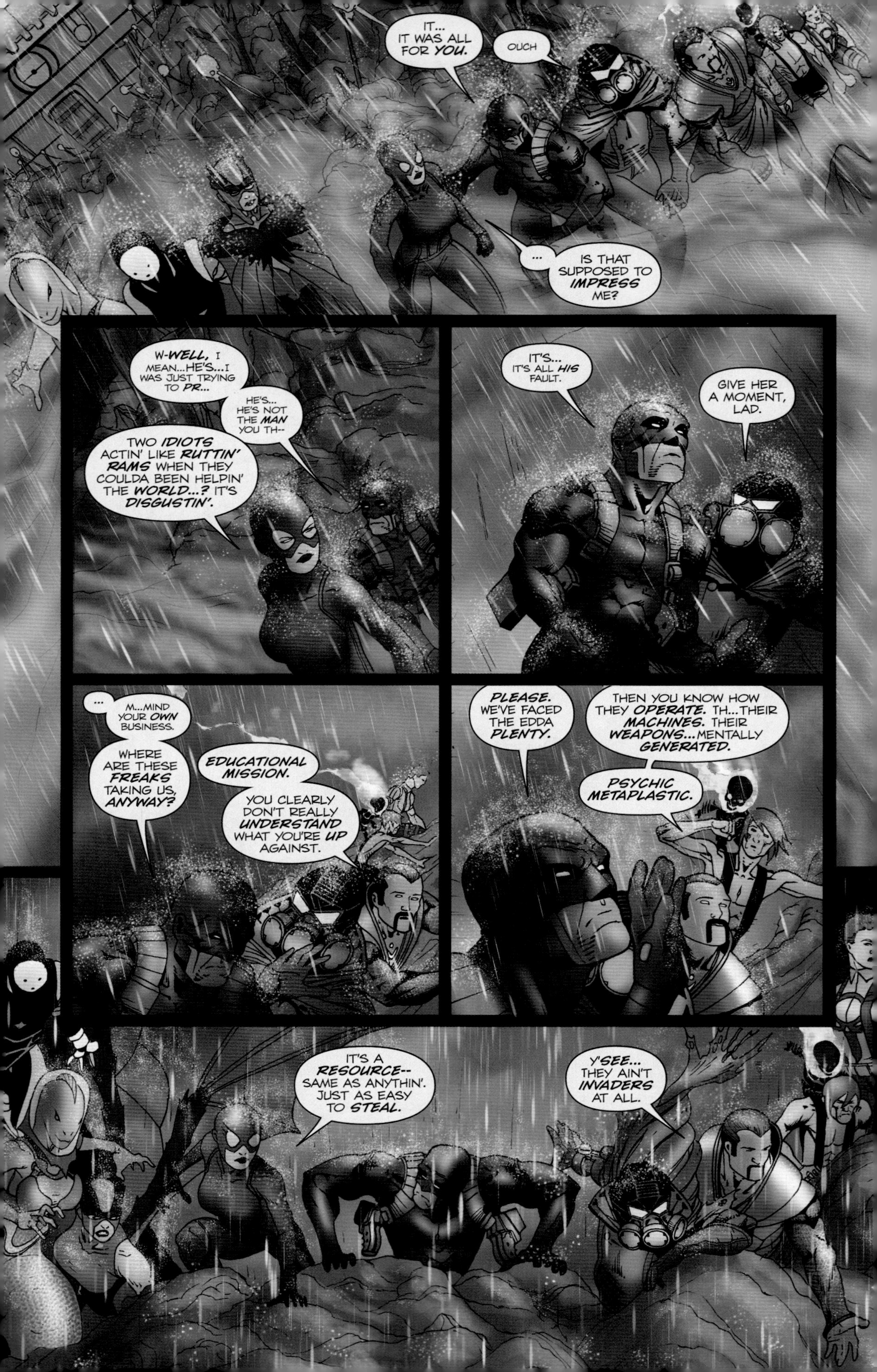
IT... IT WAS ALL FOR YOU.
OUCH
... IS THAT SUPPOSED TO IMPRESS ME?
W-WELL, I MEAN...HE'S...I WAS JUST TRYING TO PR...
HE'S... HE'S NOT THE MAN YOU TH--
TWO IDIOTS ACTIN' LIKE RUTTIN' RAMS WHEN THEY COULDA BEEN HELPIN' THE WORLD...? IT'S DISGUSTIN'.
IT'S... IT'S ALL HIS FAULT.
GIVE HER A MOMENT, LAD.
...
M...MIND YOUR OWN BUSINESS.
WHERE ARE THESE FREAKS TAKING US, ANYWAY?
EDUCATIONAL MISSION.
YOU CLEARLY DON'T REALLY UNDERSTAND WHAT YOU'RE UP AGAINST.
PLEASE. WE'VE FACED THE EDDA PLENTY.
THEN YOU KNOW HOW THEY OPERATE. TH...THEIR MACHINES. THEIR WEAPONS...MENTALLY GENERATED.
PSYCHIC METAPLASTIC.
IT'S A RESOURCE-- SAME AS ANYTHIN'. JUST AS EASY TO STEAL.
Y'SEE... THEY AIN'T INVADERS AT ALL.

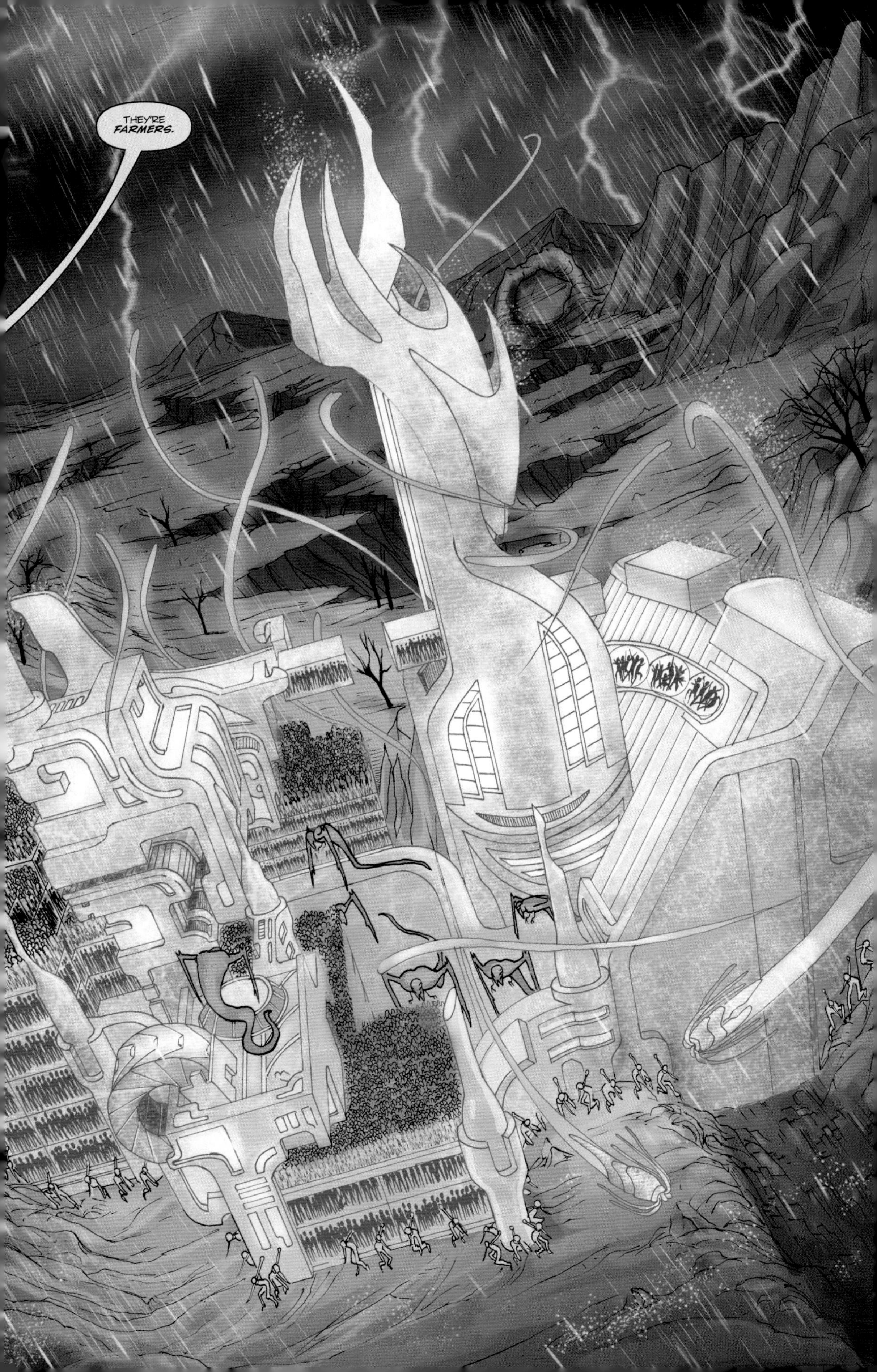
THEY'RE FARMERS.

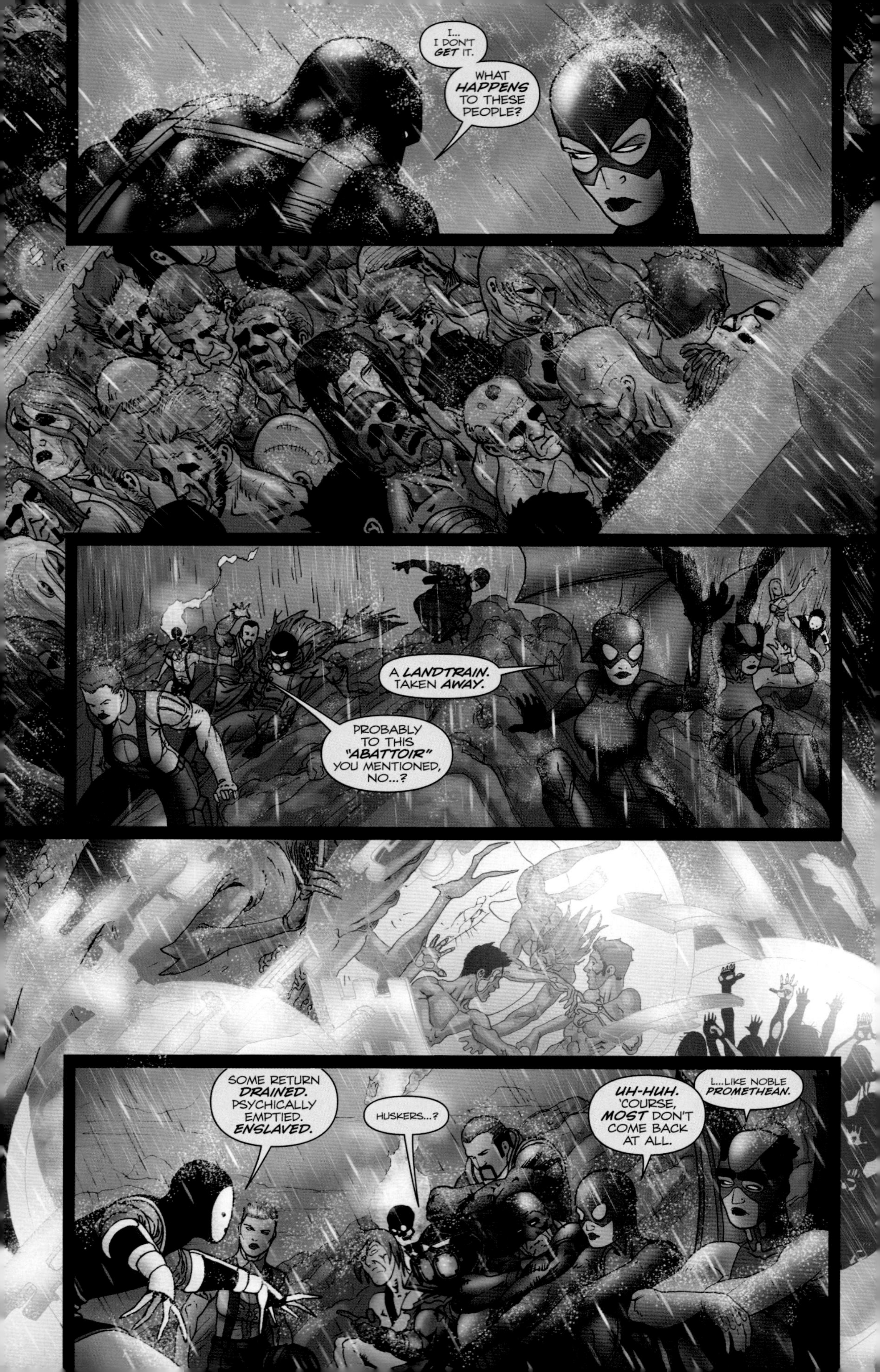
I... I DON'T GET IT.
WHAT HAPPENS TO THESE PEOPLE?
A LANDTRAIN. TAKEN AWAY.
PROBABLY TO THIS "ABATTOIR" YOU MENTIONED, NO...?
SOME RETURN DRAINED. PSYCHICALLY EMPTIED. ENSLAVED.
HUSKERS...?
UH-HUH. 'COURSE, MOST DON'T COME BACK AT ALL.
L...LIKE NOBLE PROMETHEAN.

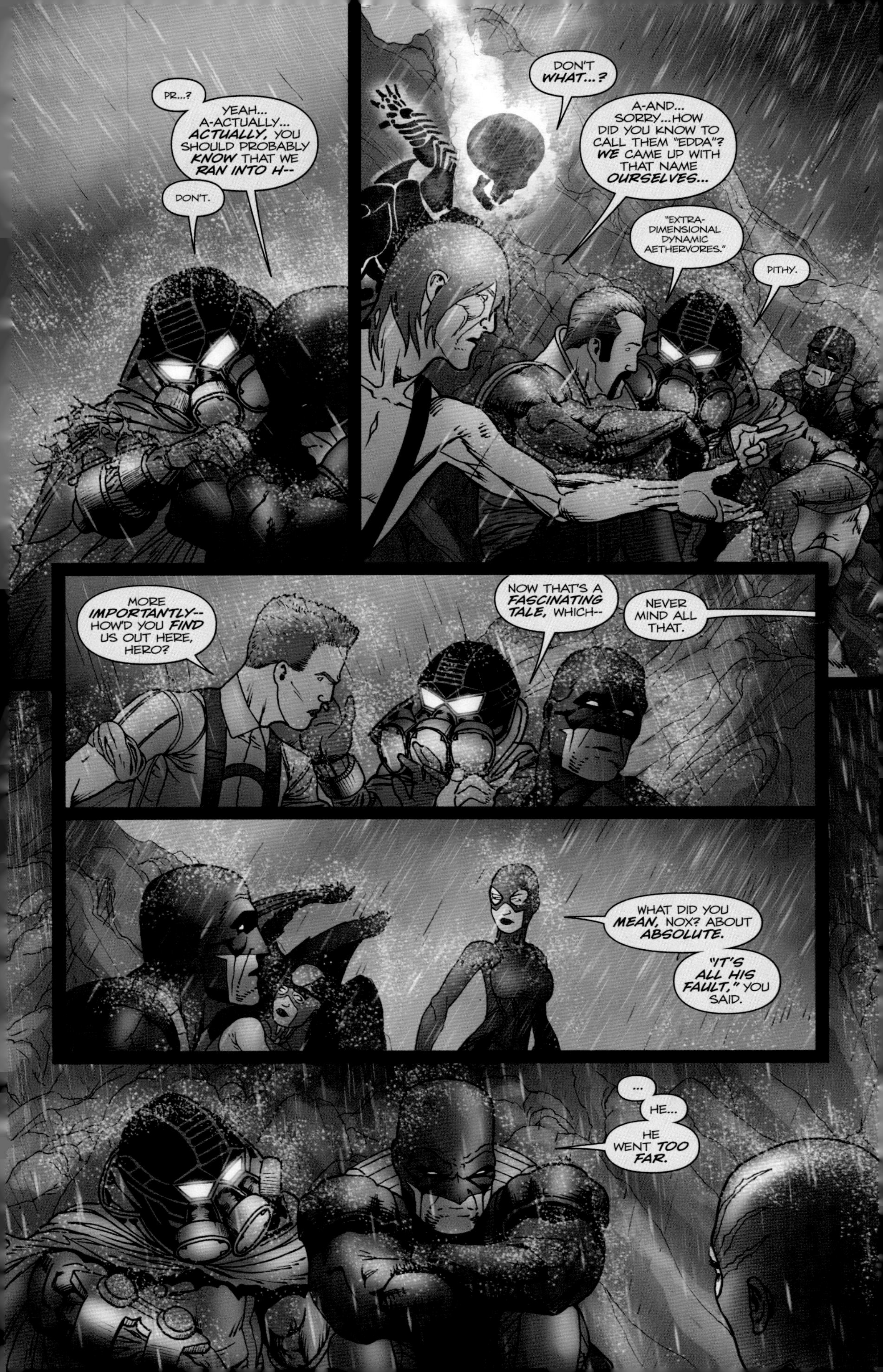
PR...?
YEAH... A-ACTUALLY... ACTUALLY, YOU SHOULD PROBABLY KNOW THAT WE RAN INTO H--
DON'T.
DON'T WHAT...?
A-AND... SORRY...HOW DID YOU KNOW TO CALL THEM "EDDA"? WE CAME UP WITH THAT NAME OURSELVES...
"EXTRA-DIMENSIONAL DYNAMIC AETHERVORES."
PITHY.
MORE IMPORTANTLY-- HOW'D YOU FIND US OUT HERE, HERO?
NOW THAT'S A FASCINATING TALE, WHICH--
NEVER MIND ALL THAT.
WHAT DID YOU MEAN, NOX? ABOUT ABSOLUTE.
"IT'S ALL HIS FAULT," YOU SAID.
...
HE...
HE WENT TOO FAR.

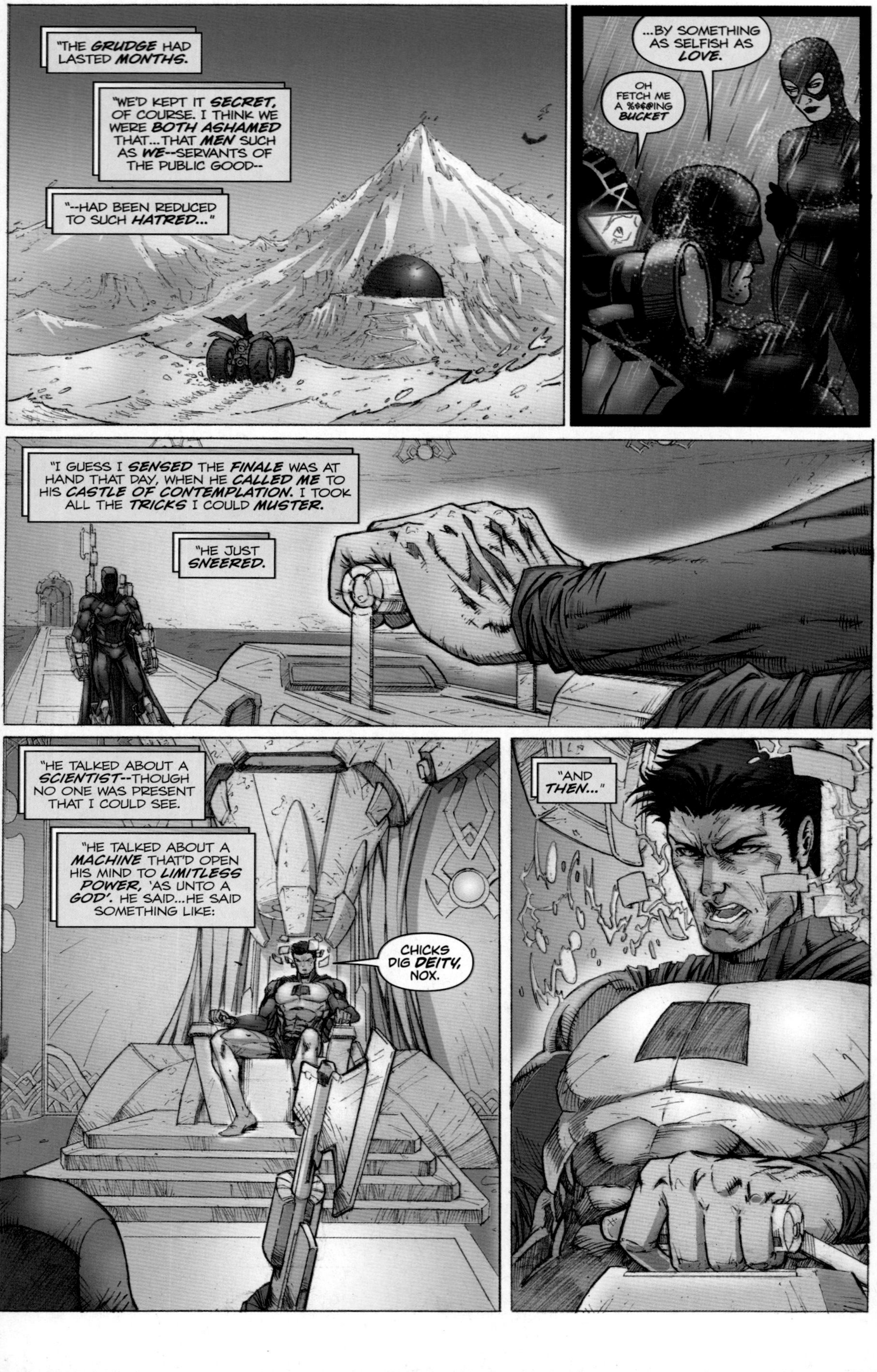
"THE GRUDGE HAD LASTED MONTHS.
"WE'D KEPT IT SECRET, OF COURSE. I THINK WE WERE BOTH ASHAMED THAT...THAT MEN SUCH AS WE--SERVANTS OF THE PUBLIC GOOD--
"--HAD BEEN REDUCED TO SUCH HATRED..."
...BY SOMETHING AS SELFISH AS LOVE.
OH FETCH ME A %$$@ING BUCKET
"I GUESS I SENSED THE FINALE WAS AT HAND THAT DAY, WHEN HE CALLED ME TO HIS CASTLE OF CONTEMPLATION. I TOOK ALL THE TRICKS I COULD MUSTER.
"HE JUST SNEERED.
"HE TALKED ABOUT A SCIENTIST--THOUGH NO ONE WAS PRESENT THAT I COULD SEE.
"HE TALKED ABOUT A MACHINE THAT'D OPEN HIS MIND TO LIMITLESS POWER, 'AS UNTO A GOD'. HE SAID...HE SAID SOMETHING LIKE:
CHICKS DIG DEITY, NOX.
"AND THEN..."

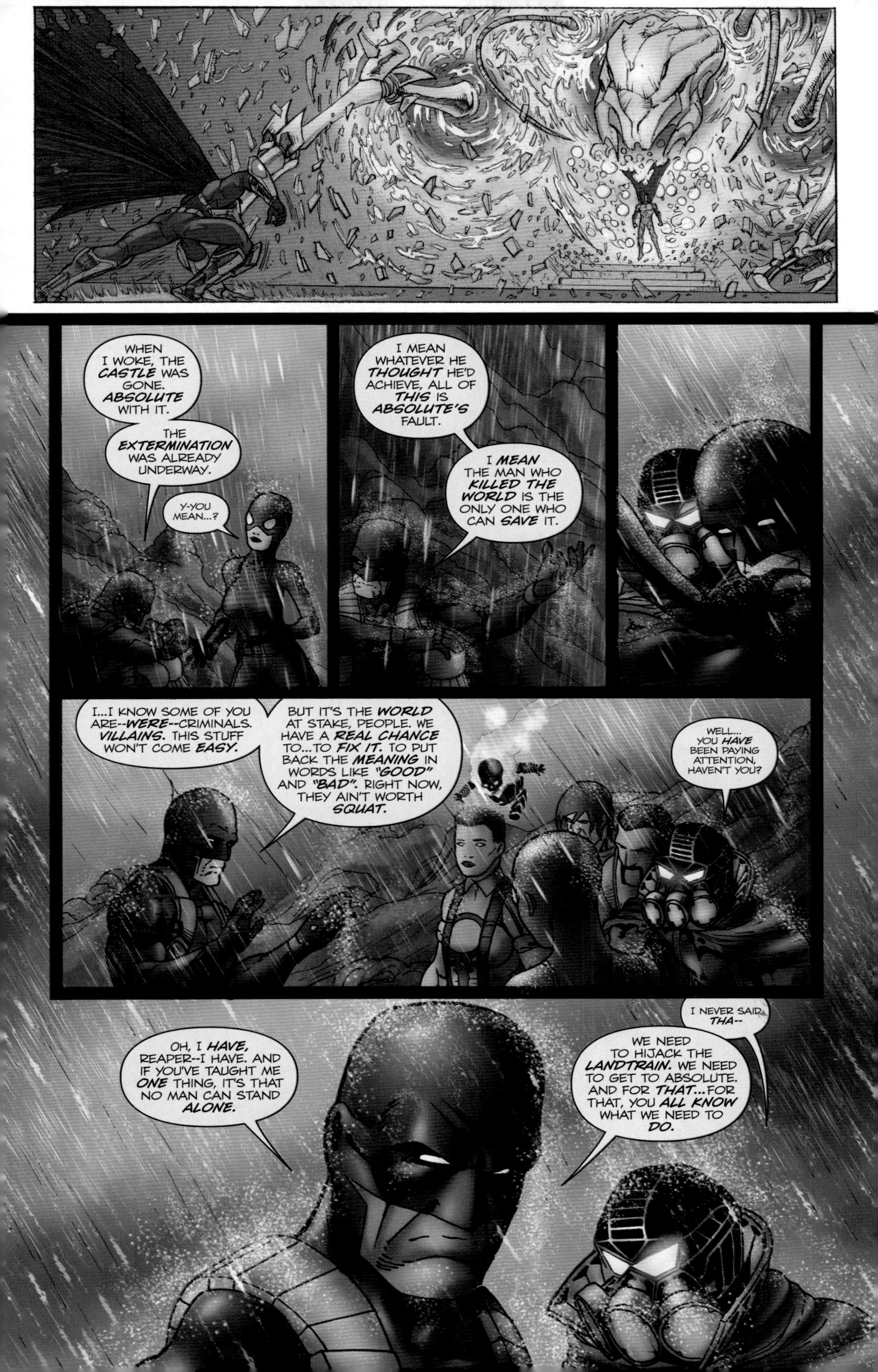
WHEN I WOKE, THE CASTLE WAS GONE. ABSOLUTE WITH IT.
THE EXTERMINATION WAS ALREADY UNDERWAY.
Y-YOU MEAN...?
I MEAN WHATEVER HE THOUGHT HE'D ACHIEVE, ALL OF THIS IS ABSOLUTE'S FAULT.
I MEAN THE MAN WHO KILLED THE WORLD IS THE ONLY ONE WHO CAN SAVE IT.
I...I KNOW SOME OF YOU ARE--WERE--CRIMINALS. VILLAINS. THIS STUFF WON'T COME EASY.
BUT IT'S THE WORLD AT STAKE, PEOPLE. WE HAVE A REAL CHANCE TO...TO FIX IT. TO PUT BACK THE MEANING IN WORDS LIKE "GOOD" AND "BAD". RIGHT NOW, THEY AIN'T WORTH SQUAT.
WELL... YOU HAVE BEEN PAYING ATTENTION, HAVEN'T YOU?
OH, I HAVE, REAPER--I HAVE. AND IF YOU'VE TAUGHT ME ONE THING, IT'S THAT NO MAN CAN STAND ALONE.
I NEVER SAID THA--
WE NEED TO HIJACK THE LANDTRAIN. WE NEED TO GET TO ABSOLUTE. AND FOR THAT...FOR THAT, YOU ALL KNOW WHAT WE NEED TO DO.

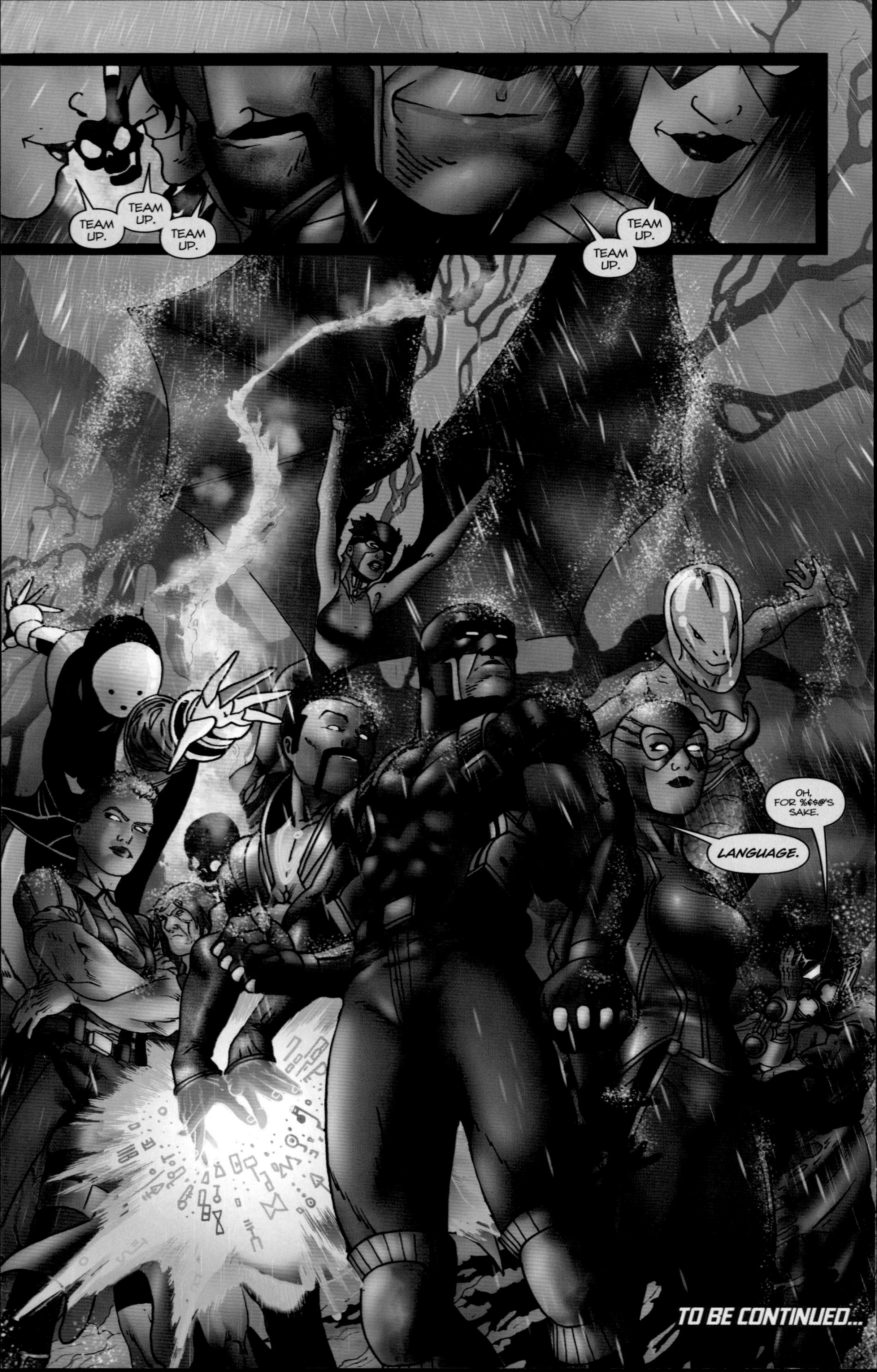
TEAM UP.
TEAM UP.
TEAM UP.
TEAM UP.
TEAM UP.
LANGUAGE.
OH, FOR %$$@'S SAKE.
TO BE CONTINUED...

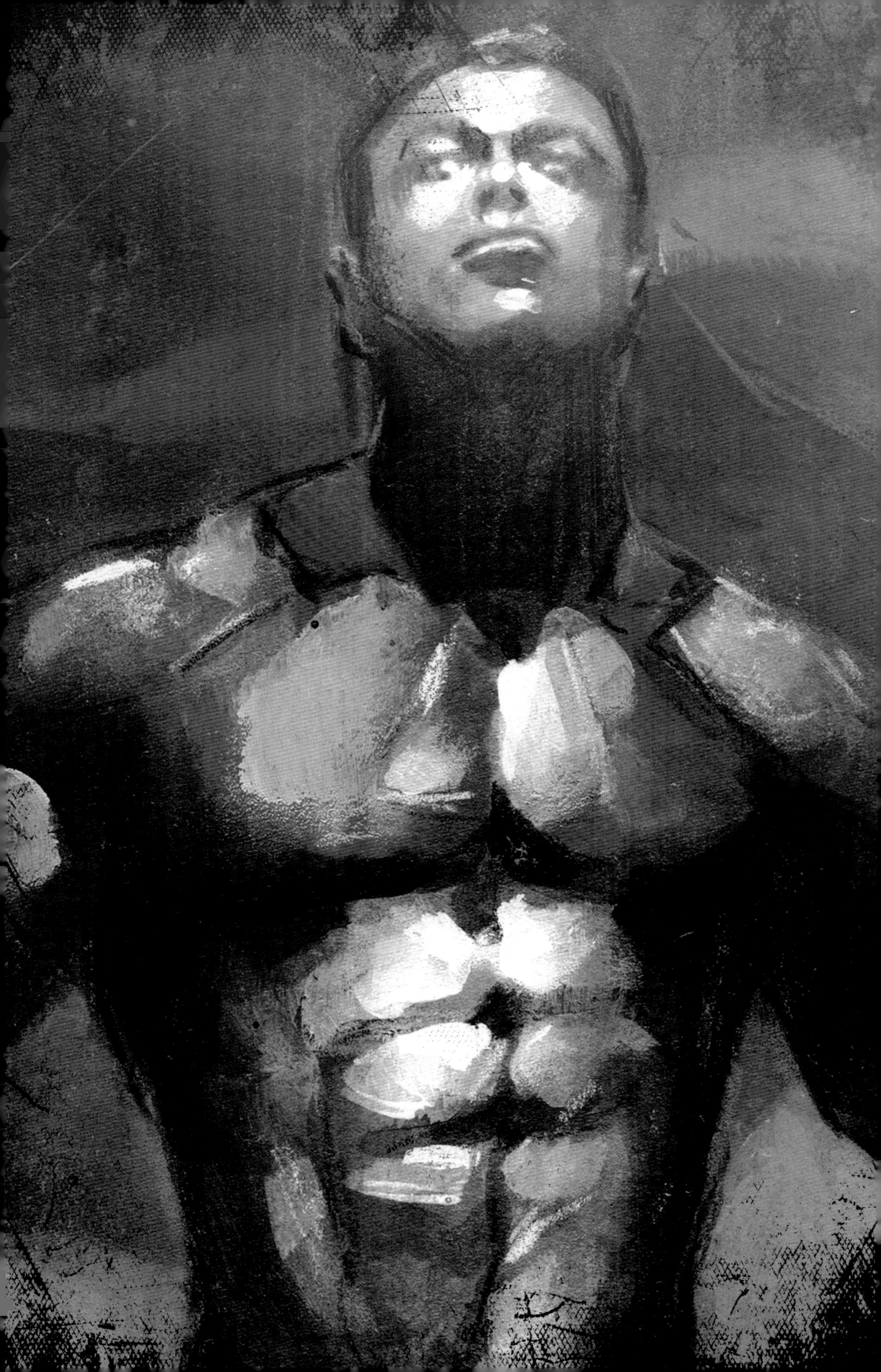

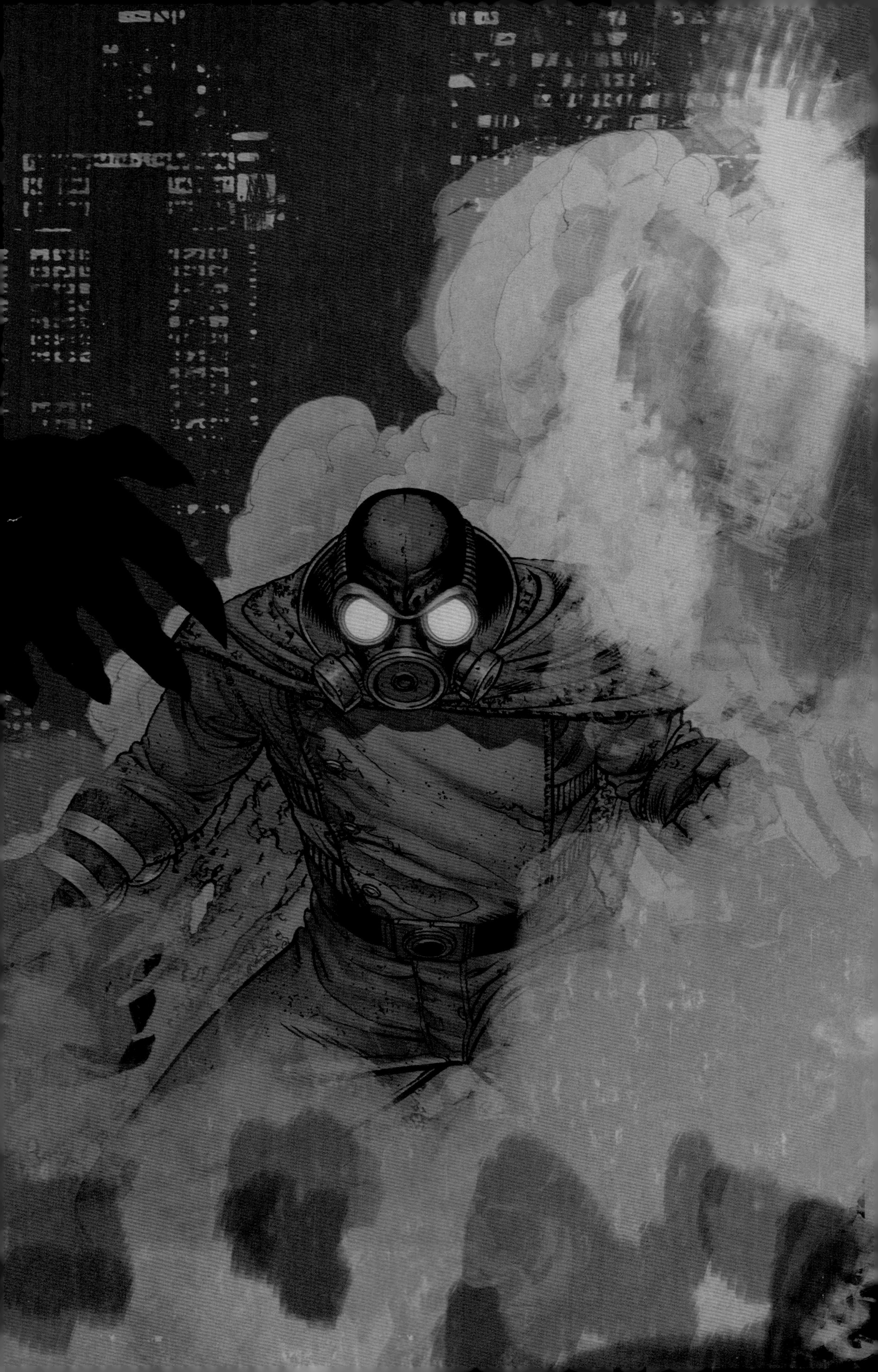

# COVER GALLERY

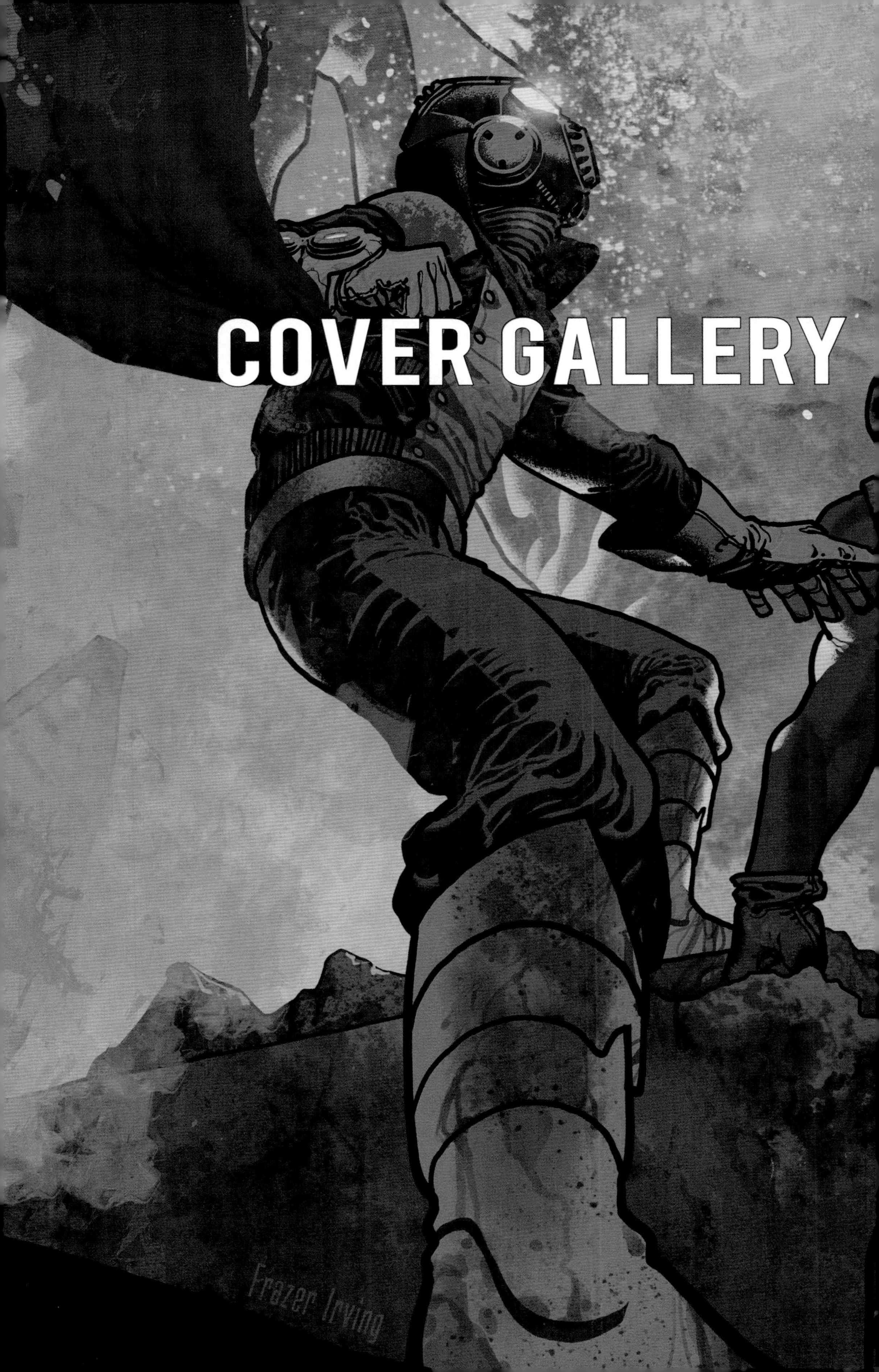
Frazer Irving

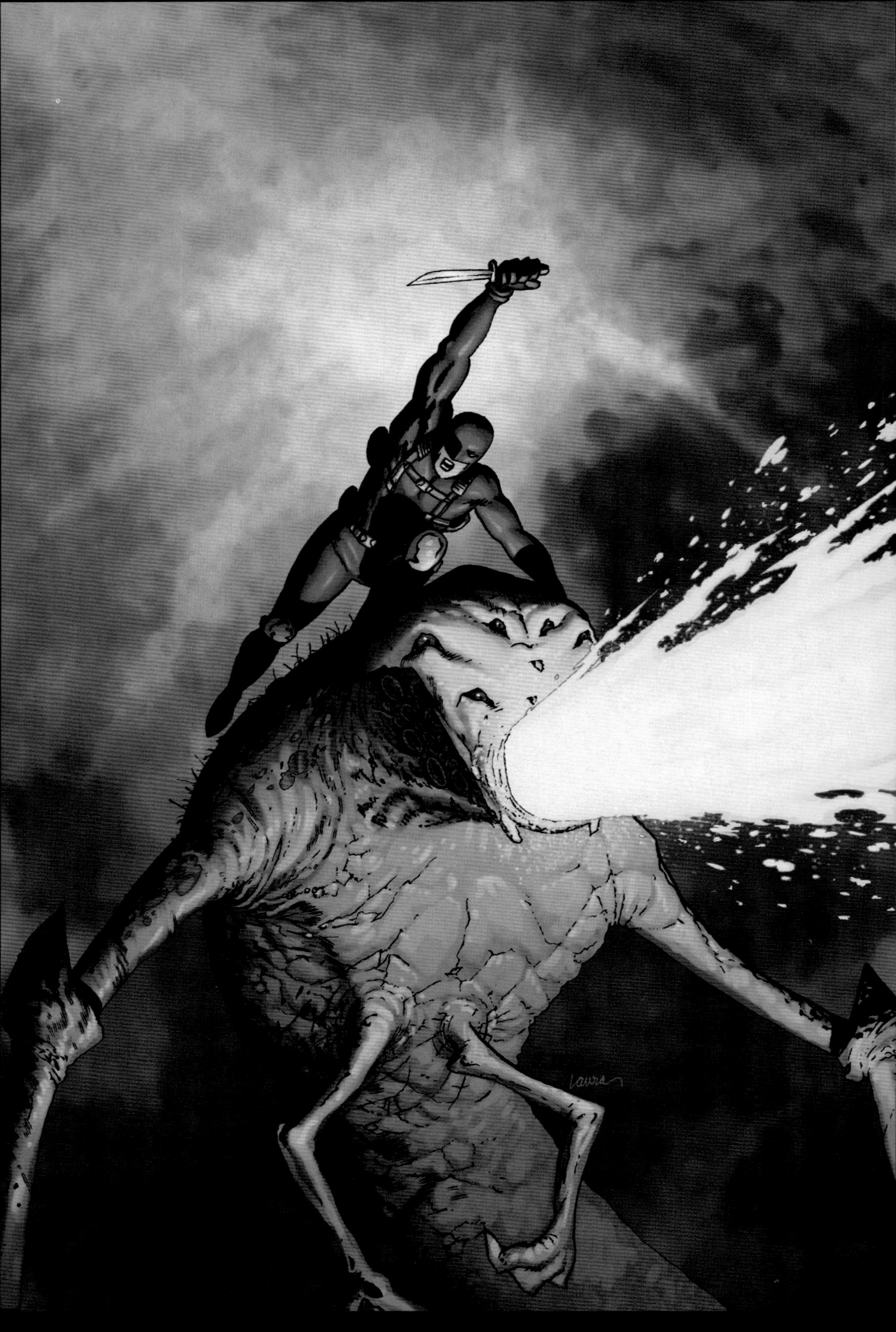
laura

ISSUE ONE: JOHN CASSADAY

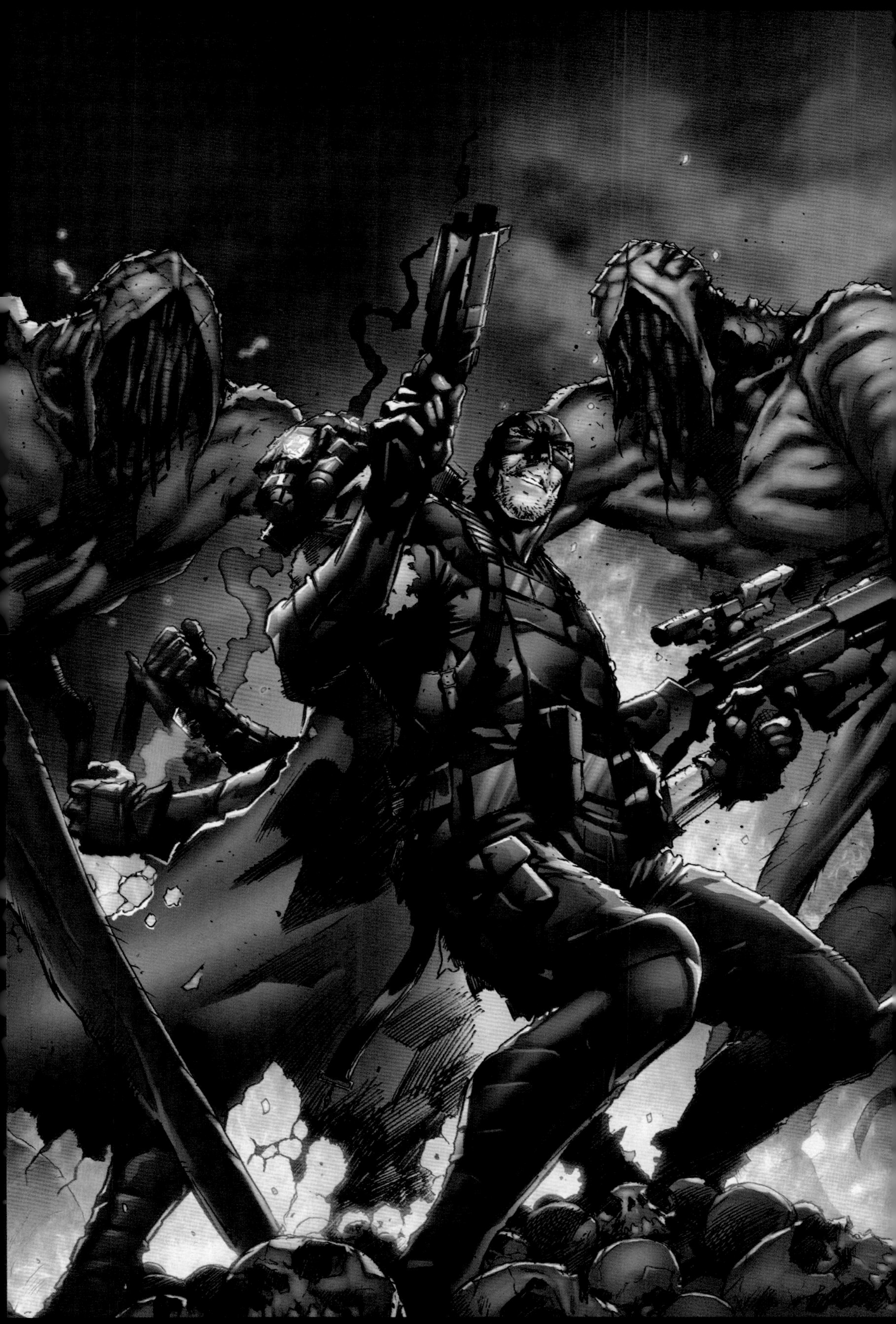

ISSUE ONE: TREVOR HAIRSIN
WITH COLORS BY BLON

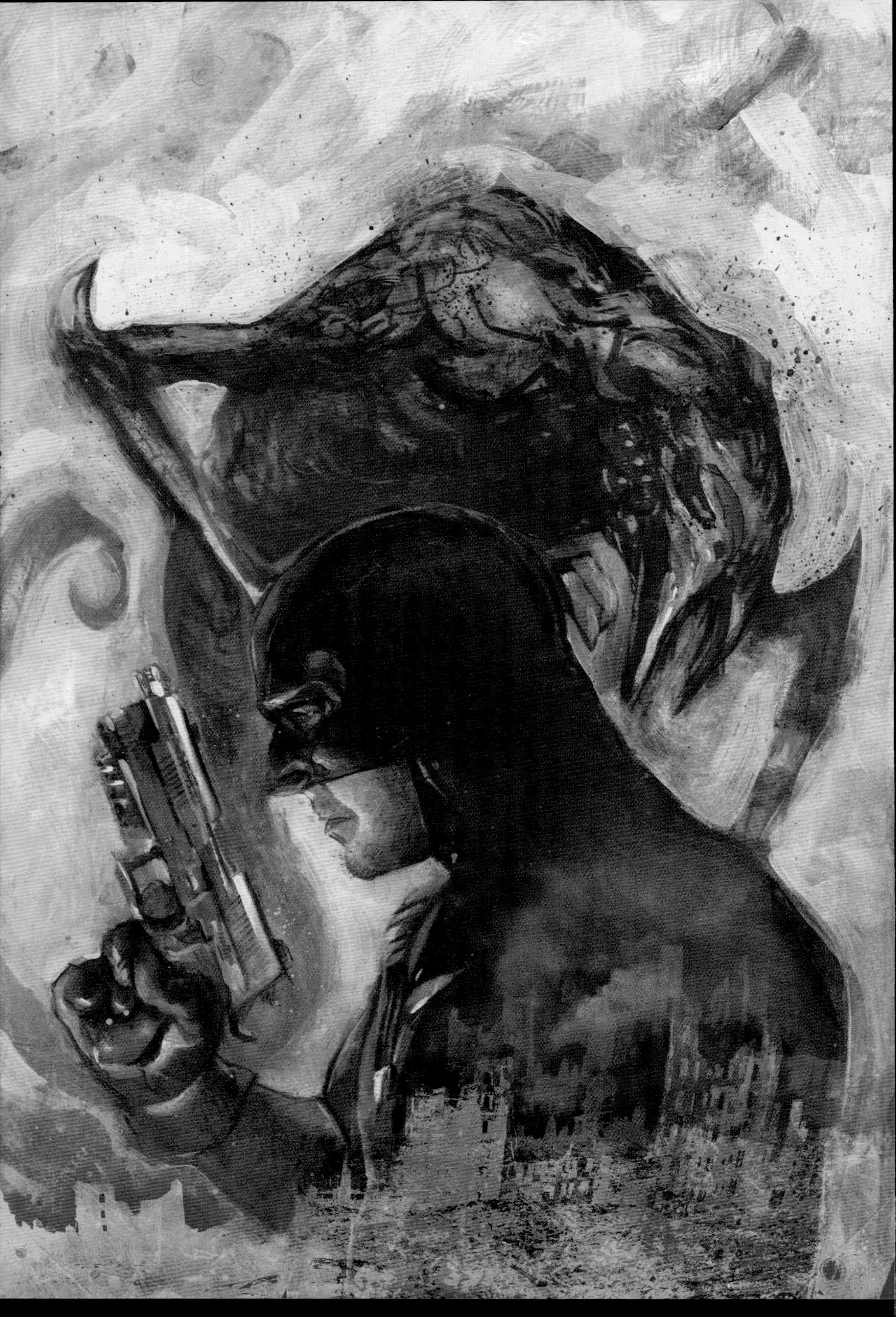

ISSUE ONE: MICHAEL GAYDOS

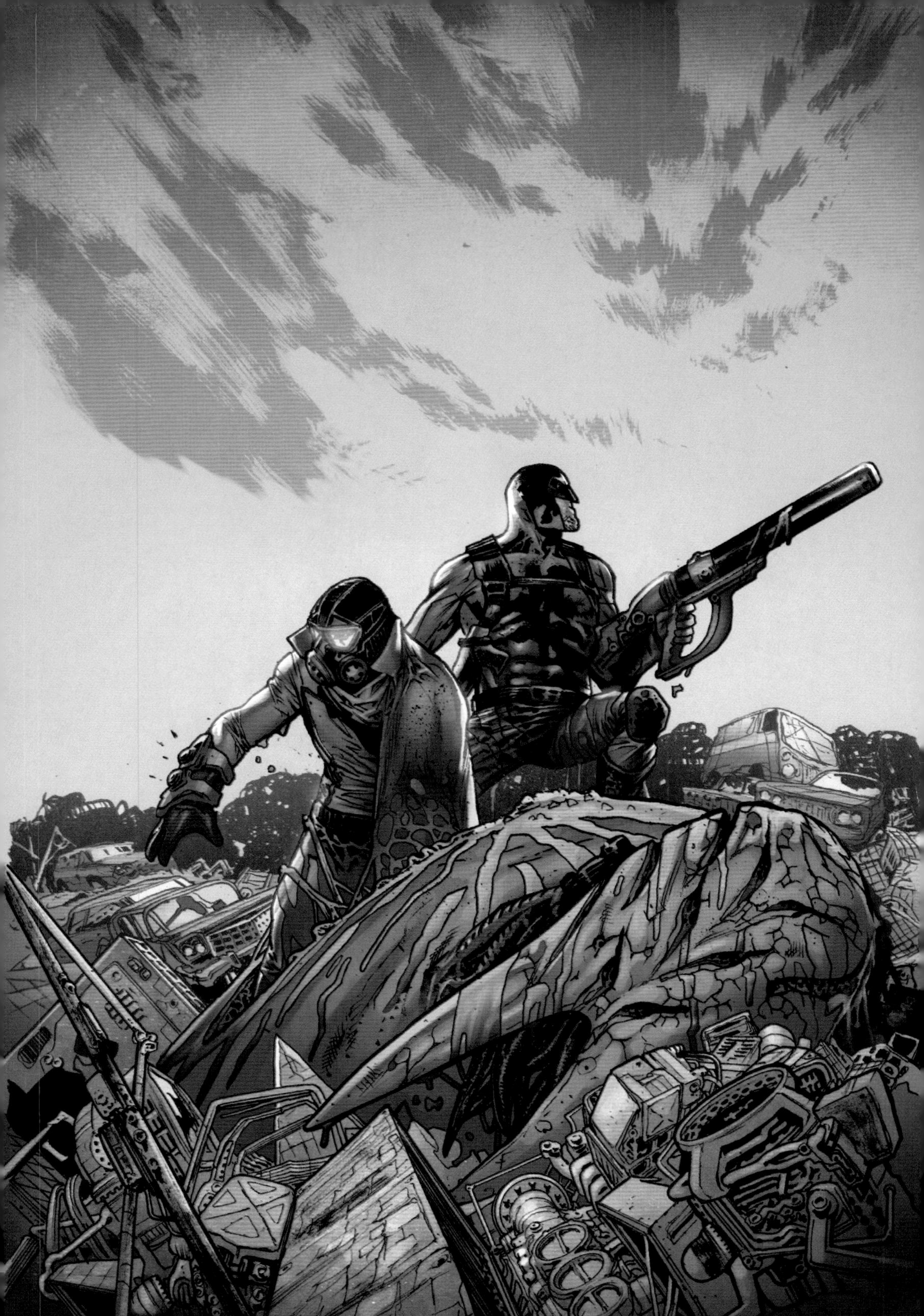

ISSUE ONE: **JAMES HARREN**

WITH COLORS BY **BLOND**

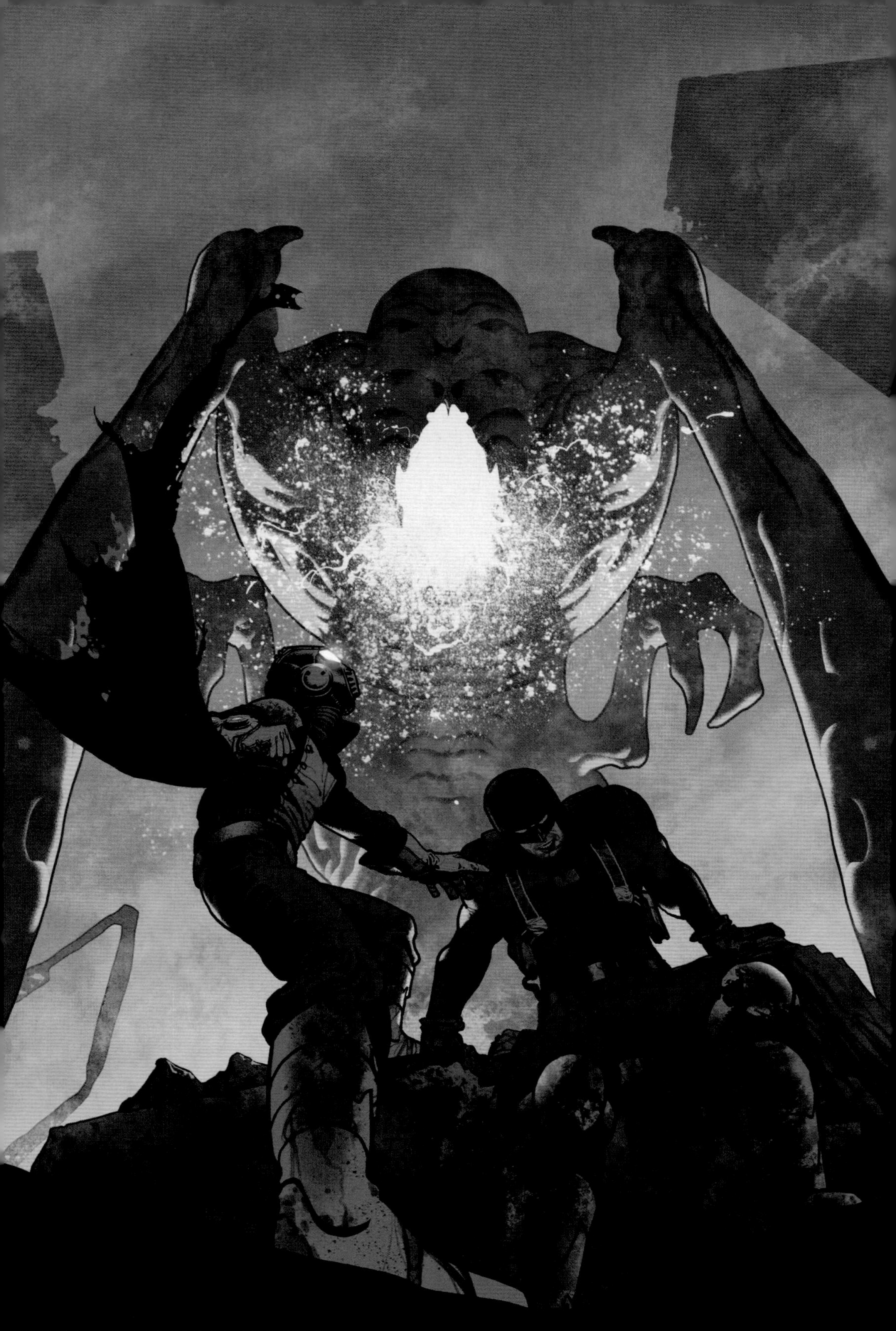

SSUE ONE-FRAZER IRVING

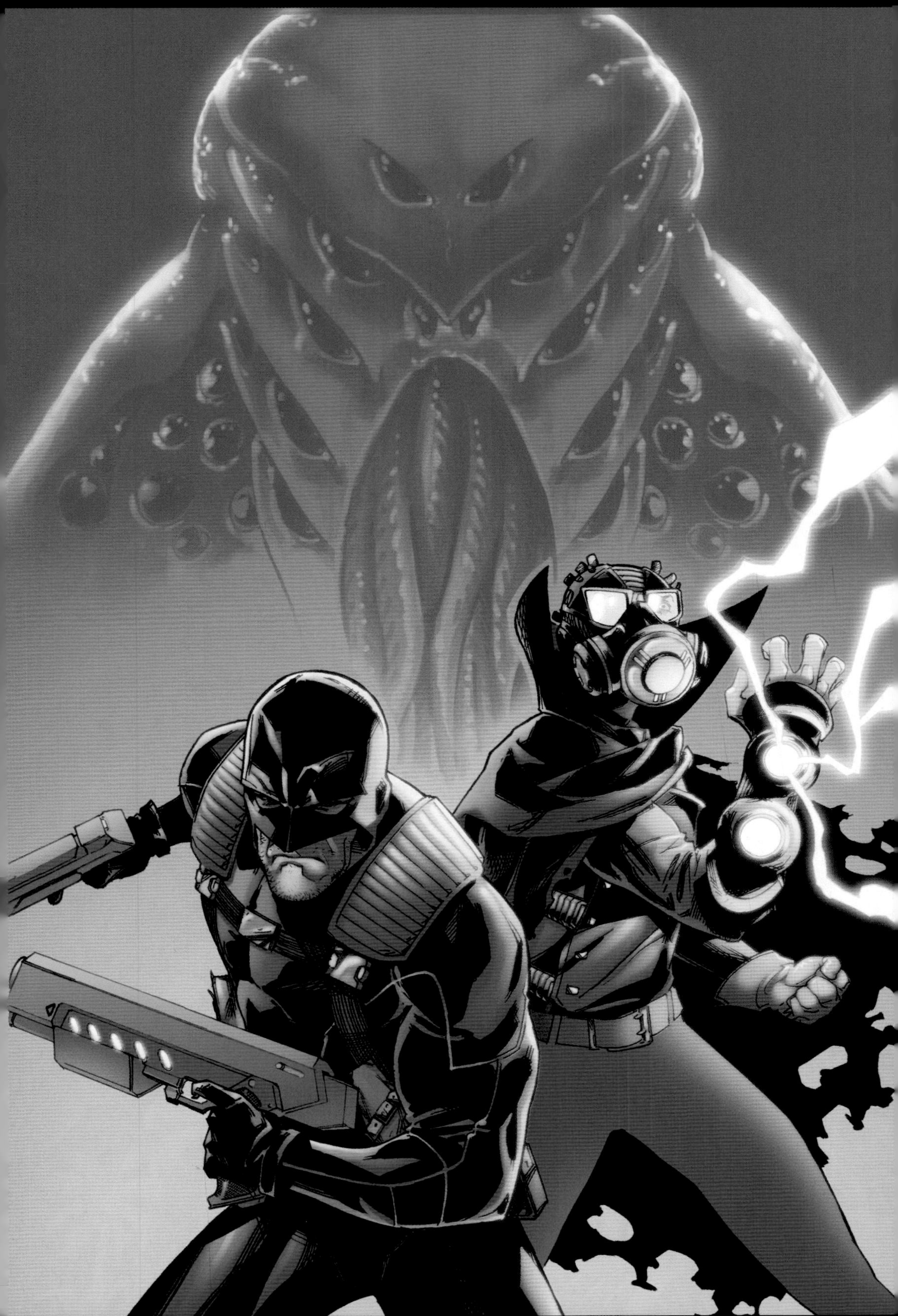

ISSUE ONE 2ND PRINT: **KALMAN ANDRASOFSZKY**
WITH COLORS BY NOLAN WOODARD

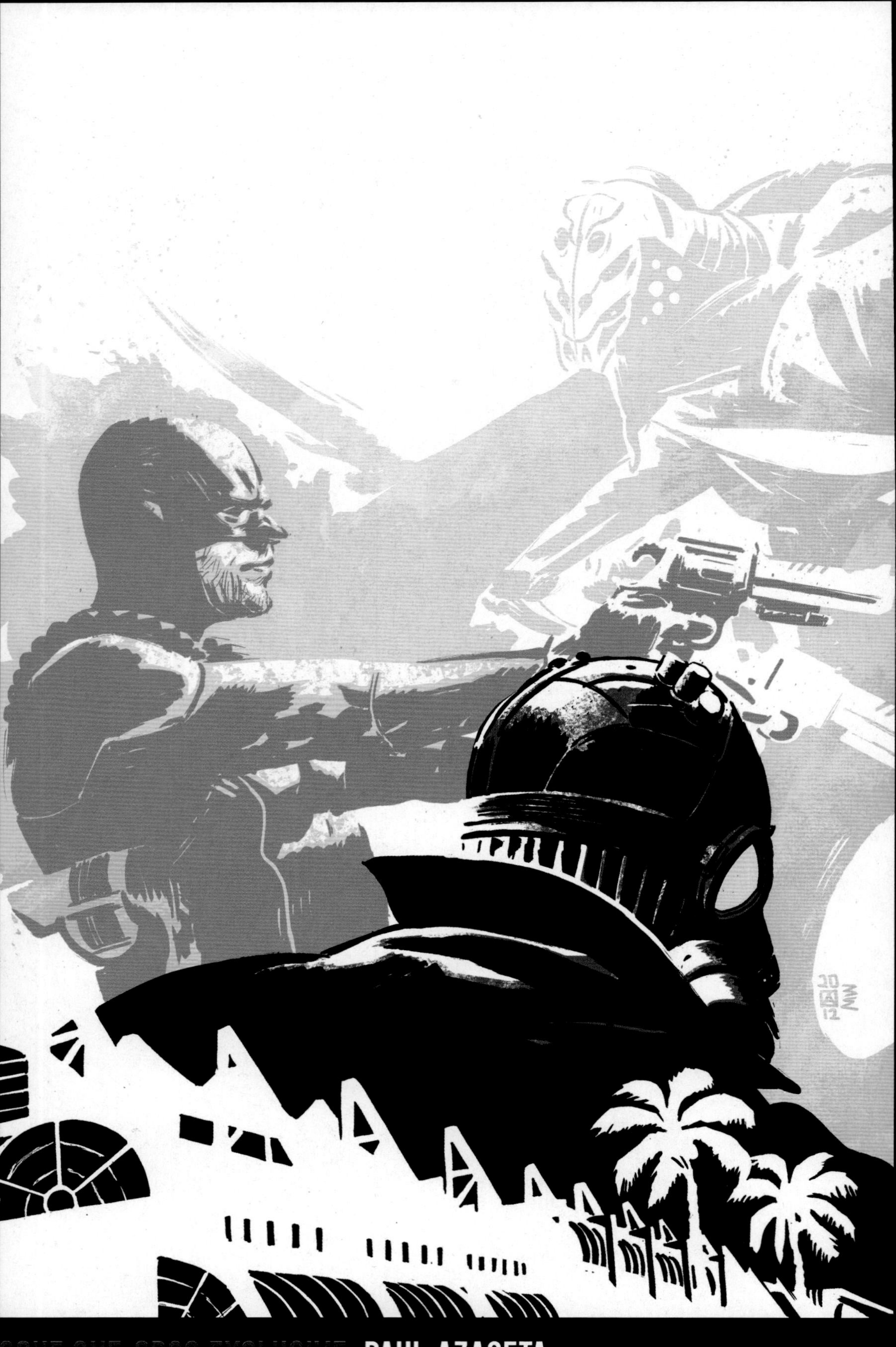

SSUE ONE SDCC EXCLUSIVE: PAUL AZACETA

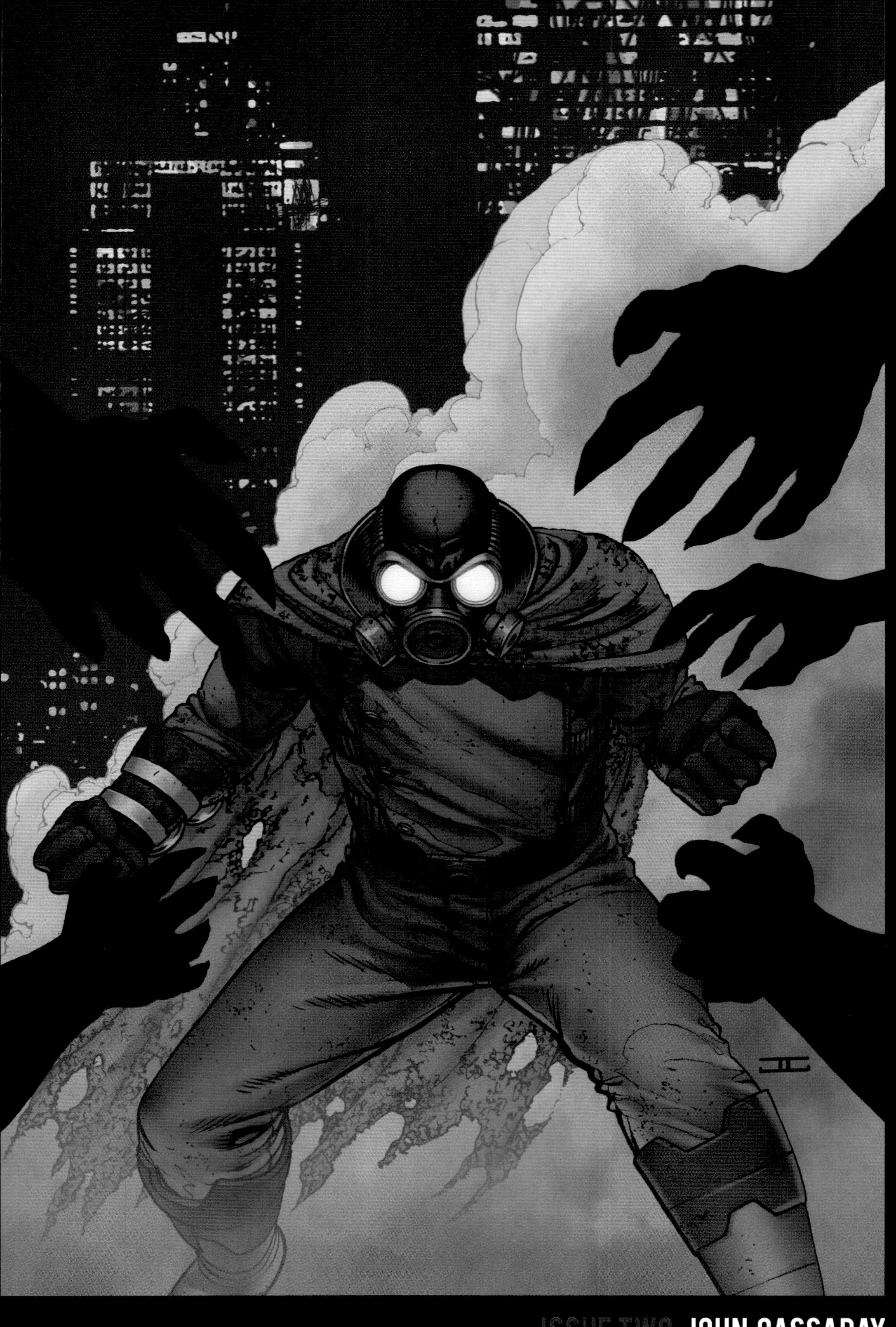

ISSUE TWO: **JOHN CASSADAY**

WITH COLORS BY LAURA MARTIN

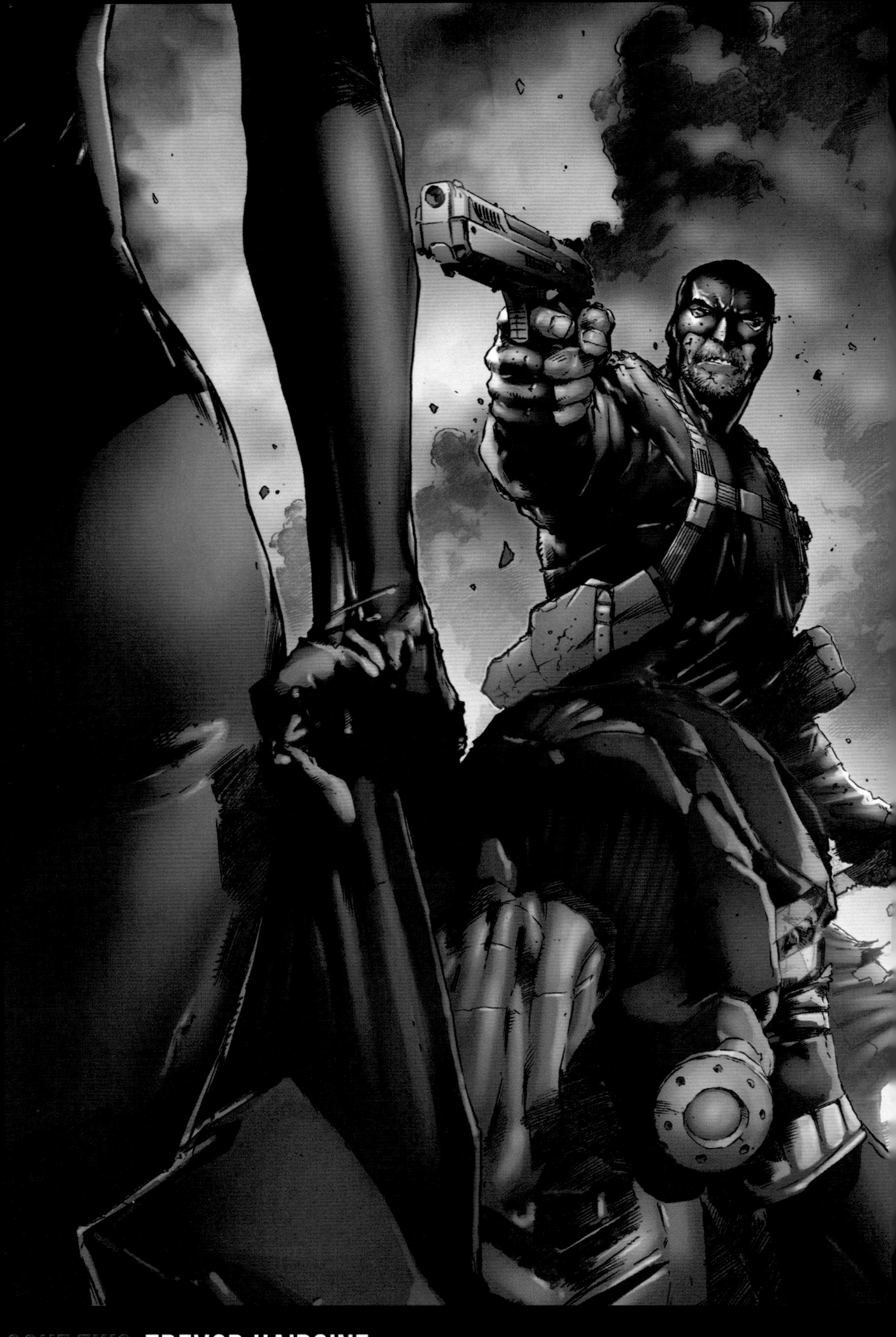

SSUE TWO: **TREVOR HAIRSINE**
WITH COLORS BY BLOND

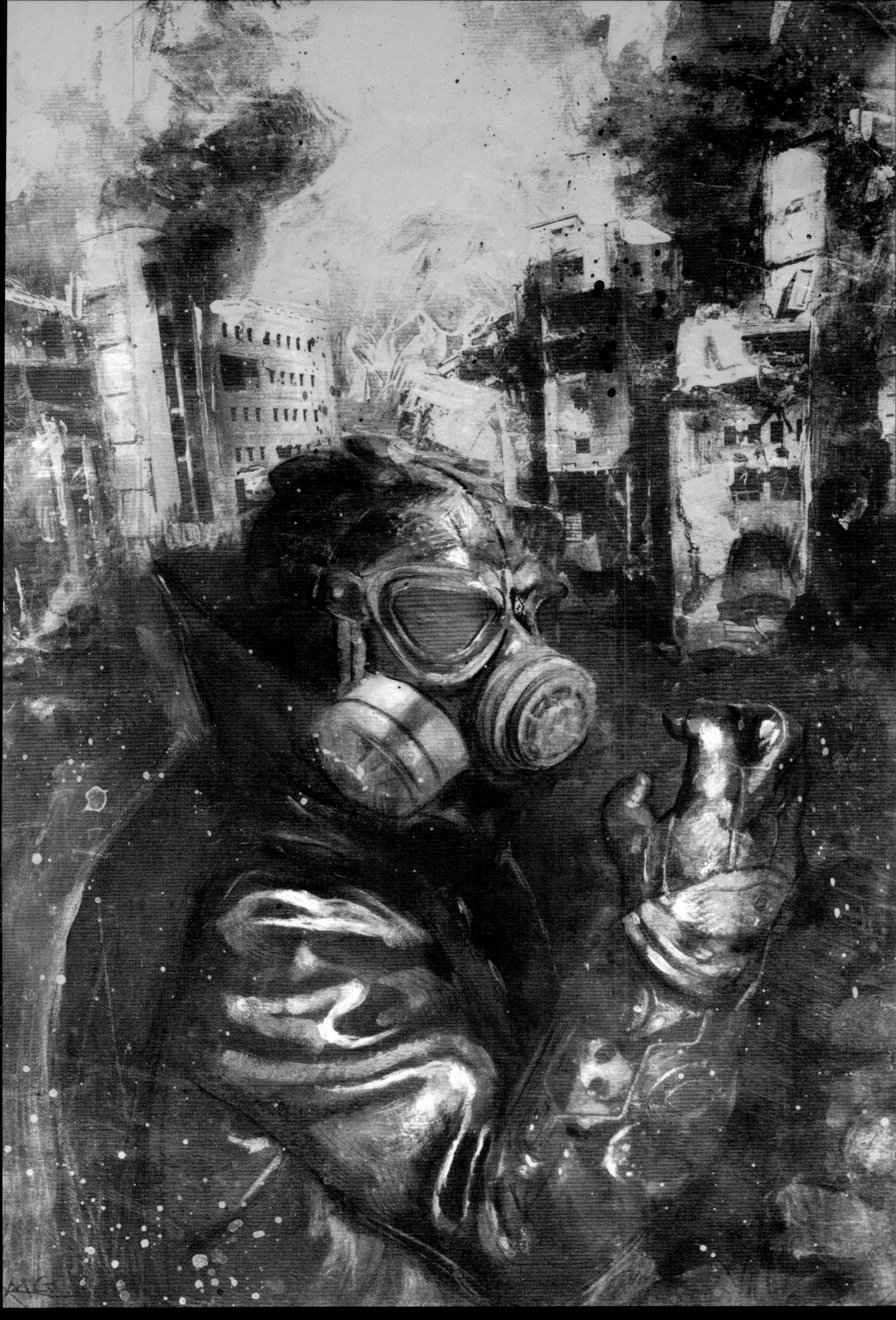

ISSUE TWO: MICHAEL GAYDOS

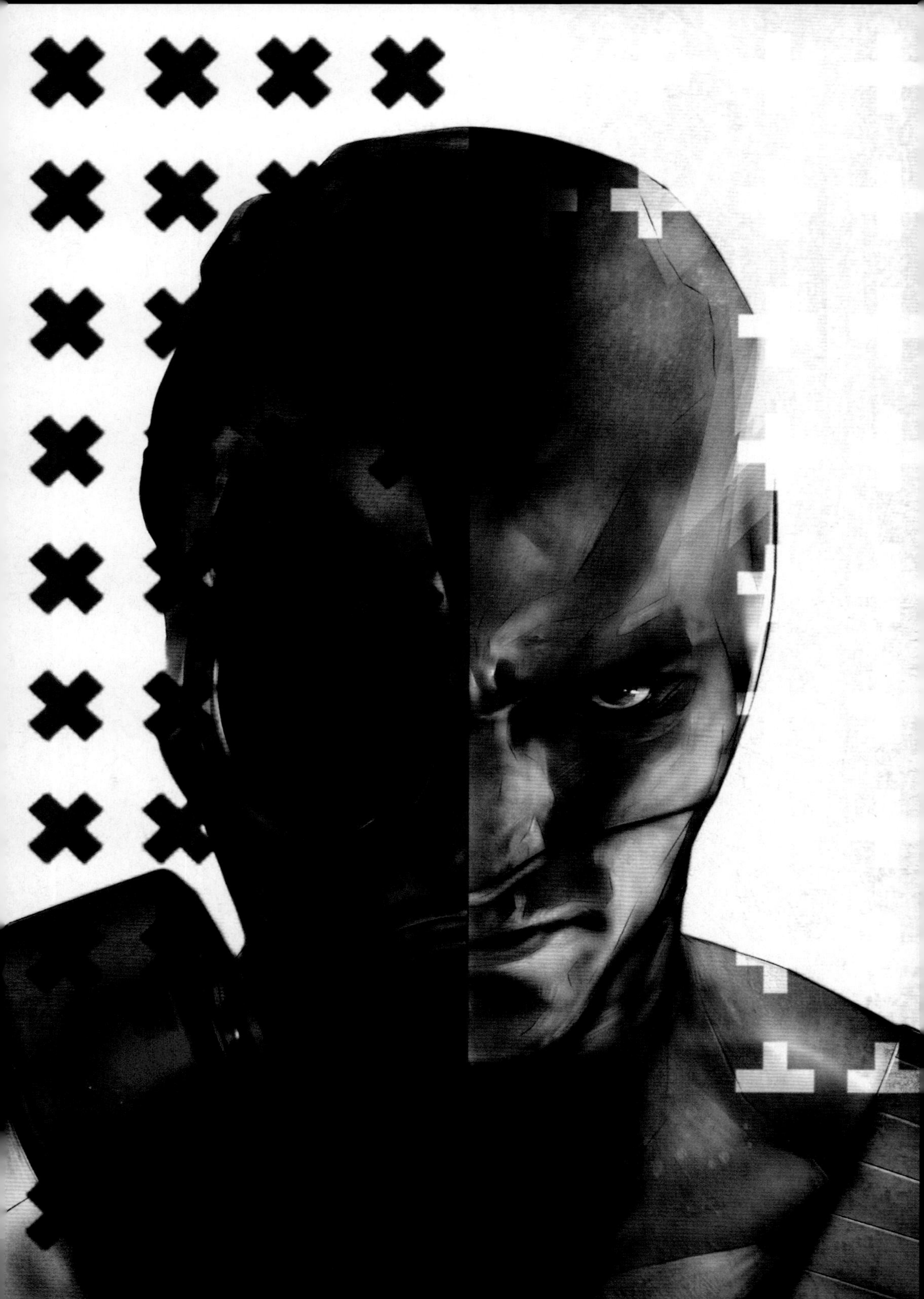

SSUE TWO: BEN OLIVER

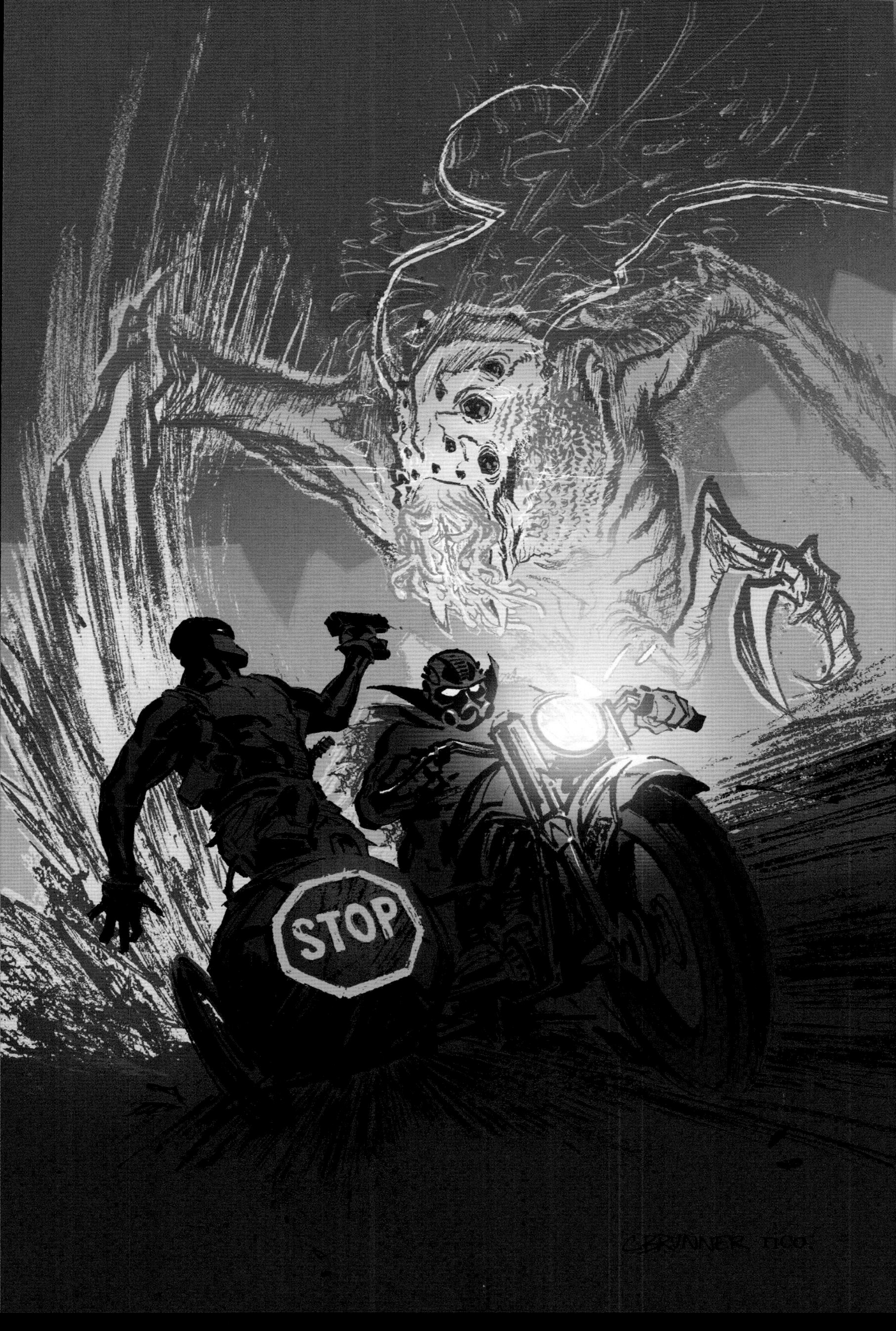
STOP
CBRUNNER 11100

ISSUE TWO 2ND PRINT: **CHRIS BRUNNER**

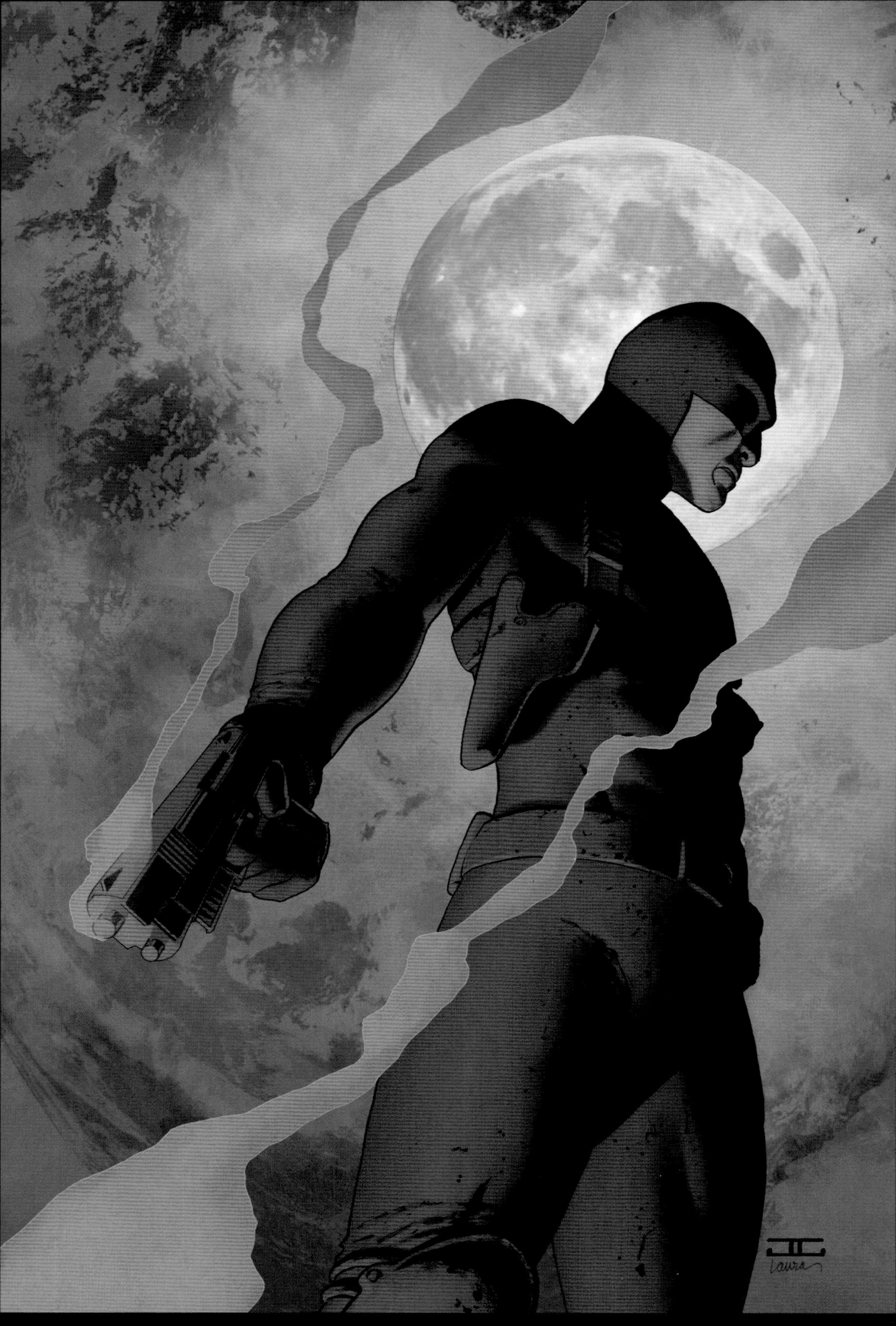
laura

ISSUE THREE: JOHN CASSADAY

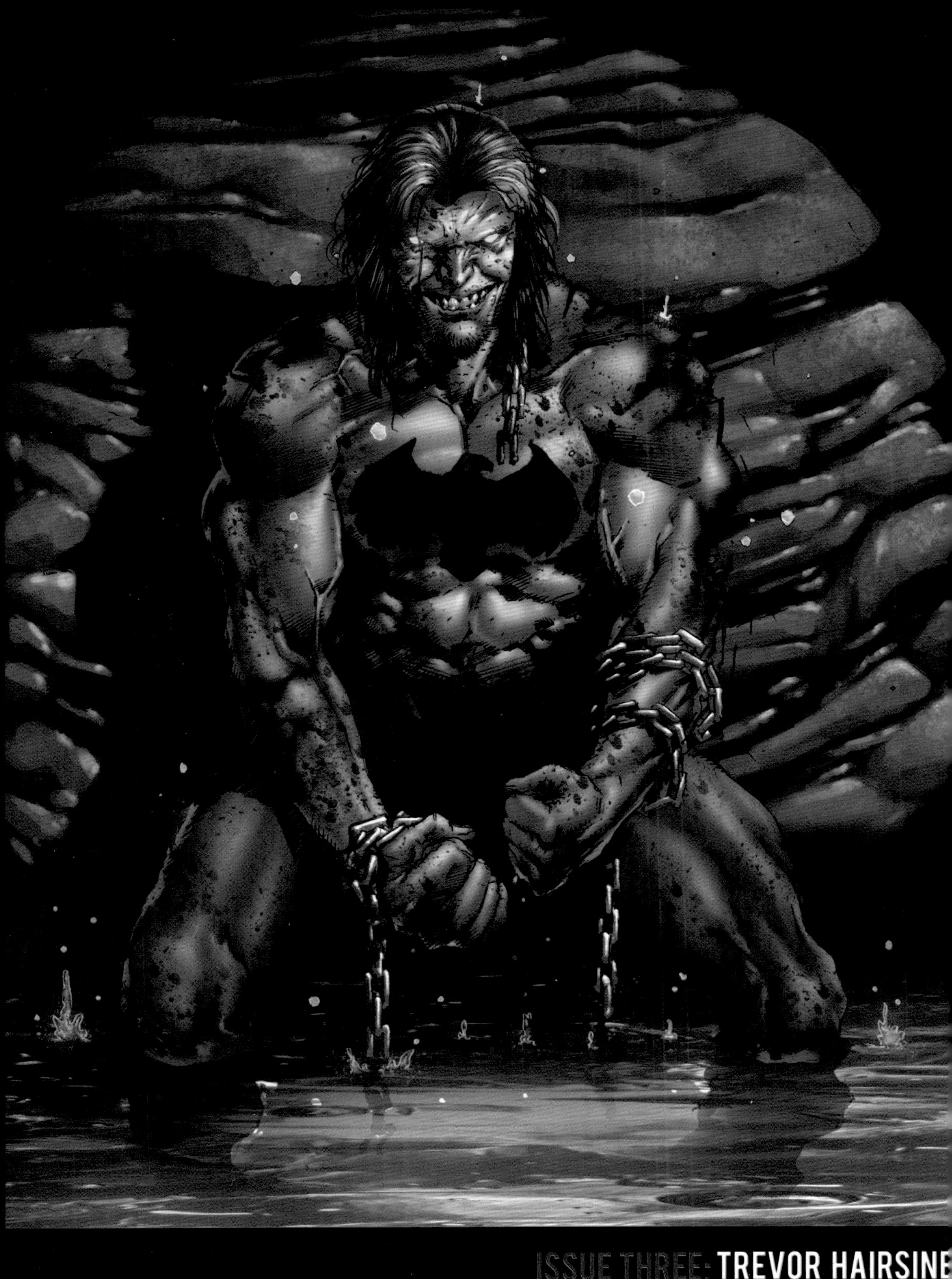

ISSUE THREE: **TREVOR HAIRSINE**
WITH COLORS BY BLOND

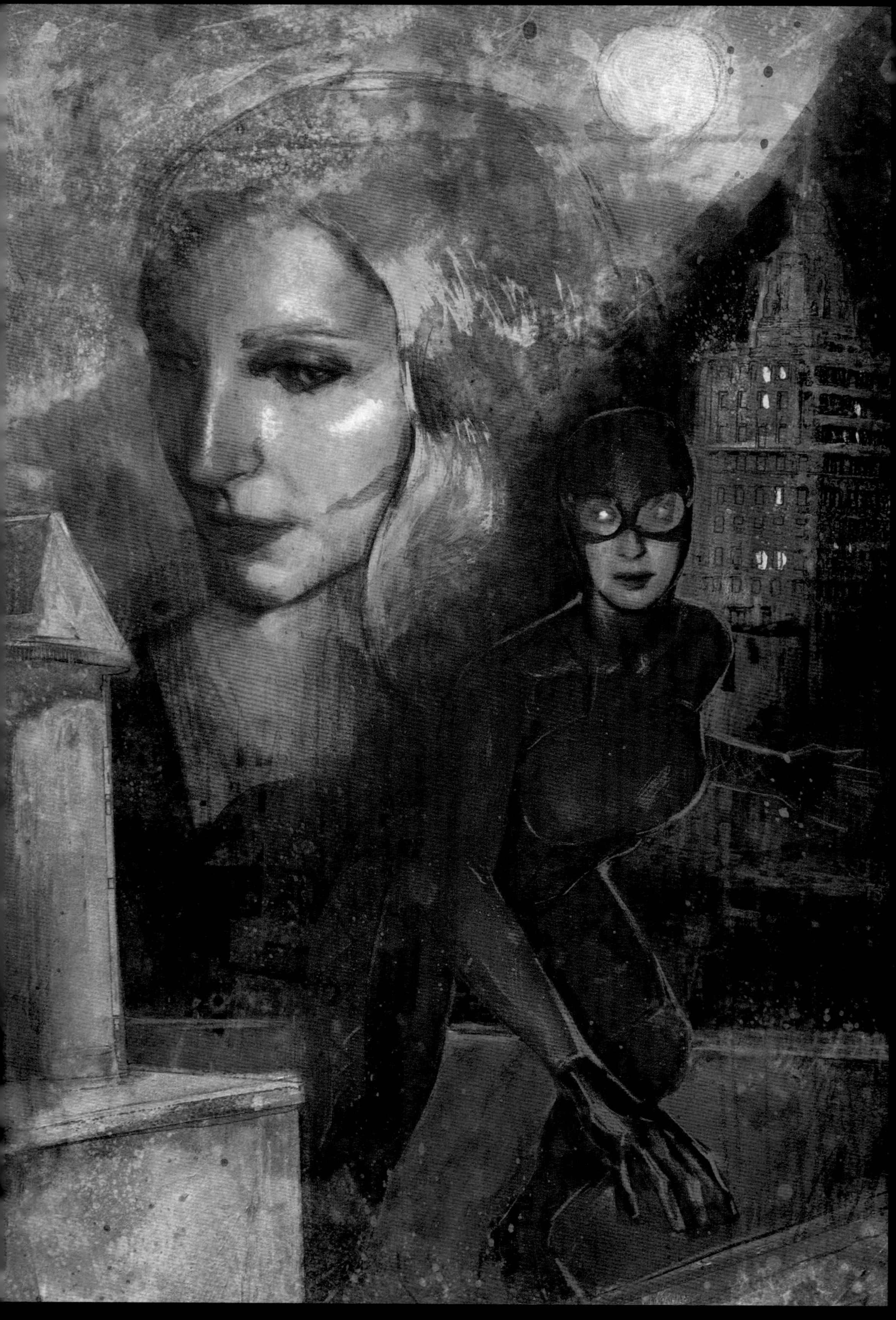

ISSUE THREE: MICHAEL GAYDOS

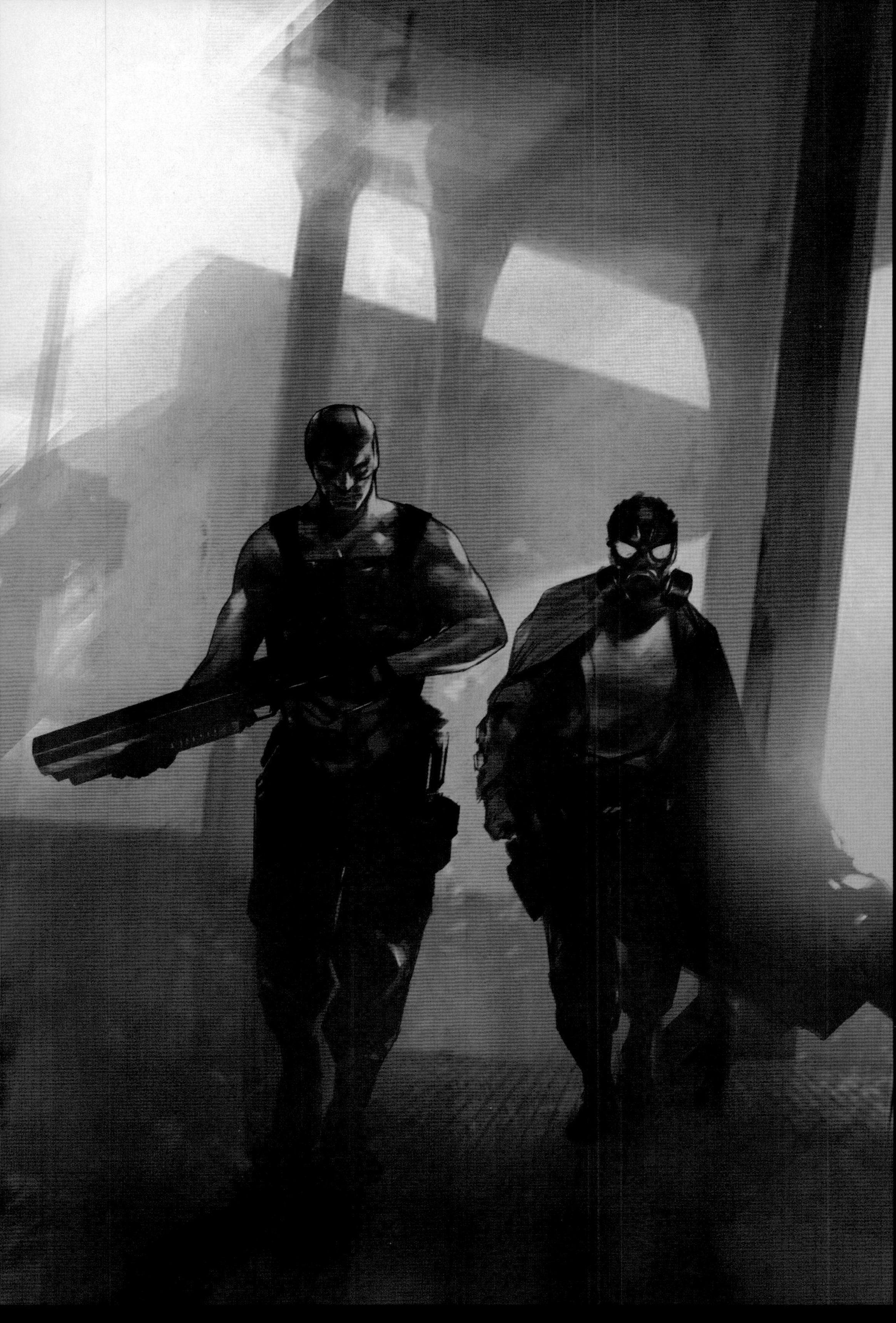

ISSUE THREE; **BEN OLIVER**

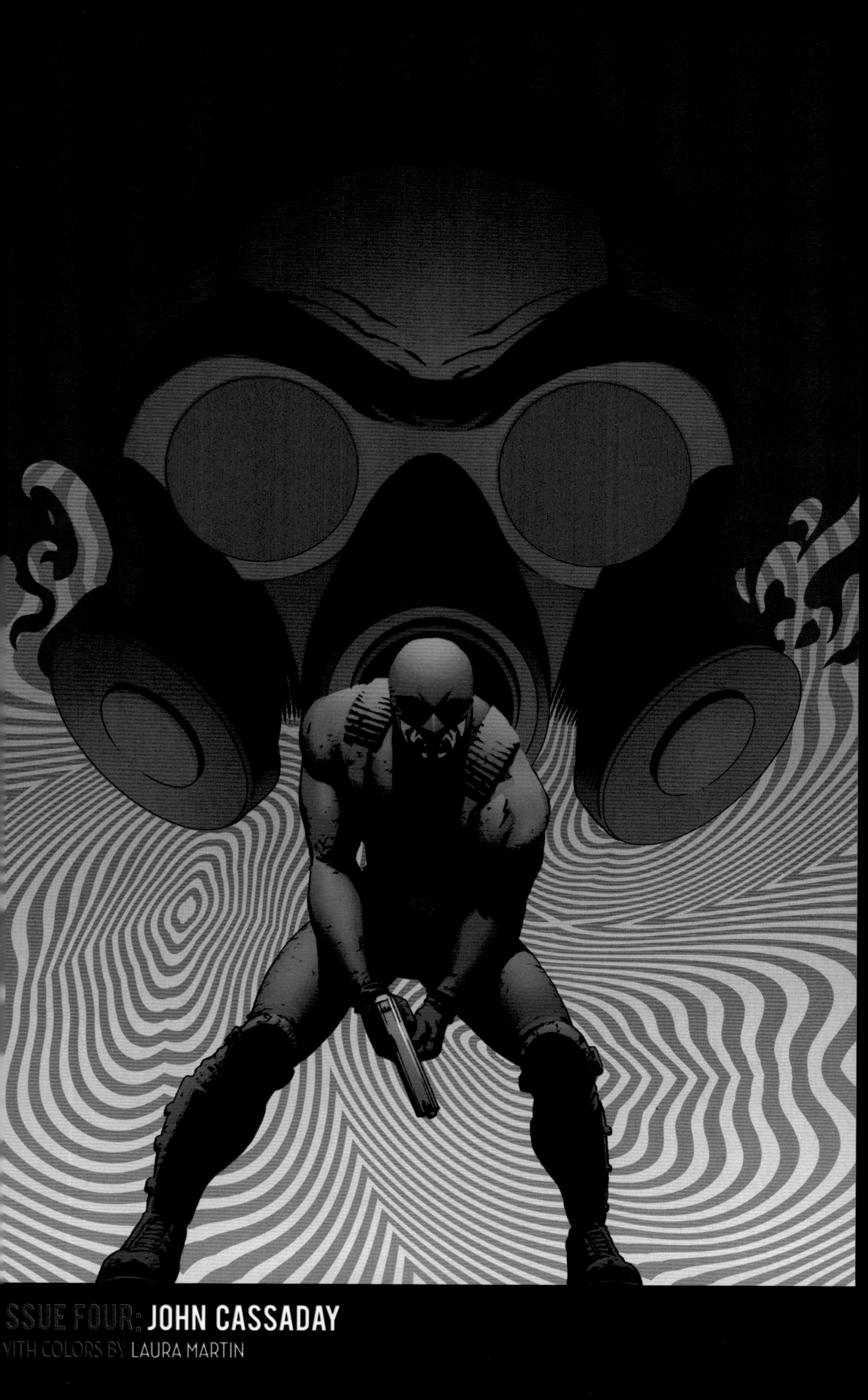

SSUE FOUR: **JOHN CASSADAY**
VITH COLORS BY LAURA MARTIN

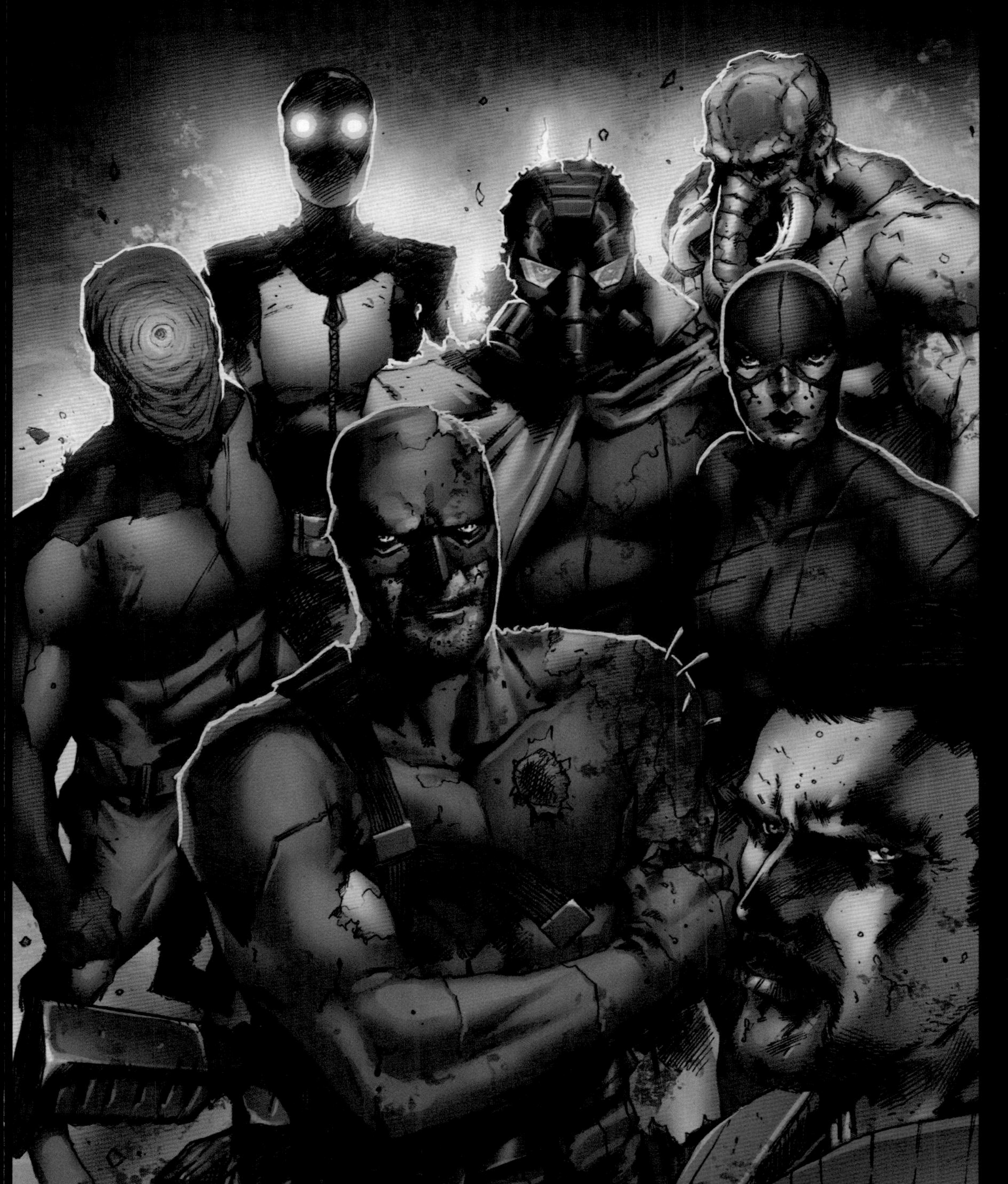

ISSUE FOUR: **TREVOR HAIRSINE**

WITH COLORS BY ARCHIE VAN BUREN

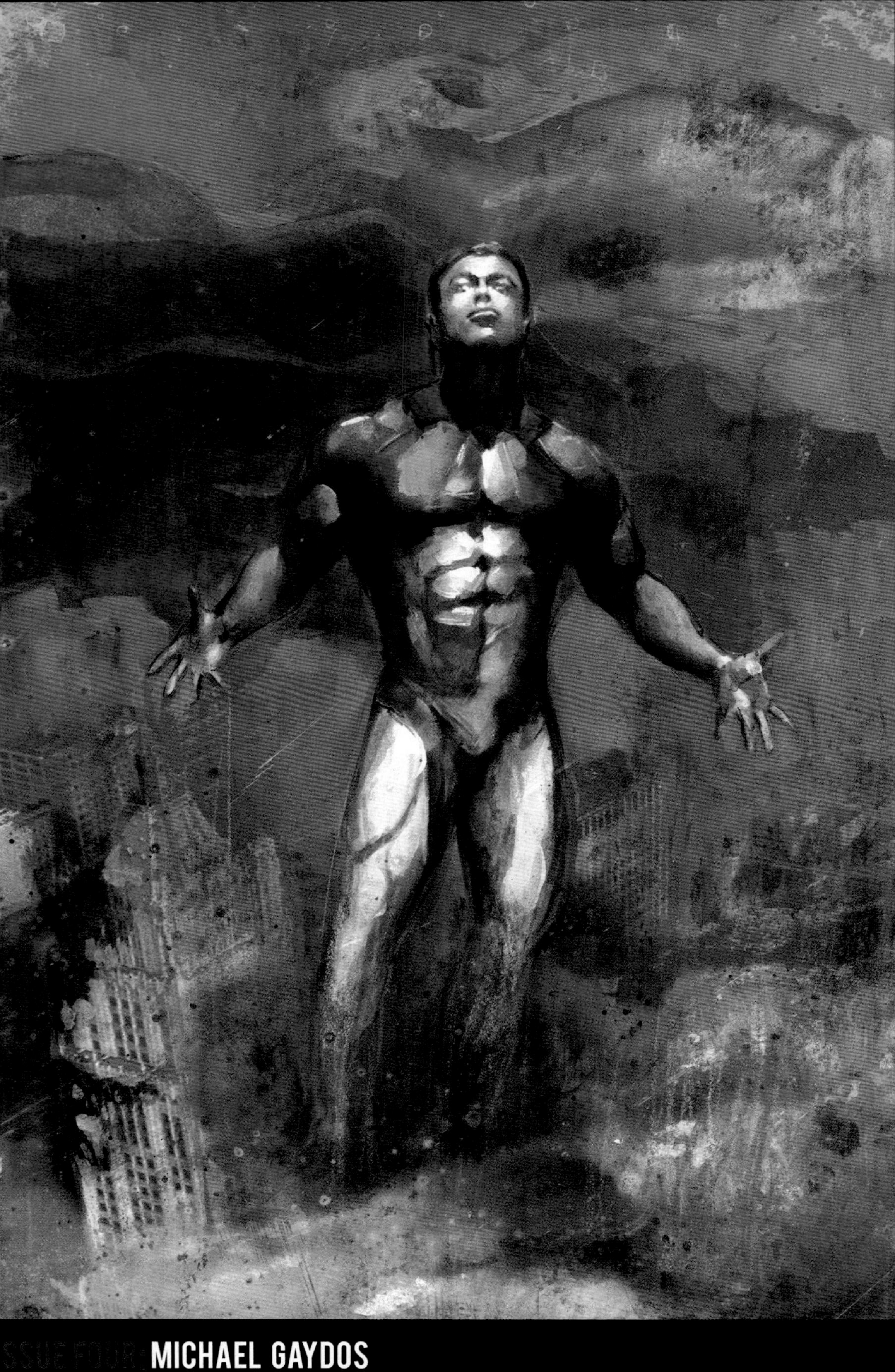

SSUE FOUR MICHAEL GAYDOS

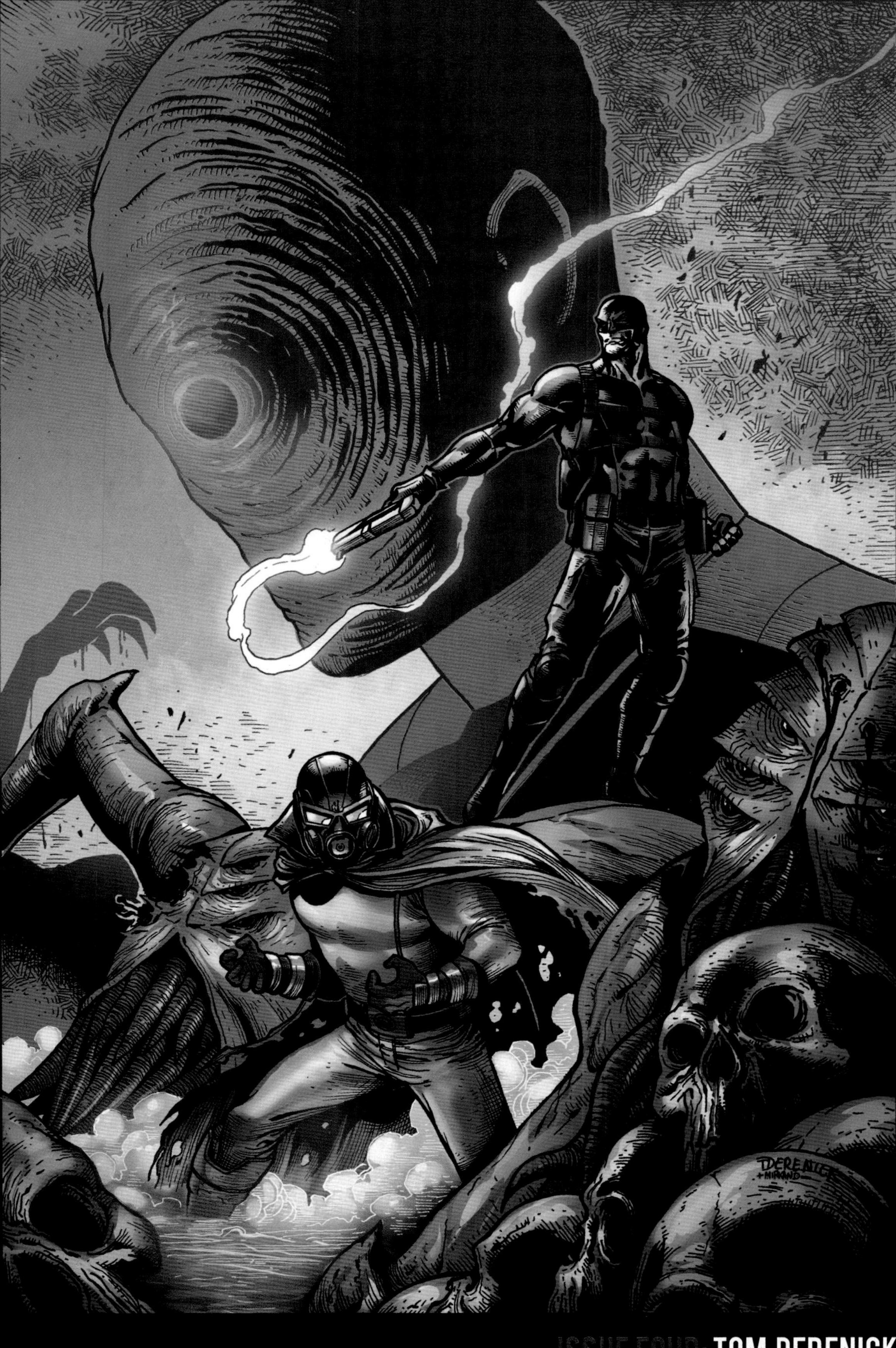

ISSUE FOUR: **TOM DERENICK**

WITH COLORS BY MIRKA ANDOLFO

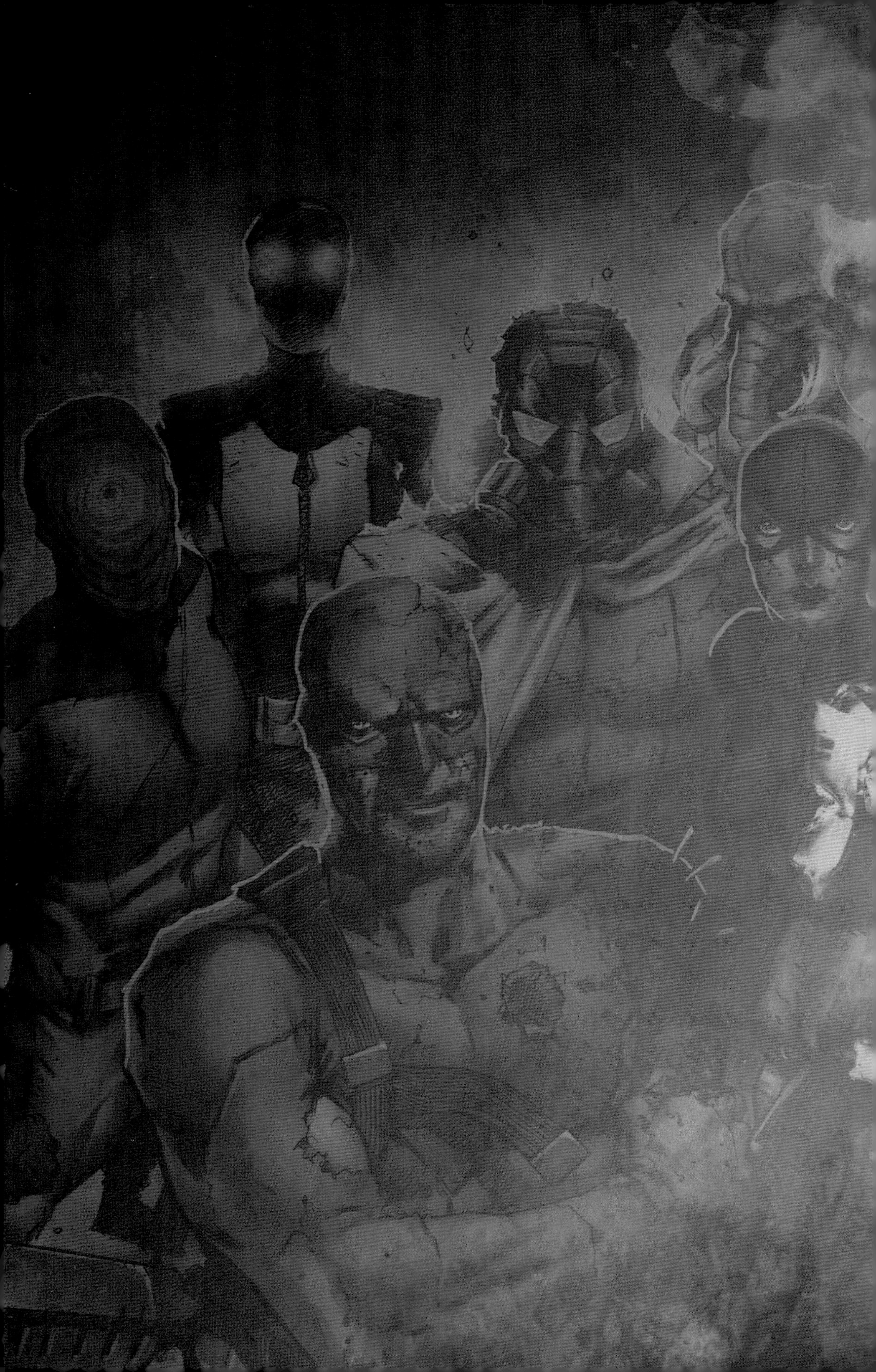

# AFTERWORD BY SIMON SPURRIER

"It's Mad Max with super-powers."

Not often does a one-line pitch conjure such a froth of images and ideas. *Extermination* lassoed my brain at the first post, bombarded me with a psi-bomb of possibilities and themes, and wrung-out my excitement-gland like an adrenaline enema. The tale which has emerged wears its High Concept on its rad-ravaged, rust-mangled sleeve, then plunges it into altogether more complex, darker and more rancid waters. It's a thing of blistering deserts, acidic snowscapes, insane salvaged machinery, hi-octane chases and seething apocalyptic alien madness... but more importantly it's a story about two people – two bitter enemies – forced together for survival and salvation.

Sometimes I think the two-tone morality of spandex comics can stray into an unhealthily simplistic view of the world – are you a Good Guy or a Bad Guy? All too often our beloved Hit-Things-Until-They're-Fixed ™ genre dodges the gorgeous, ghastly nuances of what's *truly* right and wrong. In *Extermination* we're taking Costumed Conventionality as our starting-point then stamping on it until it shrieks.

In the boldly-coloured old world our two main characters were polar opposites: the cowl-wearing vigilante <u>Nox</u> and the megalomaniacal villain <u>Red Reaper</u>. But in the new world – a world in which the psychic technologies of the astral EDDA invaders have crippled the Earth, decimated its defenses and humbled its heroes – all the old certainties must be re-evaluated. What's the good of a crime-fighter in a world without law? Where's the evil in a ruthless empire-builder on a planet-sized cinder?

Only together – despite years of shared history and hate – can the two men hope to save their tortured species. Only by travelling the ash-roads, assembling the burnt-out remnants of a bygone age, and taking the fight back to the devils who so grievously defeated them, can they heal the wounds of their world.

But both men have secrets. Both men have scores to settle and vendettas to pursue, and amidst the wreckage of civilisation nothing is as simple as it once was.

# EXTERMINATION
## CHARACTER DESIGNS

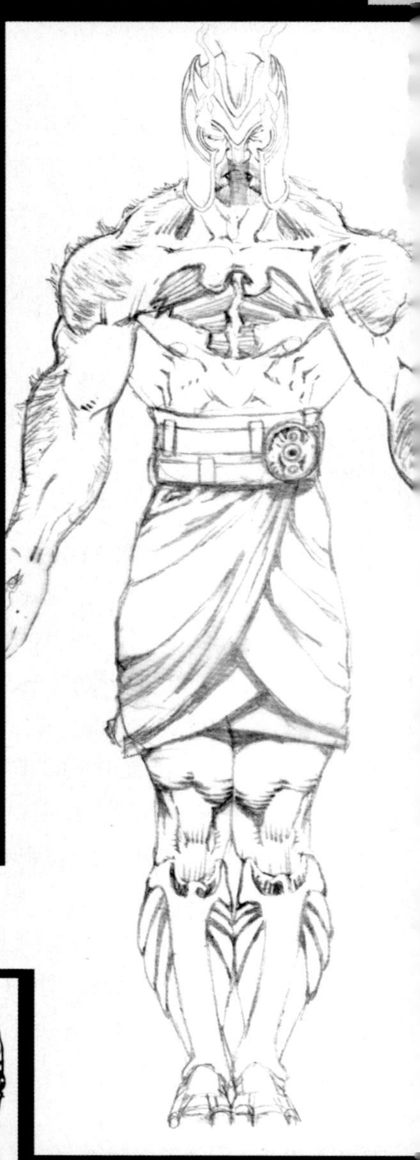

PROMETHEAN BY JEFFREY EDWARDS

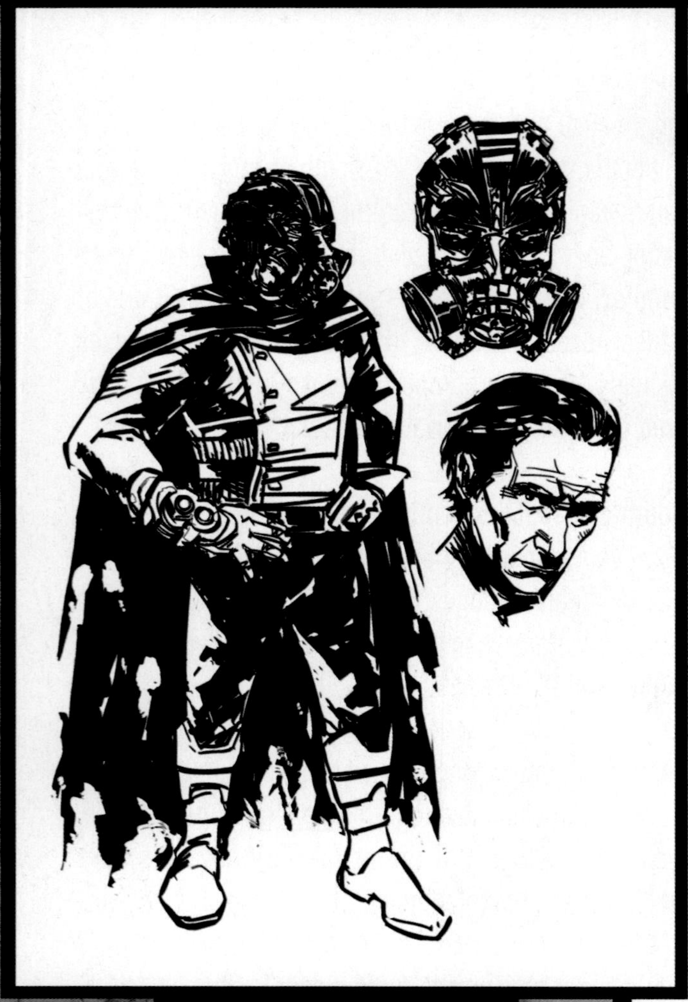

THE RED REAPER BY GARRY BROWN

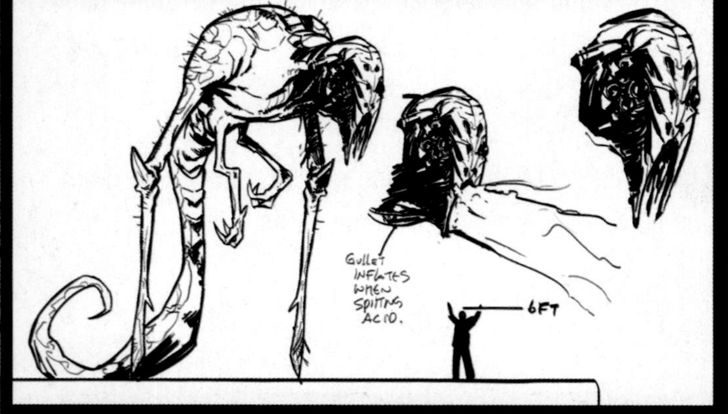
GULLET INFLATES WHEN SPITTING ACID.
6FT

EDDA BY GARRY BROWN

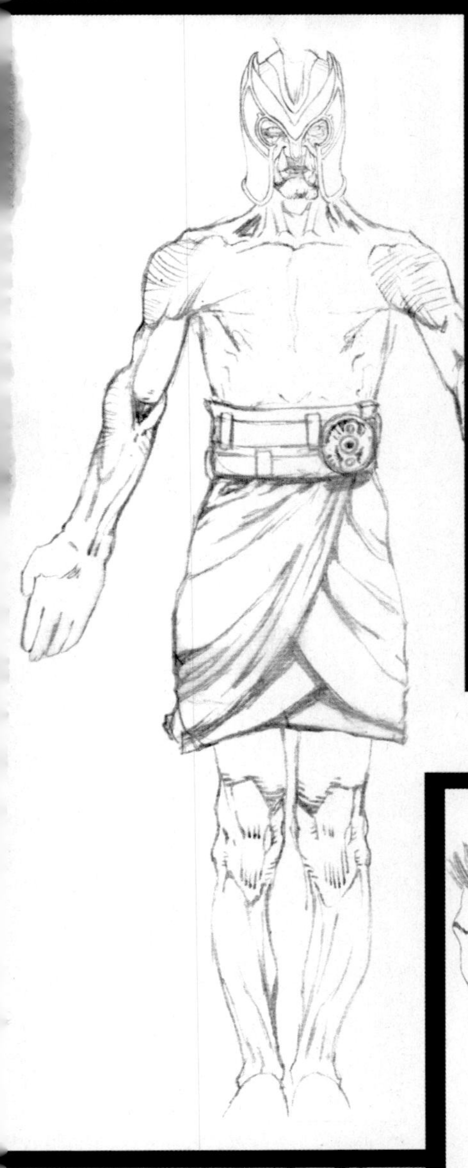

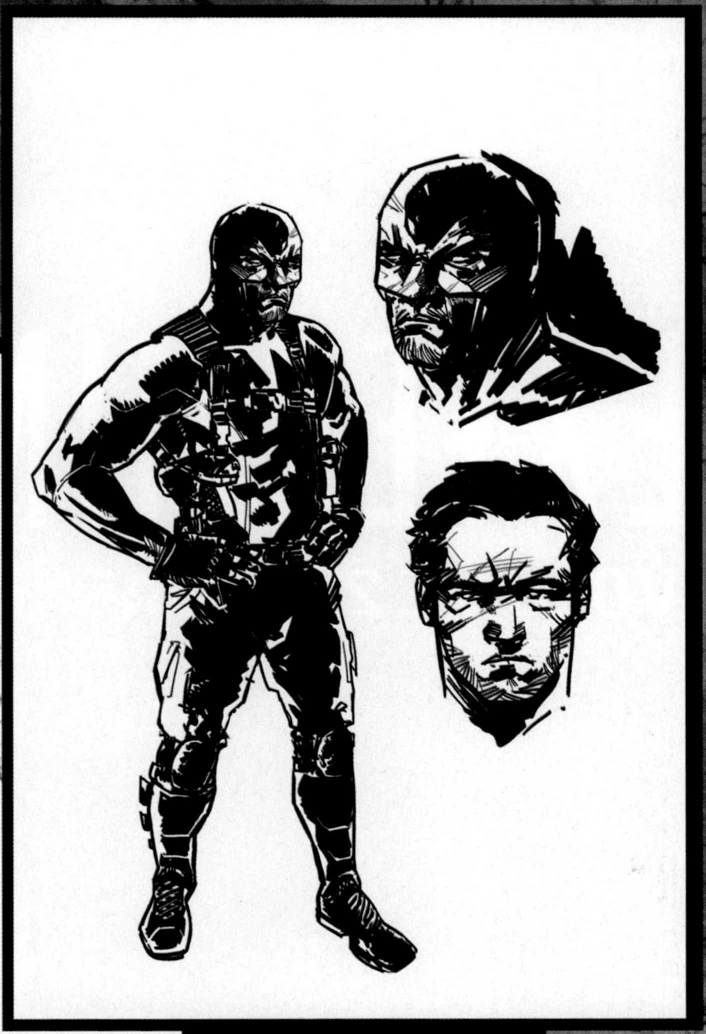

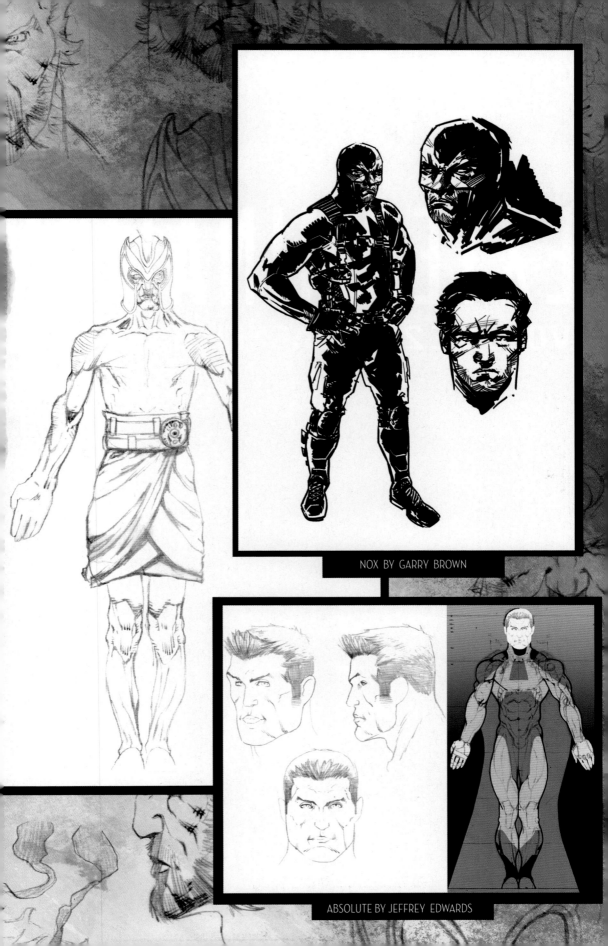

NOX BY GARRY BROWN

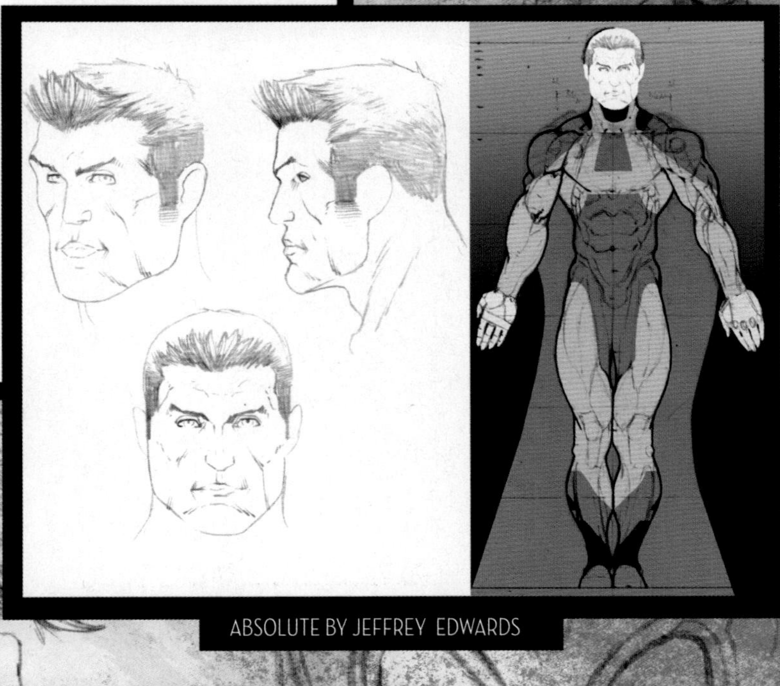

ABSOLUTE BY JEFFREY EDWARDS

# EXTERMINATION

## VOLUME 2: TO VASTER DARKNESS

## COMING SOON